Dynamic Christian Foundations

A series of studies on
Foundational Christian Truths

Ken and Alison Chant

Dynamic Christian Foundations

A series of studies on Foundational Christian Truths

Ken and Alison Chant

Copyright 2012 Ken and Alison Chant

ISBN 978-1-61529-045-1

Vision Publishing

1672 Main St. E 109

Ramona, CA 92065

1-800-9-VISION

www.booksbyvision.com

All rights reserved worldwide

No part of the book may be reproduced in any manner whatsoever without written permission of the author except in brief quotations embodied in critical articles of reviews.

A NOTE ON GENDER

It is unfortunate that the English language does not contain an adequate generic pronoun (especially in the singular number) that includes without bias both male and female. So *"he, him, his, man, mankind,"* with their plurals, must do the work for both sexes. Accordingly, wherever it is appropriate to do so in the following pages, please include the feminine gender in the masculine, and vice versa.

FOOTNOTES

A work once fully referenced will thereafter be noted either by "ibid" or "op. cit."

CONTENTS

PREFACE 5
ABOUT THESE BOOKS 7

BOOK ONE: THE WAY OF SALVATION 9

LESSON ONE: SO GREAT SALVATION 15
LESSON TWO: YOU MUST BE BORN AGAIN 25
LESSON THREE: HOW CAN WE BE BORN AGAIN? 35
LESSON FOUR: THE ATONEMENT OF
JESUS CHRIST 45

BOOK TWO: JESUS THE HEALER 57

LESSON ONE: AUTHORITY FOR DIVINE HEALING 60
LESSON TWO: HEALING IN THE ATONEMENT 79
LESSON THREE: DIVINE DELIVERANCE 89

**BOOK THREE: THE POWER OF
PENTECOST TODAY** 107

LESSON ONE: THE PERSONALITY AND POWER
OF THE HOLY SPIRIT 109
LESSON TWO: THE PURPOSE OF THE BAPTISM
IN THE HOLY SPIRIT 131
LESSON THREE: THE SPIRIT FILLED LIFE 149

BOOK FOUR: SIGNS WONDERS AND GIFTS 163

LESSON ONE: CONCERNING SPIRITUAL GIFTS 165

LESSON TWO: MORE ABOUT THE GIFTS 183

BOOK FIVE: LAW AND GRACE **197**

LESSON ONE: THE LAW OF THE LORD 199

LESSON TWO: THE NEW GLORY 215

BOOK SIX: HOW TO PRAY SUCCESSFULLY **229**

LESSON ONE: THE UNIQUE WITNESS OF PRAYER 231

LESSON TWO: THE SECRETS OF SUCCESSFUL PRAYER 250

BOOK SEVEN: THE AMAZING POWER OF FAITH **263**

LESSON ONE: THE IMPORTANCE OF FAITH 265

LESSON TWO: THE POWER OF POSITIVE BELIEVING 278

LESSON THREE: YOUR WORD OF FAITH AND AUTHORITY 302

BOOK EIGHT: WATER BAPTISM AND THE LORDS SUPPER **309**

LESSON ONE: THE GREATEST EXPERIENCE AFTER THE NEW BIRTH WATER BAPTISM 312

LESSON TWO: THE LORD'S SUPPER 333

BOOK NINE: CHRIST IS COMING **343**

LESSON ONE: THE SECOND COMING 346

LESSON TWO: CHRIST'S RETURN, THE RAPTURE, AND THE JUDGMENT 361

PREFACE

The series of books which comprise Dynamic Christian Foundations have been written as a beginner's manual for those who have never studied God's word and need something to start them on their way.

The compiling and editing of the writings by Dr. Ken Chant have been taken from his books "This We Believe" and "Asked and Answered".

I would like to thank Charlotte Fry and Julie Chant for their constant encouragement and typing skills without which these books would not have been completed.

I pray that this manual will be useful to many who wish to study the things of God and that they will benefit from these pages.

New Revised edition 2012

Alison Chant

ABBREVIATIONS

Abbreviations commonly used for the books of the Bible are

Genesis	Ge	Habakkuk	Hb
Exodus	Ex	Zephaniah	Zp
Leviticus	Le	Haggai	Hg
Numbers	Nu	Zechariah	Zc
Deuteronomy	De	Malachi	Mal
Joshua	Js		
Judges	Jg		
Ruth	Ru	Matthew	Mt
1 Samuel	1 Sa	Mark	Mk
2 Samuel	2 Sa	Luke	Lu
1 Kings	1 Kg	John	Jn
2 Kings	2 Kg	Acts	Ac
1 Chronicles	1 Ch	Romans	Ro
2 Chronicles	2 Ch	1 Corinthians	1 Co
Ezra	Ezr	2 Corinthians	2 Co
Nehemiah	Ne	Galatians	Ga
Esther	Es	Ephesians	Ep
Job	Jb	Philippians	Ph
Psalm	Ps	Colossians	Cl
Proverbs	Pr	1 Thessalonians	1 Th
Ecclesiastes	Ec	2 Thessalonians	2 Th
Song of Songs	Ca *	1 Timothy	1 Ti
Isaiah	Is	2 Timothy	2 Ti
Jeremiah	Je	Titus	Tit
Lamentations	La	Philemon	Phm
Ezekiel	Ez	Hebrews	He
Daniel	Da	James	Ja
Hosea	Ho	1 Peter	1 Pe
Joel	Jl	2 Peter	2 Pe
Amos	Am	1 John	1 Jn
Obadiah	Ob	2 John	2 Jn
Jonah	Jo	3 John	3 Jn
Micah	Mi	Jude	Ju
Nahum	Na	Revelation	Re

Ca is an abbreviation of *Canticles*, a derivative of the Latin name of the *Song of Solomon*, which is sometimes also called the *Song of Songs*.

ABOUT THESE BOOKS

This is one of a series of books which are available in two forms.

This format, which, contains all of the text, has been produced to provide a single study book

The second format is a series of 9 smaller booklets which cover each section separately.

The booklets are.

1. **The Way of Salvation**
2. **Jesus the Healer**
3. **The Power of Pentecost Today**
4. **Signs Wonders and Gifts**
5. **Law and Grace**
6. **How to Pray Successfully**
7. **The Amazing Power of Faith**
8. **Water Baptism and the Lord's Supper**
9. **Christ is Coming**

These booklets will be particularly useful for use in classes for new Christians.

Scripture references in this book are taken from the Holy Bible, New International Version (c) 1973, 1978 by the International Bible Society, used by permission of Zondervan Bible Publishers.

BOOK ONE:
THE WAY OF SALVATION

Introduction to Lesson One
Lesson One - **So Great Salvation**

Introduction to Lesson Two
Lesson Two - **Ye Must Be Born Again**

Introduction to Lesson Three
Lesson Three - **How Can We Be Born Again**

Introduction to Lesson Four
Lesson Four - **The Atonement Of Jesus Christ**

INTRODUCTION TO LESSON ONE

Newton the famous preacher and hymn writer of the 19th century was converted from a wicked and immoral life. He was a sailor and was involved in the slave trade. He gave his life to Christ during a violent storm when he despaired of any hope of rescue. He and his companions were saved just as the last of the food and water were being shared out. On shore Newton spent some time learning about his new faith and in preparing to receive communion. Some time later he sailed on another voyage and, being with his former companions, he gradually drifted away from his conversion. It was during this time he found he had no apparent strength to overcome sin.

Whenever temptation came along he would yield to it immediately. In the end, his state, if that could be possible, was worse than before. Finally he took sick with a fever, because of his immoral way of life, and lay at death's door. In desperation he cried out to God for forgiveness and mercy. After strong crying and many tears he came to a place of peace. He said that after this experience sin no longer had the same power over him. He went on to become one of the best loved pastors and hymn writers of his time.

In this first lesson we learn how Jesus has saved us from the PENALTY AND POWER of sin. Even though it is not possible for us to overcome sin on our own, Jesus has broken the power of sin for us. He has, as it were, taken away the weapons of the enemy.

> *"...and having disarmed the powers and authorities, he made a public spectacle of them, triumphing over them by the cross." Cl 2:15*

Remember each day to put on the whole armour of God that you might be able to stand against all the wiles (deceptions, tricks, enticements) of Satan. (Ep 6:10-18). Learn as much as you can of the Word of God, so that when Satan tempts you to sin you can quote Scripture as Jesus did. (Mt 4:1-11). With any temptation God has promised us a way of escape. Look for that way of escape that you might be able to stand un-ashamed in that great day when Jesus comes again. (1 Co 10:13).

We will also concentrate on the different aspects of salvation and what they mean to us in our daily lives.

SALVATION

This means -

    a. Deliverance from the power and effects of sin.

    b. Preservation from destruction or failure.

    c. Deliverance from danger or difficulty.

It is the first aspect of these that the Christian is most concerned with. We can be saved from drowning, or from a fire that is threatening our lives, by someone who is brave and resourceful, but only Jesus can save us from the power and effects of sin. He does this when we accept his sacrifice on Calvary for us. He not only frees us from all the sin we have committed in the past, but he also promises to free us from the power of sin in our lives. We need no longer feel helpless!

JUSTIFICATION

This means -

a. The act, process, or state of being justified by God.

b. Something that justifies.

When we are justified by God it simply means that he now looks on us as though we had never sinned. When he looks at us after we have received Jesus as our Saviour, he sees, not us, but Jesus. Someone once said to look at the word this way: JUST AS IF I'D NEVER SINNED. This is the meaning of justification. Remember, we are justified by faith, we simply have to believe what God says about us. (Ro 5:1).

SANCTIFICATION

This means -

a. The state of being sanctified.

b. The state of growing in divine grace as a result of Christian commitment after baptism or conversion.

While our standing before God is one of justification, we still have to go on living and developing as Christians, and this is where sanctification comes in. Our sanctification is a gradual changing and developing of our total being into the image of Jesus. It is the conscious setting apart of ourselves for the service of God. (Ro 12:1-2).

> *Rom 12:1 I therefore urge you, brothers, in view of God's mercies, to offer your bodies as living sacrifices, holy and pleasing to God, - this is your spiritual act of worship.*
>
> *Rom 12:2 Do not conform any longer to the pattern of this world, but be ye transformed by the renewing*

of your mind. Then you will be able to test and approve what God's will is-His good, pleasing, and perfect will.

LESSON ONE:
SO GREAT SALVATION

> *"...how shall we escape if we ignore such a great salvation?" He 2:3a*

WHAT IS SALVATION?

"Salvation" means being brought into a state of soundness and wholeness before God. It means coming into a place of safety: escaping the stormy winds of the wrath of heaven and entering into God's great harbor of mercy and kindness.

Salvation has three aspects:

- I am saved.
- I am being saved.
- I am about to be saved.

Or, to express it more fully ...

1. I am saved from the PENALTY of sin.

> *"...But because of his great love for us, God, who is rich in mercy, made us alive with Christ even when we were dead in transgressions - it is by grace you have been saved." Ep 2:4-5*

> *"...For the wages of sin is death, but the gift of God is eternal life in Christ Jesus our Lord." Ro 6:23*

This is the past tense of salvation, and speaks of completed freedom from condemnation for all those who have entered in and who have put their wholehearted faith in Christ as their Saviour.

2. I am being saved from the POWER of sin.

> *"...continue to work out your salvation with fear and trembling, for it is God who works in you to will and to act according to his good purpose." Ph 2:12b-13.*

> *"...Therefore, my brothers, be all the more eager to make your calling and election sure. For if you do these things, you will never fall, and you will receive a rich welcome into the eternal kingdom of our Lord and Saviour Jesus Christ." 2 Pe 1:10-11.*

This is the present tense of salvation, and speaks of the Christian entering more and more into victory over sin, and growing more and more like Christ.

3. I am about to be saved from the PRESENCE of sin.

> *"...But our citizenship is in heaven. And we eagerly await a Saviour from there, the Lord Jesus Christ, who, by the power that enables him to bring everything under his control, will transform our lowly bodies so that they will be like his glorious body." Ph 3:20-21.*

> *"...For God did not appoint us to suffer wrath but to receive salvation through our Lord Jesus Christ. He died for us so that, whether we are awake or asleep, we may live together with him." 1 Th 5:9-10.*

> *"...so Christ was sacrificed once to take away the sins of many people; and he will appear a second time, not be bear sin, but to bring salvation to those who are waiting for him." He 9:28.*

This is the future tense of salvation, and speaks of the great hope that lies before us, the second coming of Christ, the day of resurrection, and the immense reward waiting for those who have faithfully served their God.

Or we could express it this way ...

If I have accepted Christ as Saviour, and walk with him day by day, then ...

1. I have been delivered from all PAST sin - that is I am JUSTIFIED.

> *"...Therefore, my brothers, I want you to know that through Jesus the forgiveness of sins is proclaimed to you. Through him everyone who believes is justified from everything you could not be justified from by the law of Moses." Ac 13:38-39.*

> *"...Therefore, since we have been justified through faith, we have peace with God through our Lord Jesus Christ,..." Ro 5:1.*

JUSTIFICATION means that although we are guilty of gross sin and deserving of heavy punishment, God, by his own grace, has restored us to fellowship with him and reckons us to be just or righteous. Because of our trust in the atoning sacrifice of Christ, God has pardoned us of all our sin, accepts us as now being made righteous, and treats us as though we have never sinned.

2. I am being delivered from all PRESENT sin: that is, I am SANCTIFIED.

> *"...Finally, brothers, we instructed you how to live in order to please God, as in fact you are living. Now we ask you and urge you in the Lord Jesus to do this more and more. For you know what instructions we gave you by the authority of the Lord Jesus. It is God's will that you should be sanctified; that you should avoid sexual immorality; that each of you should learn to control his own body in a way that is holy and honourable,..."* 1 Th 4:1-4.

> *"...But we ought always to thank God for you, brothers loved by the Lord, because from the beginning God chose you to be saved through the sanctifying work of the Spirit and through belief in the truth."* 2 Th 2:13.

SANCTIFICATION means that although we stand legally before God as justified (released from all guilt of sin) there is still a need for us to be made actually free from the power of sin. Being justified, opportunity is then given us to separate ourselves from all unrighteousness and set ourselves apart for the service and honour of God. Whereas we are justified solely by the free kindness of God, on the basis of our faith in Christ, the work of sanctification involves the active co-operation of the believer. If we earnestly endeavour to sanctify ourselves, that is, to separate ourselves from sin, detaching our affections from the world and its defilements, and lifting them up to a supreme love for God, then we are said to be in a state of sanctification. In this state we are granted the omnipotent grace of God, the supreme power of the blood of Christ, the sharp edge of the Word of God, and the strong influence of the Holy Spirit, all designed to shatter the strength of sin, to loose the bonds that bind us, and to bring us into the glorious liberty of the sons of God!

3. I will be delivered from any PROSPECT of sin: that is, I will be GLORIFIED.

> *"...In his great mercy he has given us new birth into a living hope through the resurrection of Jesus Christ from the dead, and into an inheritance that can never perish, spoil or fade - kept in heaven for you, who through faith are shielded by God's power until the coming of the salvation that is ready to be revealed in the last time." 1 Pe 1:3b-5.*

> *"...Dear friends, now we are children of God, and what we will be has not yet been made known. But we know that when he appears, we shall be like him, for we shall see him as he is." 1 John 3:2*

In the kingdom of God sin will be no more ...

> *"...And I heard a loud voice from the throne saying, "Now the dwelling of God is with men, and he will live with them. They will be his people, and God himself will be with them and be their God. He will wipe every tear from their eyes. There will be no more death or mourning or crying or pain, for the old order of things has passed away." Re 21:3-4.*

Every Christian has a tremendous hope lying before him, a hope of honour, of reward, of eternal happiness. If we abide in Christ unto the end, then we can indeed say with Paul:

> *"...The Spirit Himself testifies with our spirit that*

we are God's children. Now if we are children, then we are heirs - heirs of God and co-heirs with Christ, if indeed we share in his sufferings in order that we may also share in his glory." Ro 8:16-18.

DEFINITION OF SALVATION

A simple definition covering the whole range of this threefold salvation would be - "Salvation embraces everything God provided for us by Jesus Christ's sacrifice at Calvary. It includes the mercy of God; adoption into the Father's family; forgiveness of all sin; victory over Satan's power; healing of body mind and spirit; a complete and free righteousness; abundant supply of every need; peace of heart and mind; a part in the resurrection; and a calling to reign as a prince with Christ when he establishes his kingdom."

Many of these outstanding benefits are considered elsewhere in these lessons, but here we are primarily concerned with the first feature, namely: I AM SAVED FROM THE PENALTY OF SIN.

This is the first fundamental. Our desperate need in the eyes of God makes it most urgently important that we should be saved from the penalty of sin. So we discover that the Bible declares every man to be ...

A DOOMED SINNER

"...for all have sinned and fall short of the glory of God." Ro 3:23.

"...For the wages of sin is death...." Ro 6:23a.

"...Therefore, just as sin entered the world through one man, and death through sin, and in this way death came to all men, because all sinned."

Ro 5:12.

ALIENATED FROM GOD

"...We all, like sheep, have gone astray, each of us has turned to his own way;" Is 53:6a.

"...But your iniquities have separated you from your God; your sins have hidden his face from you, so that he will not hear." Is 59:2.

LOST AND WITHOUT HOPE

"...There is no one righteous, not even one; there is no one who understands, no one who seeks God. All have turned away, they have together become worthless; there is no one who does good, not even one." Ro 3:10-12.

"...The wrath of God is being revealed from heaven against all the godlessness and wickedness of men who suppress the truth by their wickedness." Ro 1:18.

IN SPIRITUAL DARKNESS

"...For from within, out of men's hearts, come evil thoughts, sexual immorality, theft, murder, adultery, greed, malice, deceit, lewdness, envy, slander, arrogance and folly. All these evils come from inside and make a man unclean." Mi 7:21-23.

It is also true that:

"...The man without the Spirit does not accept the

> *things that come from the Spirit of God, for they are foolishness to him, and he cannot understand them, because they are spiritually discerned." 1 Co 2:14.*

These things all clearly indicate the utter inability of man to break through the power of sin by himself. It is impossible for anyone to shake himself free from the result of his sin. This desperate situation demanded that God should either wipe out the whole human race or else work out a way of salvation whereby man could be completely recreated. In his immense love the Father chose the second alternative, and so we read -

> *"...For God so loved the world that he gave his one and only Son, that whoever believes in him shall not perish but have eternal life. For God did not send his Son into the world to condemn the world, but to save the world through him." Jo 3:16-17.*

So Jesus came that we, who are already born into sin, might be born again into the kingdom and righteousness of God; so the Lord said -

> *..."I tell you the truth, no one can see the kingdom of God unless he is born again." Jo 3:3.*

INTRODUCTION TO LESSON TWO

It is not enough to believe in the 'new birth' or in being 'born again'. We must have a personal relationship with Jesus Christ. Being 'born again' is not just believing the facts that are expressed in the Word of God. It is getting to know the Lord Jesus Christ. Christianity not only consists in believing in something, but in receiving someone! Your Christian experience will not mean much to you if it is just a matter of mental assent to the Word of God. You must have an experience with God and come into a personal relationship with Jesus.

When you have done that, by believing in your heart and confessing with your mouth, (Ro 10:9-10), then you must continue to have fellowship with the Lord every day. This will keep your experience alive. It is very hard to carry on a relationship with someone to whom we do not speak and to whom we do not listen. If we tried the relationship would eventually die.

In this lesson we learn about Nicodemus and his search for the truth. He was a Pharisee and a member of the Sanhedrin. The Pharisees were one of the most important of the Jewish sects. The name Pharisee is thought to come from the HEBREW word meaning 'separatist'.[1] If this is the true meaning it would explain why the Pharisees were given this name, because in practice they did keep themselves separate from everyone. They believed in life after death, in contrast to the Sadducees, who did not.

The Sanhedrin to which Nicodemus belonged was the Jewish council of supreme authority which met in Jerusalem. The

---

[1] Zondervan' Pictorial Encyclopedia

Sanhedrin is also referred to in the New Testament as the 'Council of Elders'. See Lu 22:6 and Ac 22:5.

The main argument of this lesson is that Jesus Christ is the only way of Salvation. When Peter spoke to: "the rulers, elders, and teachers of the law, along with Annas, Caiaphas, John, Alexander and the other members of the High Priest's family," he spoke boldly about Jesus:

> *"...Salvation is found in no one else, for there is no other name under heaven given to men by which we must be saved." Ac 4:12.*

And again Paul confirms this in his letter to Timothy:

> *"...For there is one God and one mediator between God and men, the man Christ Jesus," 1 Ti 2:5.*

We must come to God through Jesus, there is no other way.

LESSON TWO:
YOU MUST BE BORN AGAIN

Following on from the previous lesson we ask ...

WHAT IS THE NEW BIRTH?

This may best be answered by stating firstly what it is not! It is obvious from the Word of God that being born again does not mean a mere reformation, turning over a new leaf. Nor is the new birth found in baptism, nor in the dedication of infants, nor in church membership. A person can be a church member all his life and yet not be born again! This can be illustrated by one of the best known stories in the entire Bible, the visit of Nicodemus to Jesus late one night. See Jn 3:1-9.

Nicodemus was a Pharisee. He was one of the rulers of the Jews, a man who was rich and powerful, a member of the great Sanhedrin which was the supreme judicial body in ancient Jewry. Jesus called him 'a master' of Israel. He was a brilliant, gifted man, a counsellor whose ministry and wisdom was widely sought.

As one of the leading teachers in Israel, he had a thorough grasp of the Scriptures. Nicodemus knew the Old Testament prophecies. He believed the Scripture to be inspired and, from the prophecies, he knew that the time for the Messiah's birth was already past. He knew that the Messiah should now be a grown man; and he wondered if Jesus of Nazareth was indeed the Christ, the Messiah sent from God as so many people acclaimed him.

Nicodemus was determined to find out the truth, so he made diligent inquiries, discovering when he could find Jesus alone, and went to see him late one night.

He came to the Lord Jesus Christ with his brilliant mind, his strong logic, and began to reason with the Lord:

> *"...Rabbi, we know you are a teacher who has come from God. For no one could perform the miraculous signs you are doing if God were not with him." Jn 3:2.*

But before Nicodemus could go any further into his argument with the Lord, Jesus interrupted him and struck home to the real need in the life of this great man. Bluntly, forcefully, Jesus said to Nicodemus:

> *"...No one can see the Kingdom of God unless his is born again." Jn 3:3*

At no time did Jesus speak words that were more arresting then these, especially when we see them in the light of the man against whom they were thrust ...

- He was a ruler
- He was rich
- He was a great preacher
- He was active in religious affairs
- He believed in the Scripture
- He respected Jesus

YET HE WAS NOT SAVED

CHURCHIANITY IS NOT CHRISTIANITY

It is the same today: people are relying on their social standing, or their Bible knowledge, or their respect for God, or their church activities, to bring them eternal life. But the Bible says that:

> *"...All of us have become like one who is unclean, and all our righteous acts are like filthy rags; we all shrivel up like a leaf, and like the wind our sins sweep us away." Is 64:6.*

It is impossible for the natural man to do anything pleasing in the sight of God; all our self-activities are stained by sin and made unpleasant to the Lord. No man by his own self-effort or good works can gain the kingdom of God. Salvation, eternal life, entrance into the kingdom of God, can be gained only by faith in Christ. So we discover in the following references.

THE ONLY WAY TO SALVATION

> *"...Through him every one who believes is justified from everything you could not be justified from by the law of Moses." Ac 13:39.*

> *"...Therefore no one will be declared righteous in his sight by observing the law; rather, through the law we become conscious of sin." Ro 3:20.*

> *"...For we maintain that a man is justified by faith apart from observing the law." Ro 3:28.*

> *"...For it is by grace you have been saved, through faith and this not from yourselves, it is the gift of God - not by works, so that no one can boast." Ep 2:8-9.*

> "...God, who has saved us and called us to a holy life - not because of anything we have done but because of his own purpose and grace. This grace was given us in Christ Jesus before the beginning of time,..." 2 Ti 1:9.

> "...At one time we too were foolish, disobedient, deceived, and enslaved by all kinds of passions and pleasures. We lived in malice and envy, being hated and hating one another. But when the kindness and love of God our Saviour appeared, he saved us, not because of righteous things we had done, but because of his mercy. He saved us through the washing of rebirth and renewal by the Holy Spirit whom he poured out on us generously through Jesus Christ our Saviour, so that, having been justified by his grace, we might become heirs having the hope of eternal life." Tit 3:3-7.

We conclude that salvation, the experience of the new birth, is not something which a man, of his own will, can produce within himself: far from it - the new birth is a divinely wrought change of heart making one a new creation in Christ.

So we read -

> "...Therefore, if anyone is in Christ, he is a new creation; the old has gone, the new has come!" 2 Co 5:17.

THE URGENCY OF THE NEW BIRTH

Returning to the story of Nicodemus we can easily see the vast importance of being truly saved by faith in Christ alone. See Jn 3:5-7

Jesus said:

> "...I tell you the truth no one can enter the Kingdom of God unless he is born of water and the Spirit."

and again:

> "...You should not be surprised at my saying, 'You must be born again"

Then Jesus laid down the reason for this strong injunction: and it is this -

> "...flesh gives birth to flesh, but the Spirit gives birth to spirit." Jn 3:5-7

Across the ages of human history man has ever chosen the way of the flesh, not the way of the Spirit of God. Adam and Eve chose the fleshy tree of knowledge rather than the tree of life. So God was compelled to pronounce the sentence of death upon them. Adam was made 'a living soul' but when he fell the Lord said to him,

> "...for dust you are and to dust you will return." Ge 3:19b.

This judgment has passed down upon the whole human race. And now the scripture says:

> "...The man without the Spirit does not accept the things that come from the Spirit of God, for they are foolishness to him, and he cannot understand them, because they are spiritually discerned." 1 Co 2:14.

> "...I declare to you, brothers, that flesh and blood

> *cannot inherit the kingdom of God, nor does the perishable inherit the imperishable." 1 Co 15:50.*

> *"...God is Spirit, and his worshipers must worship in spirit and truth." Jn 4:24.*

Only Christ can lift us from the dust of mortal life into the eternal reality of the kingdom of God.

So we see the absolute necessity for a man to be born again. It is only by the new birth that we can receive spiritual life, and so enter the kingdom of God. This spiritual life can only be received as we believe in the Lord Jesus Christ and are born from above by the Holy Spirit, born into the heavenly realm just as surely as we were once born into the earthly realm.

WHAT IS THE NATURE OF THE NEW BIRTH?

The words of the Lord Jesus Christ to Nicodemus show that regeneration is the spiritual counterpart of our natural birth. The Master said, 'You must be born again!'

Now Nicodemus heard these words and immediately he saw their implication. He changed his whole line of approach to the Master, and in earnest inquiry asked the Lord a question and then used an illustration to enforce his question. He asked the Lord,

> *"...How can a man be born when he is old?" Jn 3:4a.*

Then he illustrated it by saying to the Lord,

> *"...Surely he cannot enter a second time into his mother's womb to be born!" Jn 3:4b.*

This is what Nicodemus meant. He saw that Jesus said a man's whole life had to be changed, that he had to become like a new born child; but Nicodemus asked, 'How can a man be born when he is old? How can his whole life start again? How can the past be eradicated? How can he change the habits and the way of life which have been formed over the years.'

This great man saw the startling significance of Jesus' words. With all his heart he longed that it might be so, but yet he asked how could it possibly be?

Now Jesus answered Nicodemus' query in two ways.

Firstly he stated the fact again and he told Nicodemus that, while no man could understand the mystery of the new birth, ALL MEN COULD FEEL ITS POWER. So Jesus said again to Nicodemus:

> *"...I tell you the truth, no one can enter the Kingdom of God unless he is born of water and the Spirit." Jn 3:5.*

Despite its mystery, the fact is clearly established by the Lord that no person can enter the kingdom of God unless they are first born again.

Secondly, Jesus confirmed the mystery and power of the new birth by an illustration of his own. He said,

> *"...The wind blows wherever it pleases. You hear its sound, but you cannot tell where it comes from or where it is going. So it is with everyone born of the Spirit." Jn 3:8.*

With all their vast knowledge, men today still do not really understand the way of the winds. No man knows exactly where the wind comes from, nor where it will go. But while men do not understand the winds, they nevertheless feel the force of the wind and use its power in countless ways - to pump their water, to drive their ships across the lakes and oceans, to cool their homes.

So it is with the new birth. No one is able to understand it, but all who will may experience its power to radically change the whole life, to blot out the memory of the past, to give a man or woman a new start in life.

In speaking of being born of 'water and of the Spirit' Christ was contrasting our first birth from a human mother with the new birth from above. By the one we are born into the realm of the flesh, by the other into the realm of the Spirit. 'Born of water' may also have reference to the vital part the Word of God has in our regeneration.

So we read -

> *"...You are already clean because of the word I have spoken to you." Jn 15:3.*
>
> *"...Christ loved the church and gave himself up for her to make her holy, cleansing her by the washing with water through the word." Ep 5:25b-26.*
>
> *"...He saved us through the washing of rebirth and renewal by the Holy Spirit." Tit 3:5.*

In the three phrases emphasised we plainly see the thought of Jesus re-expressed:-

'born of water', (washing of regeneration) and 'born of the Spirit', (re-newing of the Holy Spirit). Together bringing to the life of the believer an abundant salvation.

INTRODUCTION TO LESSON THREE

Are you content with your Christian life as it is? Are you quite sure that you have had a genuine experience of salvation? If so, are you satisfied with the depth of your experience, or do you feel that you would like a deeper, more satisfying relationship with the Lord?

Has your faith been any more than just a mental assent to the words of scripture? Have you just been following in the footsteps of your peer group, or your family, or have you worked out what you believe? Can you say with Paul the Apostle,

> *"I know whom I have believed, and am convinced that he is able to guard what I have entrusted to him for that day." 2 Ti 1:12b.*

If you can say, 'Yes, I do believe, I have accepted Jesus as my own personal Saviour, and I have told some of my friends and family of my experience. I know what I believe, and why I believe it, and I know who it is that I believe in; Jesus Christ my Saviour and Lord.' Then you can be sure that Jesus has also confessed that you are his before his Father in heaven, and that the angels have rejoiced over your decision.

In this third lesson we learn who Jesus is, why he had to die, and what it means to believe. We also discover the benefits of believing.

Remember, to keep the joy of your salvation fresh and vital, it is necessary to acknowledge Jesus, not only as your Saviour, but as your Lord. Because of this it is necessary to be obedient to him each day, following in his steps, and obeying the scripture that he lays on your heart. As Jesus was obedient to the Father, so we must be also. This is the secret to a happy Christian life.

Do not think that you have to choose, between God's will for your life, and happiness.

Nothing could be further from the truth. It is as you are obedient to the Father's will that you find true happiness.

LESSON THREE:
HOW CAN WE BE BORN AGAIN?

1. HOW IS THE NEW BIRTH GAINED?

To Nicodemus, the rich preacher who was yet unsaved, Jesus said,

> *"...You must be born again."*

Then he told Nicodemus how he could be born again:

> *"...Just as Moses lifted up the snake in the desert, so the Son of Man must be lifted up, that everyone who believes in him may have eternal life." Jn 3:14-15.*

Jesus was the Son of man and he was lifted up on the cross to die for your sins that you might believe in him and not perish. He did this because God loves you; and so Jesus went on to say,

> *"...For God so loved the world that he gave his one and only Son, that whoever believes in him shall not perish but have eternal life." Jn 3:16.*

Still further Jesus declared that he had not come into the world to judge it or to destroy it; he came to bring abundant life -

> *"...For God did not send his Son into the world to condemn the world, but to save the world through him." Jn 3:17.*

On the other hand, if any man or woman fails to believe on the Lord Jesus Christ they will have to face him when he returns to this earth; and when he comes again it will be to judge, not to save.

So with all solemnity the Master said,

> "...Whoever believes in him is not condemned, but whoever does not believe stands condemned already because he has not believed in the name of God's one and only Son." Jn 3:18.

But for you today Jesus Christ has been lifted up, forgiveness of all your sins is freely offered. You may still be young in years, but it makes no difference - you need to be born again.

And though you may be old, you can be born again. The record of the past, the stain of the past, the domination of the past can all be taken from you. You can begin a more abundant life if you will believe in the Lord Jesus Christ.

So we read -

> "...for there is no other name under heaven given to men by which we must be saved." Ac 4:12b.

And again -

> "...Yet to all who received him to those who believed in his name, he gave the right to become the children of God." Jn 1:12.

> "...If you confess with your mouth, 'Jesus is Lord', and believe in your heart that God raised him from the dead, you will be saved." Ro 10:9.

2. WHO IS THE SAVIOUR WHO HAS SECURED FOR US THIS GREAT SALVATION?

His name is Jesus -

> *"...And you are to give him the name Jesus, because he will save his people from their sins."* Mt 1:21b.

He is the eternal son of God.

> *"...He is the image of the invisible God, the first born over all creation. For by him all things were created; things in heaven and on earth...all things were created by him and for him...and through him to reconcile to himself all things...by making peace through his blood, shed on the cross."* Cl 1:15-20.

He came to bear away the sins of the world.

> *"...Look, the Lamb of God, who takes away the sin of the world!"* Jn 1:29b.

> *"...Here is a trustworthy saying that deserves full acceptance: Christ Jesus came into the world to save sinners."* I Ti 1:15.

He took the punishment that should have fallen on us, and died in our place on the cross.

> *"...You see, at just the right time, when we were still powerless, Christ died for the ungodly...God demonstrates his own love for us in this: While we were still sinners, Christ died for us."* Ro 5:6,8.

> *"...He himself bore our sins in his body on the tree, so that we might die to sins and live for righteousness; by his wounds you have been healed."* 1 Pe 2:24.

He poured out his life's blood that we might be washed clean of every mark of sin.

> *"...and without the shedding of blood there is no forgiveness... He 9:22b*
>
> *...But now he has appeared once for all at the end of the ages to do away with sin by the sacrifice of himself." He 9: 26b.*
>
> *"...For you know that it was not with perishable things,..." 1 Pe 1:18a*
>
> *...but with the precious blood of Christ." 1 Pe 1:19a*
>
> *"...The blood of Jesus, his Son, purifies us from all sin." 1 Jn 1:7b.*

He rose from the dead after three days. And thus forever broke the power of sin and of death, providing sure hope of resurrection and eternal life for all who believe in him.

3. HOW DO WE COME TO KNOW THE LORD JESUS CHRIST AND BE 'BORN AGAIN'?

By the scriptures! For they testify or tell of Jesus Christ.

> *"...These are the scriptures that testify about me," Jn 5:39b.*

So we read -

> *"...every good and perfect gift is from above, coming down from the Father of heavenly lights,*

> *who does not change like shifting shadows. He chose to give us birth through the word of truth, that we might be a kind of first fruits of all he created." Ja 1:17-18.*

And again the powerful words of Peter -

> *"...For you have been born again, not of perishable seed, but of imperishable, through the living and enduring word of God. For, 'all men are like grass, and all their glory is like the flowers of the field; The grass withers and the flowers fall, but the word of the Lord stands for ever' And this is the word that was preached to you." I Pe 1:23-25.*

4. WHAT DOES IT MEAN TO BELIEVE?

Firstly, the word translated 'believe' in the New Testament means much more than to give a mere mental assent to the truth. It means to RELY UPON, to ADHERE TO, or to COMMIT ONESELF TO. Believe, as the New Testament uses the word, means much more than a head knowledge. It is a heart knowledge. It means committing oneself wholeheartedly, unreservedly, to what is believed. It means 'burning your bridges behind you' and acting your faith in the promises of God.

Because many people do not understand what it means to believe in the Bible way, they go on hoping for salvation, yet never arriving at a definite experience and never receiving the assurance of their salvation.

Secondly, we must CONFESS our faith in Jesus Christ. As we put our faith into words and declare before men that we believe in the Lord Jesus Christ, our faith is crystallised. After all Jesus said -

> *"...For out of the overflow of his heart his mouth speaks." Lu 6:45.*

Sooner or later, we express with our mouths what we really believe in our hearts.

If you definitely believe in God's promises of salvation, and you confess with your mouth that Jesus Christ is your Lord and Saviour, the Bible declares that you are saved. Jesus said -

> *"...Whoever acknowledges me before men, I will also acknowledge him before my Father in heaven. But whoever disowns me before men, I will disown him before my Father in heaven." Mt 10:32-33.*

5. WHAT ARE WE TO BELIEVE AND CONFESS

The texts we have quoted have answered that question for us. No church can save us and no man can save us. We are saved by Jesus Christ alone. Therefore it is Jesus Christ on whom we must believe and whom we must confess. Jesus Christ died for our sins, taking our guilt upon himself. After three days he was raised from the dead and received back into the presence of God. He did not do this for himself: he had no sins of his own for which to die; it was as our substitute that he suffered and 'poured out his life unto death'. (Is 53:12).

Therefore repenting of our sins, we turn to Jesus Christ and trust in him as our only Saviour. We confess our faith that he was our sin-bearer, who died in our stead, rose again for our justification, and ever lives to keep us by his power.

WE CAN BE SAVED AND KNOW IT, free from every disturbing doubt and fear. We must come the Bible way, and enjoy a Bible salvation through faith in the Lord Jesus Christ. If you have not already settled this question then it is imperative that you do so without delay: it is urgent for only this moment is yours.

We are warned,

> "...Do not boast about tomorrow, for you do not know what a day may bring forth." Pr 27:1.

> "...I tell you, now is the time for God's favour, now is the day of salvation." 2 Co 6:2b.

6. WHAT ARE THE BENEFITS OF THE NEW BIRTH?

If any man will sincerely repent of his sin, turn back to God, wholeheartedly believe scripture, and place his utmost faith in Jesus Christ as personal Saviour, then God has promised that the Holy Spirit will work a mighty work of salvation in that man.

The benefits of this great salvation are described in the following terms -

His sins, though they were as scarlet, will be utterly removed and he will have peace as a quiet river; all things will become new; he will know that he has eternal life; he will be a member of God's family; he will have joy unspeakable and full of glory; he will have the witness of God's Spirit that he is born of God.

So we read -

> "...The Spirit himself testifies with our spirit that we are God's children." Ro 8:16.

Being born of God and becoming a member of God's family, we are born into the inheritance of that family, an inheritance splendid beyond all imagination.

> "...since you are a son, God has make you also an heir." Ga 4:7b.

and again -

> "...I consider that our present sufferings are not worth comparing with the glory that will be revealed in us." Ro 8:18 (See also 2 Co 4:17-18; 1 Pe 1:3-5).

To conclude this lesson we can do no better than quote the powerful words of John -

> "...Anyone who believes in the Son of God has this testimony in his heart. Anyone who does not believe God has made him out to be a liar, because he has not believed the testimony God has given about his Son. And this is the testimony: God has given us eternal life, and this life is in his Son. He who has the Son has life; he who does not have the Son of God does not have life." 1 Jn 5:10-13.

INTRODUCTION TO LESSON FOUR

There have been many great and honourable men who have given everything to serve their Lord and Saviour, Jesus Christ of Nazareth.

One of these was David Livingstone, that great missionary explorer of the 19th century, a man who suffered greatly to bring the message of salvation to the African nations. Listen to this description of him by Stanley:

"His gentleness never forsakes him; his hopefulness never deserts him. No harassing anxieties, distraction of mind, long separation from home and kindred can make him complain. He thinks 'all will come right at last;' he has such faith in the goodness of Providence[2]

Another great man of God, Father Damien, a Belgian priest, lived among the lepers in Molokai. He built them a church, which they loved, he built them houses, he nursed them, he dressed their dreadful wounds, he comforted them when they were dying and he dug graves for them when they were dead. One day he realised that he too had contracted leprosy but he would not leave his people to seek medical help. He remained in Molodai, continuing his ministry, until death finally overcame him. He was only 48 years of age when he died.

But there has never been any one who suffered as Jesus suffered. We cannot comprehend what it meant to him to leave the brightness of heaven for this sinful earth and to suffer such a

---

[2] David Livingstone, "His Life and Letters", George Seaver Copyright 1957, Harper & Brothers N.Y.

dreadful death as Calvary must have been. Apart from his physical suffering, he endured the incredible agony of separation from his Father during those last agonising moments on the cross. This is something that we cannot even begin to understand.

All this to offer himself in our place, to make atonement for us. He has restored us to favour with God and we did not have to do anything to deserve it. There was nothing we could do. It is hard for us as human beings to accept what Jesus did for us and not attempt to add to his sacrifice by trying to do something toward our own salvation.

We cannot! We must not try! It must all be from God the Father and from Jesus the Son. "Nothing in my hand I bring, Simply to thy cross I cling." [3]

The hymn writer of long ago understood the secret of acceptance without reservation yet still people everywhere are attempting to assist God in their own redemption. There is nothing you can do toward your salvation! Simply accept the sacrifice and rejoice in it. In this way you will enter in and receive forgiveness.

In this fourth lesson we will study "Atonement", (satisfaction given for wrong doing or injury: Webster's Dictionary), and what it meant to Jesus and to God the Father.

---

[3] "Rock of Ages Cleft For Me" A.M. Toplady

LESSON FOUR:
THE ATONEMENT OF JESUS CHRIST

Calvary stands central in the Bible.

The cross is the focal point of divine revelation, the pivot around which all Christian experience revolves.

At Golgotha Jesus died to make atonement for the whole sin of the whole world. Had Jesus Christ not died we would have remained eternal enemies of God, but in his death reconciliation (or atonement) was made, so that you and I could be at peace with God.

Jesus was born that he might die. He died that he might redeem us from the slavery of sin. His whole life was given over to this tremendous purpose. The work of redemption began with his birth and was finally accomplished at his ascension into heaven where he now reigns in glory, seated on the right hand of the Majesty on high.

Jesus Christ wrought out this great salvation then, in four stages -

1. By His HUMILIATION:

> *"...Who, being in very nature God, did not consider equality with God something to be grasped, but made himself nothing, taking the very nature of a servant, being made in human likeness. And being found in appearance as a man, he humbled himself and became obedient to death- even death on a cross!" Ph 2:5-8.*

2. By His OBEDIENT LIFE:

> "...For just as through the disobedience of the one man the many were made sinners, so also through the obedience of the one man the many will be made righteous." Ro 5:19.

3. By His SUFFERING And DEATH On The Cross:

> "...By his wounds you have been healed." 1 Pe 2:24B

> "...In him we have redemption through his blood, the forgiveness of sins." Ep 1:7a

4. By His RESURRECTION, ASCENSION And INTERCESSION Before God:

> "...Therefore his is able to save completely those who come to God through him, because he always lives to intercede for them." He 7:25.

In this lesson we are especially concerned with the central part of this drama of redemption, that is the atonement for sin made by Jesus Christ in his sufferings and death on the cross.

THE MEANING OF ATONEMENT:

Basically the word 'atonement' means to 'make at one with', that is, to restore to favour, to reconcile, to appease. In describing the outworking of atonement the Bible uses a number of terms such as - sacrifice, ransom, redemption, propitiation, reconciliation, pardon, disannul, and so on.

All of these expressions forcibly convey the thought of estrangement between heaven and earth. What has caused this separation? On man's side, it is the direct consequence of his sin. On God's side, it is the direct consequence of his holiness. Because he is holy, God cannot be indifferent to sin, his wrath must rest upon the disobedient.

But moving against all this is the love of God: His eternal compassion which leads him to draw close to man and to want to rid man of his sin and of the penalty of his sin. Thus it was that the Lord devised a means of atonement which would be no means condone sin but sufficiently punish it, permitting the sinner to go free.

This atonement was finally made by the Lord Jesus Christ on the cross, but it was prefigured for many centuries on the blood-stained altars of ancient Israel.

SACRIFICE OLD AND NEW

THE OLD TESTAMENT SACRIFICES

The most important celebration in the calendar of ancient Israel was the great Day of Atonement. On this day the High Priest made atonement for the sins of the people. He took two goats, and presented them before the Lord in the presence of the whole congregation. One goat was chosen by lot to be a sin-offering; this was known as the offering 'for the Lord'; the other was named the 'scape-goat'. In choosing the goats himself the Lord demonstrated his unalienable right to set forth the proper sacrifice for sin. This God did when he chose Jesus Christ as a ransom for the whole world, and none may choose another Saviour. Then the goat for the sin-offering was killed, and its blood sprinkled around the sanctuary. During these ministrations, no man save the High Priest was permitted to enter the tabernacle. So also Jesus stood alone when he sacrificed his own life and made atonement for your sins and mine: he said -

> "...I have trodden the wine press alone, from the nations no one was with me." Is 63:3a.

> "...After he had provided purification for sins, he sat down at the right hand of the Majesty in heaven." He 1:3b.

SIN AND ITS PENALTY REMOVED

The first goat took away the penalty of sin. It suffered death in place of the people. Then the second goat was brought forward. In type, this goat would take away the sins of Israel. The High Priest put both his hands on the head of the scape-goat, confessed over it all the wickedness of the people, and then called upon a 'fit man' to lead the goat away into the wilderness.

> "...The goat will carry on itself all their sins to a solitary place; and the man shall release it in the desert." Le 16:22.

Here, terrified and alone, the poor animal soon perished at the claw of some wild beast.

As the goat was sent into the wilderness, so Jesus went 'outside the camp' and was crucified and buried 'in a solitary place'. In this, he too carried our sins far away:

> "...as far as the east is from the west, so far has he removed our transgressions from us." Ps 103:12.

> "...You will again have compassion on us; you will tread our sins underfoot and hurl all our iniquities

into the depths of the sea." Mi 7:19.

There are many laws concerning the sacrifices the people were to make in atonement for their sins. All of them involved the suffering, death and blood of the intended victim. When offered correctly the Old Testament sacrifices involved -

- An awareness of sin on the part of the worshipper.
- Bringing a victim to atone for that sin.
- Laying of the hand of the offerer upon the victim's head.
- Confession of sin by the offerer.
- Slaying the beast.
- Sprinkling or pouring the blood upon the altar.
- The consequent forgiveness of sin and acceptance of the worshipper.

We may say that these old sacrifices were:

- By divine appointment.
- To satisfy the command of God that sin be punished.
- The substitution of the innocent victim to bear the deserved suffering, death and sin of the guilty one, so that the offender might go free.

However it is

"...because it is impossible for the blood of bulls and goats to take away sins." He 10:4.

There is a vast difference between the value of a man and the value of a beast. Therefore, all of these old sacrifices were only types or shadows, just symbols of the one perfect sacrifice which was finally to be made of Jesus Christ. In the life blood of Jesus there is a value beyond all human measure -

> *"...For you know that it was not with perishable things such as silver or gold that you were redeemed from the empty way of life handed down to you from your fore-fathers, but with the precious blood of Christ, a lamb without blemish or defect. He was chosen before the creation of the world, but was revealed in these last times for your sake." I Pe :18-20.*

THE SACRIFICE OF JESUS CHRIST

Just how desperately we each one need an atoning sacrifice, unless we are to die in our sins, is shown by these verses:

> *"...For all have sinned and fall short of the glory of God." Ro 3:23*
>
> *"...There is no one righteous not even one." Ro 3:10*
>
> *"...The wages of sin is death but the gift of God is eternal life." Ro 6:23a.*

What is sin? How sorely has it gripped us?

Sin is lawlessness. It is the refusal on man's part to remain in subjection to the law of God. And, beyond question, we have all shared in this refusal, in fact, a spirit of disobedience seems to be ingrained in our very nature. Each act of sin causes us to be separated from God. In fact each act of sin widens the gulf further. For each act of sin weakens the will, and makes a man the increasing slave of his sin. And each act of sin brings fresh guilt and so adds new terror to the curse of the law; it deepens a man's defilement, and so makes him shrink away from the presence of God.

The end of sin is always death.

But Jesus Christ who was innocent, took our sin on himself so that we who were guilty might be set free.

> *"...God made him who had no sin to be sin for us, so that in him we might become the righteousness of God." 2 Co 5:21.*

THE COST OF CALVARY

The cost of the atonement is represented from two sides. Firstly as it affected the Father, who

> *"...did not spare his own Son, but gave him up for us all." Ro 8:32*

and secondly, as it affected the Son, who suffered for you

> *"...By his wounds you have been healed." 1 Pe 2:24b.*

1. The Cost to The FATHER

It is impossible for us to conceive what infinite sorrow the humiliation and pain of Jesus must have caused the Father. The Bible maintains a reverent and perfect silence concerning this greatest agony of eternity. The Father's anguish is lost in his own heart, submerged beneath the overwhelming love and compassion for fallen man that caused him to drive Jesus to the cross with all its horror and pain.

2. The Cost to The SON

   a.   He suffered in his body.

The sufferings of Jesus in the flesh were human sufferings. We are able to understand them - at least in some measure.

The agonies he endured at Calvary were a direct result of his open acceptance of all the consequences that fall on us as a result of our sin.

His pain culminated, on the one side, in an agonising and shameful death. On the other side, and more sharply, he sank into a fathomable depth of spiritual suffering. The Father turned away from the awful sight. And gathered into his own breast all the despair of all men. The victim cried out:

> *"...My God, my God, why have you forsaken me?"*
> *Mk 15:34b*

> *"...he poured out his soul unto death..." Is 53:12b*

dying such a death as no man has ever died -

> *"...Who gave himself as a ransom for all men..."*
> *1 Ti 2:6a.*

   b.   He sacrificed his blood.

Peter said that we are redeemed by his 'precious blood'. The word precious has two meanings:

   1. Of great cost to purchase.

   2. Of great value to the owner.

So we have: -

The precious blood - that is, the blood of Jesus, the Son of God, the eternal

> *"...Lamb of God, who takes away the sin of the world!" Jn 1:29b*

This is the blood that

> *"...speaks a better word than the blood of Abel." He 12:24b*

The cry of Abel's blood caused God to work for it - in judgment upon Cain. How much more will the cry of Jesus' blood cause God to work for us in unlimited blessing.

It is the blood that speaks better things than did that of bulls and goats. Think of this for a moment. The dollar value of the hundreds of thousands of animals and birds that were slain on Israel's altars over fifteen centuries must have totalled untold millions.

But this is like a child's penny set alongside the treasures of a great kingdom when compared with the cost and value of the blood of Jesus.

His blood was of great cost - the wealth of the entire universe could not be measured against it. (He 1:2-3, 10-12). The heavens and the earth, the whole sweep of the skies, every mountain and valley, were all fashioned by his hand: and the day is coming when he will fold them all up as an old garment, and cast them aside. Yet he gave his life to save us who live as the small dust of the balance on our tiny earth: and more than that, he became himself a man despised, small in the eyes of the world.

His blood was of great value - it is of great value to us -

Firstly, because it is a love gift, freely given and greatly treasured.

> *"...Come, all you who are thirsty, come to the waters; and you who have no money, come, buy and eat! Come, buy wine and milk without money and without cost. Why spend money on what is not bread, and your labour on what does not satisfy? Listen, listen to me, and eat what is good, and your soul will delight in the richest of fare." Is 55:1-2.*

Secondly, because once gained, and then lost, it can never be recovered.

> *"...Anyone who rejected the law of Moses died without mercy on the testimony of two or three witnesses. How much more severely do you think a man deserved to be punished who has trampled the Son of God underfoot, who has treated as an unholy thing the blood of the covenant that sanctified him, and who has insulted the Spirit of grace." He 10:28-31.*

Thirdly, because of the great things it achieves on our behalf.

> *"...The blood of goats and bulls and the ashes of a heifer sprinkled on those who are ceremonially unclean sanctify them so that they are outwardly clean. How much more, then will the blood of Christ, who through the eternal Spirit offered himself unblemished to God, cleanse our consciences from acts that lead to death, so that we may serve the living God!" He 9:13-14.*

"...Just as man is destined to die once, and after that to face judgment, so Christ was sacrificed once to take away the sins of many people; and he will appear a second time, not to bear sin, but to bring salvation to those who are waiting for him." He 9:27-28.

BOOK TWO: JESUS THE HEALER

Introduction to Lesson One
Lesson One - **Authority For Divine Healing**

Introduction to Lesson Two
Lesson Two - **Healing In The Atonement**

Introduction to Lesson Three
Lesson Three - **Divine Deliverance**

INTRODUCTION TO LESSON ONE

Down through the ages there have been many great men of God who have experienced healing and who have believed it to be God's will to heal the sick.

John Wesley, the founder of Methodism, had tuberculosis at the age of 27; he had it for eleven years. When he was in the third stage of this dreadful disease God miraculously healed him over a period of three months.[4] John Wesley was certainly and permanently healed as this testimony of his life shows!

1. He traveled 250,000 miles on horseback, averaging 20 miles per day for 40 years.

2. He preached 40,000 sermons and produced hundreds of books: he knew ten languages.

3. At the age of 83 he was concerned that he could not write more than 15 hours a day without hurting his eyes and was ashamed he could not preach more than twice a day. He noted at this time in his journal that there was an increasing tendency to lie late in bed in the morning - until 5:30 a.m. (J. Boyd Nicholson).

What can we do as Christians to help produce a climate of faith which will see God moving in healings and miracles?

---

[4] "Healing Rays", George Jeffreys. Henry E. Walter LTD., London. Third Ed., 1932. This ref. Pg. 71.

1. We can encourage our faith by reading of the healings and miracles in God's Word. This will produce faith.

2. We can look back to our fore-fathers in the faith and read of their miraculous healings and deliverances.

3. We can confess who we are in Christ, and what God has wrought for us by thesacrifice of Jesus.

4. We can spend time in communion and prayer with God.

In this next study we begin to learn about the healing ministry.

LESSON ONE:
AUTHORITY FOR DIVINE HEALING

DIVINE HEALING IN THE OLD TESTAMENT:

GOD AS CREATOR

The Lord God is the creator of the heavens and the earth, and of all that inhabits them. He made man.

> *"...he knows how we are formed,..." Ps 103:14a*

This being so, it is surely not unreasonable to suppose that he who made us is able to mend us.

THE LORD THAT HEALS

But we do not need to rest on supposition, for God declares himself to be the healer. So we read:

> *"...I will not bring on you any of the diseases ... for I am the Lord who heals you." Ex 15:26b*
>
> *"...I will take away sickness from among you..." Ex 23:25b*

These two references could be multiplied by many examples throughout the history of Israel.

TESTIMONIES

Those who loved him most and know him best in Old Testament days referred to God as their healer.

David was a man whom God loved. He called him a man after his own heart and the Bible says that he was,

> *"...the man exalted by the Most High, the man anointed by the God of Jacob, Israel's singer of songs." 2 Sa 23:1b*

and he said,

> *"...Praise the Lord, O my soul, and forget not all his benefits. Who forgives all your sins and heals all your diseases; he redeems your life from the pit..." Ps 103:2-4a*

In another place David spoke about some sick people who called on the Lord for healing. He described it this way -

> *"...They loathed all food and drew near the gates of death. Then they cried to the Lord in their trouble, and he saved them from their distress. He sent forth his word and healed them; he rescued them from the grave." Ps 107:18-20*

RAISING THE DEAD

The Bible gives us record of times when the Lord God raised the dead; so surely he is able to heal the living.

By the power of the prophet Elijah the son of a poor widow was brought to life again. Then some years late the prophet Elisha prayed for the son of the Shunamite and raised him out of death and restored him to his mother. (1 Kg 17; 2 Kg 4)

On another occasion a dead soldier, who was being taken for burial, was hastily cast into the tomb of the prophet Elisha. As soon as the dead man fell and struck the bones of the prophet, he was brought back to life again, and crept out of the tomb to join his friends. In this way God honoured the faith of the great prophet, and showed his willingness to work a miracle of healing and deliverance. (2 Kg 13:21). If God, through the bones of a dead prophet, could restore a soldier to life, how much easier it must be for him, using the hands and faith of his living servants, to bring simple healing to those who call upon him.

The issues of life and death belong to God, and it is our privilege to trust him for life and life more abundant.

> *"...Our God is a God who saves; from the Sovereign Lord comes escape from death." Ps 68:20*

DIVINE HEAING IN THE OLD TESTAMENT

There are many examples of God healing the sick in the Old Testament -

In response to the prayer of Abraham, the Lord healed king Abimeleck and his wife and the women folk of his household. (Ge 20:17-18)

Moses cried to the Lord, and Miriam was healed of leprosy. (Nu 12:13-15)

And again when the thousands of Israel were dying from the poison of the fiery serpents of the wilderness, Moses believed God for deliverance: the brazen serpent on the pole was set up and,

> *"...When anyone was bitten by a snake and looked at the bronze snake, he lived." Nu 21:9b*

How easily Naaman, *"Captain of the host of the king of Syria"* was healed of his dreadful leprosy simply by dipping seven times in the river Jordan. (2 Kg 5:1-4)

When king Jereboam repented of his anger against the prophet of God, the Lord graciously healed him of a withered hand, making his arm normal again. (1 Kg 13:1-6)

There was another time when king Hezekiah was stricken with a deadly disease and was at death's door, but with all his faith he called to the Lord, and God delivered and healed him. So willing was the Lord to heal Hezekiah that he shook the foundations of the whole heaven, and caused the shadows to go back 10 degrees. The Lord God moved heaven and earth just to prove to one man that the Lord would heal him. (2 Kg 20:1-11)

A MAN WHO DIED

The Old Testament contains one small but sombre account of a man who failed to trust in the healing power of God. His feet became diseased and gradually sickness spread through his whole body. (2 Ch.16:12). His fault was not that he sought the physicians but that he sought only the physicians and did not seek the Lord at all.

THE UNCHANGING GOD

Once God has made a promise he does not carelessly change it.

> *"...God is not a man, that he should lie, nor a son of man, that he should change his mind. Does he speak and then not act? Does he promise and not fulfil?" Nu 23:19*

Whatever God has promised he is both able and bound to do, else he would no longer be God. Abraham knew this, and it is recorded of him that he was -

> *"...fully persuaded that God had power to do what he had promised." Ro 4:21*

Neither is God a respecter of persons -

> *"...how true it is that God does not show favouritism..." Ac 10:34b*

It is clear then that the healing power of the Lord was not a foreign thing in the days of Israel. From that early revelation of himself as 'the Lord that heals you' God went on to prove the fact by healing thousands of his people across the years as they called upon him in distress.

DIVINE HEALING IN THE NEW TESTAMENT

1. Jesus The HEALER

If you read the New Testament without looking for secondary meanings, taking everything just as it is recorded, it becomes plainly evident that healing the sick was the most prominent part of the ministry of the Lord Jesus Christ. The four gospels record 33 outstanding miracles performed by Jesus with 24 of them miracles of healing. This is apart from the number of other references to the crowds surrounding Jesus and beseeching him to heal their sick. Again and again it is recorded that

> *"...all who touched him were healed." Mt 14:36b*

In fact the total number of healing miracles performed by Jesus in the three years of his public ministry must run into many thousands.

The Bible says:

> *"...Jesus went throughout Galilee, teaching in their synagogues, preaching the good news of the kingdom, and healing every disease and sickness among the people." Mt 4:23*

Including palsy, dropsy, paralysis, haemorrhage, leprosy, withered limbs, blindness, deafness, dumbness, restoring new limbs and raising the dead to life.

And not only did Jesus heal every kind of disease, but he healed every person who came to him: so we read

> *"...(He) healed all the sick." Mt 8:16b*

> *"And when the men of that place recognised Jesus, they sent word to all the surrounding country. People brought all their sick to him and begged him to let the sick just touch the edge of his cloak, and all who touched him were healed." Mt 14:35-36*

Great crowds came to him, bringing the lame, the blind, the crippled, the mute and many others, and laid them at his feet; and he healed them. (Mt 15:30-31; 19:2; 21:14, etc.)

2. Is God WILLING And ABLE

There are two basic questions people ask concerning healing: Is God WILLING to heal; Is God ABLE to heal? The Lord answered both those questions very plainly. To the leper who said

> *"...If you are willing you can make me clean."*

Jesus moved with compassion, said emphatically -

> *"...I am willing, be clean!" Mk 1:40-42*

And immediately the leprosy vanished and the man was healed.

Then on another occasion an anguished father pleaded for his sick son and said

> *"...If you can do anything, take pity on us and help us." Mk 9:22*

In mighty power Jesus spoke a few words and the tormented boy was at once delivered and restored to his father.

For all time the Lord Jesus Christ has established that he is WILLING and ABLE to heal all who believe.

3. The PURPOSE Of Healing

There are several reasons why Jesus placed so much emphasis on healing the sick. All of these reasons are as relevant today as they were then. Here are some of them ...

He healed to prove that he was the long promised Messiah of Israel.

> *"...Rabbi, we know you are a teacher who has come from God. For no-one could perform the miraculous signs you are doing if God were not with him." Jn 3:2*

> *"...But if I drive out demons by the finger of God, then the kingdom of God has come to you."*

Lu 11:20

He healed to prove that he was the Son of God.

> *"...Simon Peter answered, You are the Christ, the Son of the living God." Mt 16:16*

> *"...Jesus said to them, If God were your Father, you would love me, for I came from God and now am here. I have not come on my own; but he sent me." Jn 8:42*

> *"...Do not believe me unless I do what my Father does. But if I do it, event though you do not believe me, believe the miracles, that you may know and understand that the Father is in me, and I in the Father." Jn 10:37-38*

He healed to fulfill prophecy.

> *"...When evening came, many who were demon-possessed were brought to him, and he drove out the spirits with a word and healed all the sick. This was to fulfill what was spoken through the prophet Isaiah. He took up our infirmities and carried our diseases." Mt 8:16-17*

He healed because the ability to heal the sick and cast out devils is evidence of a genuine ministry.

> *"...Then they brought him a demon-possessed man who was blind and mute, and Jesus healed him, so that he could both talk and see. All the people were astonished and said, 'Could this be the son of David?'" Mt 12:22-23 (See also verses 24-32).*

He healed because healing was 'the children's bread' - that is the rightful property of the children of God.

> *"...First let the children eat all they want, he told her, for it is not right to take the children's bread and toss it to their dogs." Mk 7:27*

He healed to bring glory to God.

> *"...Great crowds came to him, bringing the lame, the blind, the crippled, the mute and many others, and laid them at his feet; and he healed them. The people were amazed when they say the mute speaking, the crippled made well, the lame walking and the blind seeing. And they praised the God of Israel." Mt 15:30-31*

But perhaps most basic and important of all, he healed out of sheer compassion for suffering and afflicted mankind.

Let these tremendous statements sink into your heart:

> *"...When Jesus landed and saw a large crowd, he had compassion on them and healed their sick." Mt 14:14*

> *"...Jesus had compassion on them and touched their eyes. Immediately they received their sight and followed him." Mt 20:34*

> *"...Filled with compassion, Jesus reached out his hand and touched the man. I am willing, he said, Be clean! Immediately the leprosy left him and he was cured." Mk 1:41*

"...he healed those who needed healing." Lk 9:11b

I am convinced that human need is as great now as it ever was. I am also convinced that the compassion of the Son of God is no less now than ever it was. I can believe no other than that he is as willing to heal today as he was yesterday.

4. Further Proof That Jesus HEALED Because the People NEEDED Healing.

The Bible tells us that Christ was so burdened with the desperate need of the people that he enlisted the help of as many as he could in his healing ministry, and besought his disciples to pray that still others would have his compassion and go forth in faith to heal the sick as he did.

So we read:-

> *"...Jesus went through all the towns and villages, teaching in their synagogues, preaching the good news of the kingdom and healing every disease and sickness. When he saw the crowds, he had compassion on them, because they were harassed and helpless, like sheep without a shepherd. Then he said to his disciples, 'The harvest is plentiful but the workers are few. Ask the Lord of the harvest, therefore, to send out workers into his harvest field.' He called his twelve disciples to him and gave them authority to drive out evil spirits and to heal every disease and sickness."* Mt 9:35; 10:1

This being so in the past must be the same today; the nature of God cannot change

> *"...JESUS CHRIST is the same yesterday and today*

and forever." He 13:8

We also read:

> *"...But the plans of the Lord stand firm for ever, the purposes of his heart through all generations."* Ps 33:11

And again -

> *"...I the Lord, I do not change."* Mal 3:6a

And again -

> *"...Every good and perfect gift is from above, coming down from the Father of the heavenly lights, who does not change like shifting shadows."* Ja 1:17

Whatever the Lord was in the past he will be today.

Each of the above reasons is a powerful argument for the reality of divine healing today: taken all together they give us overwhelming proof in favour of the fact that God will heal the sick now just as willingly, just as fully, as he has done in the past.

5. The DISCIPLES Commissioned To Heal

During his public ministry in Palestine and before his crucifixion, the Lord Jesus Christ gave many of his disciples the right to heal the sick even as he did. The record is given to us in this-

> *"...Calling the Twelve to him, he sent them out two by two and gave them authority over evil spirits. .Mk6:7*

> *"... They went out and preached that people should repent. They drove out many demons and anointed many sick people with oil and healed them."*
> Mk 6: 12-13

Again we read -

> *"...When Jesus had called the Twelve together, he gave them power and authority to drive out all demons and to cure diseases, and he sent them out to preach the kingdom of God and to heal the sick."*
> Lu 9:1-2

A complete stranger heard the Lord giving this commission and took it to himself and went out to do likewise. The disciples tried to prevent him, but Jesus rebuked them for it and encouraged the man to continue healing the sick and casting out devils. (Lu 9:49-50)

If this unknown man (and the seventy other disciples whom Jesus appointed Lu 10:1-9, 17) were able to go out in the name of Jesus and heal the sick, then present day disciples who have faith and courage enough to do the same will see the same result.

6. The CHURCH Commissioned

Some will say that all this applied while Jesus was here in person but no longer applies since his death and resurrection. However, the scripture tells us that Christ renewed this healing commission after his resurrection, just prior to his ascension into heaven.

> *"...Go into all the world and preach the good news to all creation. Whoever believes and is baptized will be saved, but whoever does not believe will be condemned. And these signs will accompany those*

> *who believe: In my name they will drive out demons; they will speak in new tongues; they will pick up snakes with their hands; and when they drink deadly poison, it will not hurt them at all; they will place their hands on sick people, and they will get well. After the Lord Jesus had spoken to them, he was taken up into heaven and he sat at the right hand of God. Then the disciples went out and preached everywhere, and the Lord worked with them and confirmed his word by the signs that accompanied it." Mk 16:15-20*

The disciples took the Lord at his word, and the Acts of the Apostles abound with references to the great number of mighty miracles wrought in the ministry of the early church. See Ac 3:6-8; 5:12-16; 6:8; 14:3; 19:11-12; 28:8-9; etc.

As confirming evidence we may also remember the astonishing words of Jesus:

> *"...I tell you the truth, anyone who has faith in me will do what I have been doing He will do even greater things than these, because I am going to the Father. And I will do whatever you ask in my name, so that the Son may bring glory to the Father. You may ask me for anything in my name, and I will do it." Jn 14:12-14*

This chapter in the gospel of John contains many wonderful promises which are happily and gratefully claimed by Christians everywhere. They should also accept those just quoted: What were the works that Jesus did? His whole ministry is summed up in these words -

> *"...Jesus went through all the towns and villages, teaching in their synagogues, preaching the good news of the kingdom and healing every kind of disease and sickness." Mt 9:35*

These are the works we are to do too, and greater than these. Jesus' ministry was confined to Palestine whereas the church is to go to the whole world.

7. HEALING In The Epistles

Divine healing is not only found in the historical accounts of the New Testament. We find also that the doctrinal epistles of Paul and James set down healing as an established doctrine and practice of the church.

Healing is spoken of as a gift of the Spirit set in the church (1 Co 12:7-9, 28), and James gives an express command to the sick - a command which is just as emphatic as any to be found in the Bible...

> *"...Is any one of you sick? He should call the elders of the church to pray over him and anoint him with oil in the name of the Lord. And the prayer offered in faith will make the sick person well; the Lord will raise him up. If he has sinned he will be forgiven. Therefore confess your sins to each other and pray for each other so that you may be healed. The prayer of a righteous man is powerful and effective." Ja 5:14-16*

8. HEALING Comes From God

However it must be made clear that no man in himself has power to heal the sick. Authority to deliver those who are bound is given only as we act in Jesus' name. Jesus said -

> "...In my name they will lay hands on sick people and they will get well." Mk 16:18

This is more than just casually speaking the name of Jesus, it is acting in the consciousness of his divine power, as his representative on earth. Doing what he would do if he were here in the flesh. There is immense power in the name of Jesus: yet how little his name means to most Christians. This was not so in the days of the early church. After performing a mighty miracle of healing on a crippled man, Peter said to the crowd which came running to see for themselves what had been done -

> "...Men of Israel, what does this surprise you? Why do you stare at us as if by our own power or godliness we had made this man walk? By faith in the name of Jesus, this man whom you see and know was made strong. It is Jesus' name and the faith that comes through him that has given this complete healing to him, as you can all see." Ac 3:2,16; 4:10

Some people would have us believe that the apostles had a special power that is not given to the church today. But Peter plainly disclaimed any such power or holiness and said simply that faith in the name of Jesus had brought healing to the man. Surely this same faith in his unchanging name will bring the same results today?

Jesus said -

> *"...You may ask me for anything in my name, and I will do it."* Jn 14:14

The Jews recognized the power in the name of Jesus and they warned the disciples not to speak to anyone in his name. (Ac 4:17; 5:28 and 40)

The apostles were flogged, but they rejoiced that they were counted worthy to suffer shame for his name (Acts 5:41) and they only prayed more fervently that God would grant them more boldness in preaching, and that miraculous signs and wonders might be done in the name of Jesus. They prayed also that God would stretch out his hand to heal the sick, acknowledging that God was the healer, but that they were the instruments through which his healing power was conveyed as they laid their hands on the sick in the name of Jesus. (Ac 4:29-30)

The pattern is the same today for all those who are bold enough to believe!

INTRODUCTION TO LESSON TWO

No one reading the four Gospels can deny that the ministry of Jesus was predominantly a healing ministry.

Over and over we are told,

> *"He healed them all."*

Why then are there some who are not healed?

Many healing books list reasons why people are not healed, however, the final reason has to be lack of faith. Either on the part of the one who prays or on the part of the one who is being prayed for. Anyone who studies healing seriously must come to this conclusion.

There is an element of mystery in healing. It cannot be solved by human reasoning or even human experience, we must base our beliefs on scripture.

The only time Jesus was unable to bring healing was at Nazareth, and that was because of unbelief on the part of the people. No one who had faith was ever disappointed when Jesus prayed!

Jesus came to reveal God's will to us. If healing was not God's will then why did Jesus spend so much of his time bringing healing and deliverance to the people? Did Jesus ever bring sickness and disease to anyone? No! Then we cannot believe that it is God's will for any person to be sick.

Two things we must be sure of:

   1. It is God's will to heal us.

2. He has the power to do it. (Mt 21:22)

If we can believe that it is God's will to heal everyone within the boundaries of healing then limitless possibilities are open to us.

WHAT ARE THESE BOUNDARIES?

1. Healing is not given to allow us to have eternal youth.

2. Healing does not ordinarily restore missing organs. This would take a miracle.

3. Healing does not take the place of the natural processes of life.

4. Human infirmities - divine healing retards but does not arrest the processes of age.(5)

In the next study we see that healing is in the atonement, that it was purchased for us by Jesus Christ on the cross. Let us seek to take freely and gratefully the healing that Jesus suffered so much to gain for us.

---

[5] "Bible Days Are Here Again" Gordon Lindsay. 1949. Ref. Ch. 22.

LESSON TWO:
HEALING IN THE ATONEMENT

IT IS NOT ENOUGH TO KNOW THAT GOD WILL HEAL THE SICK. WE MUST ALSO KNOW THE GROUNDS ON WHICH HEALING IS BASED. FOR THIS ALONE WILL DETERMINE THE QUESTION OF GOD'S WILLINGNESS TO HEAL ALL WHO ARE SICK.

Is healing selective, is it just for a privileged few, or is it freely offered to all who will believe?

We can establish the fact that healing is freely offered to all people, everywhere without exception, by proving that health of the body as well as health of the soul was purchased for us by Jesus Christ at Calvary.

We teach, and rightly so, that all men may be saved from their sin because Jesus Christ died for all. The Bible says he carried our sins upon the cross that he might remove them from us. If we can show that in the same manner he carried our sicknesses upon the cross then we have established that Jesus Christ not only died to save all who will believe, but also to heal all who will believe.

It is very simple to prove that Jesus carried our sicknesses as well as our sins upon the cross. It is simple to prove because the Bible states the fact in so many words.

CHRIST DIED FOR OUR SICKNESSES

There is a remarkable prophecy in the book of Isaiah. The prophet said -

> *"...But he was pierced for our transgressions, he was crushed for our iniquities; (that is Jesus Christ took our sins upon himself at the cross) the punishment that bought us peace was upon him, and by his wounds we are healed." (that is Jesus Christ took our sicknesses upon himself at the cross) Is 53:5*

It is stated even more clearly in these words -

> *"...Surely he took up our infirmities and carried our sorrows." Is 53:4a*

Those two words 'infirmities' and 'sorrows' are very expressive. They refer primarily to physical diseases. The word 'infirmities' means 'maladies' or 'diseases'.

It is the same word used of King Asa who was diseased, and who died in his sickness because he sought only the physicians and not the Lord for his healing. 2 Ch 16:12 It is used again of Jehoram, who was smitten with an incurable disease and who again failed to seek the Lord and so died. 2 Ch: 21:18

The word sorrow could be rendered anguish, affliction or pain. So we have it in Job 33:19 where a sick man is described in this way-

> *"...a man may be chastened on a bed of pain with constant distress in his bones."*

This was a man who sought the Lord, and God mightily delivered him from all his pain and healed him. (See Jb 33:19-26)

But all doubt that this prophecy of Isaiah refers to healing of physical disease is removed by reference to the gospel of Matthew where we read the following words -

> *"...When evening came, many who were demon-possessed were brought to him, and he drove out the spirits with a word and healed all the sick. This was to fulfill what was spoken by the prophet Isaiah: He took up our infirmities and carried our diseases."* Mt 8:16-17

Here it is conclusively shown that Jesus healed the sick in specific fulfilment of the words of Isaiah.

But when did Jesus TAKE our infirmities, when did he CARRY our sorrows?

Obviously the answer is, on the cross. This is demonstrated by the other phrase used by Isaiah -

> *"...By his wounds (the terrible scars of the Roman lash) we are healed."*

Peter gave the words this meaning when he quoted Isaiah's prophecy -

> *"...He himself bore our sins in his body on the tree... by his wounds you have been healed."*
> 1 Pe 2:24

Some would try to tell us that the word 'healed' in this reference has a spiritual significance and speaks only of healing the soul from sin. But if this is so it is the only place in the entire New Testament where the word is so used. In all other frequent occurrences of the word it always speaks of healing actual physical diseases. In fact the Greek word here translated 'healing' means specifically 'to cure diseases'. (See for example Mt 8:8 & 13; Mk 5:29; Lu 6:17 & 19; Acts 28:8; Ja 5:16 etc).

SALVATION AND HEALING TOGETHER

Further proof may be seen in the use of the Greek word 'sozo' in the New Testament. This word occurs frequently and is usually translated by one of the following words- 'healed', 'preserve', 'save', 'do well', 'be whole', 'made whole'. It is used interchangeably of both healing of soul and body. The basic meaning of 'sozo' is 'to make whole, safe and sound'; it may refer to a person being made whole from unrighteousness or from disease.

"SOZO" AND SIN

The word is used in reference to salvation from sin in the following passages:

> *"...you are to give him the name Jesus, because he will save his people from their sins." Mt 1:21b*

> *"...For the Son of Man came to seek and to save what was lost." Lu 19:10*

> *"Whoever believes and is baptized will be saved..." Mk 16:16a*

> *"...For God did not send his Son into the world to condemn the world, but to save the world through him." Jn 3:17*

> *"...And everyone who calls on the name of the Lord will be saved." Acts 2:21*

> *"...Christ Jesus came into the world to save sinners...." 1 Ti 1:15b*

"SOZO" AND SICKNESS

The word is used in reference to healing from sickness in the following passages -

> *"...If I only touch his cloak I will be healed."* Mt 9:2b

The woman, who had been bleeding, was healed. And Jesus said to her

> *"...your faith has healed you..."* Mt 9:22b

At another time he said,

> *"...be freed from your suffering."* Mk 5:34b

And again a vast crowd of sick people -

> *"...begged him to let them touch even the edge of his cloak, and all who touched him were healed."* Mk 6:56

To blind Bartimaeus whose sight was restored, Jesus said -

> *"Go... your faith has healed you."* Mk 10:52b

To Jairus, who was desperate because his daughter was dying, the Lord said -

> *"...don't be afraid; just believe, and she will be healed."* Lk 8:50b

A leper put his trust in Christ to heal him, and Jesus responded with -

> *"...Rise and go; your faith has made you well."*
> Lk 17:19

These references leave us in no doubt that in the minds of those who wrote the New Testament, people had as much right to claim healing from God as they did to claim forgiveness of sin. By faith we are saved: by faith we are healed.

Some theologians try to limit the meaning of 'sozo' to forgiveness of sin, healing of the soul. But this is completely unreasonable in the light of the use of the word in the Bible. Strictly, 'sozo' should not even be given the two distinct groupings set out above. It is an all embracive word which tells us simply that when Jesus died on the cross he purchased for us this 'sozo', that is, full salvation of body, soul and spirit: freedom from sin, freedom from fear, freedom from sickness. Christ came to give us a more abundant life; on the cross he bore away our sins and our sicknesses; and if we believe, he says to us as he said then -

> *"...Your faith has made you well!"*

Unbelief alone divides the meaning of 'sozo' and limits its effect in our lives, but faith in the full salvation and divine deliverance purchased for us at Calvary unleashes the mighty power of God to make us whole in every way!

> *"...For the message of the cross is foolishness to those who are perishing, but to us who are being saved it is the power of God."* 1 Co 1:18

(As final evidence that healing of diseases and forgiveness of sin should go together compare the following passages -; Mk 2:5-12; Jn 5:8 and 14, Ja 5:16

CONCLUSION

Let us echo the words of Jeremiah

> "...*Heal me, O Lord, and I will be healed; save me and I will be saved, for you are the one I praise."*
> *Je 17:14a*

Other proofs can be presented, but these scriptures are entirely sufficient to establish the fact that healing of our bodies was purchased for us by Jesus Christ in his atoning death on the cross.

Sickness is a result of sin. Our community is sinful, therefore our community is sick. (That is sick, generally speaking. I do not mean to imply that in individual cases sickness is always the direct result of sin.)

But Jesus Christ died:

> "...*Christ redeemed us from the curse of the law by becoming a curse for us, for it is written.' Cursed is everyone who is hanged on a tree.' Ga 3:13*

The Lord has redeemed us - paid the price to buy us out of the slave market of sin and sickness. He has paid the price for every man, and all who will believe can find in him their all sufficient Saviour and Healer, and may go free from the bondage of sin and the fetters of sickness.

INTRODUCTION TO LESSON THREE

The following is the testimony of a young lady delivered during the revival of the early 1900's.

DEVILS CAST OUT

I feel it would be for the glory of God for me to tell how God so wonderfully delivered me from the power of Satan. For five years I was devil possessed. During these five years it was almost impossible for my own loved ones to live with me. I was so abusive and did everything that the devil wanted me to do. Many times I attempted to take my own life, and sought the life of others, but God in his love and mercy kept his hand upon me, and kept me from committing any rash deed.

I was taken to Sister Etter's meeting in Chicago and began to quiet down a little and felt that God was there, and began to feel my sins and awful condition. They tried to take me to the chair to be prayed for. Immediately I got angry and began to curse and swear, the devils taking full possession. It took five men to hold me.

Sister Etter began to rebuke the insane and all the other devils to come out. The power of Satan got broken. The devils came out screaming. The police came in to make arrests, thinking that someone was being killed or was crazy. The truth was the insane demon had gone out. I was clothed in my right mind; my mind came back clear and sound, for the first time in five years. I began to praise the Lord for my wonderful deliverance and stepped forward near the pulpit filled with the Glory of God, and told the excited people what great things God had done. Many wept for joy. The police looked glad and were convinced something great had happened. I continued to attend the meetings till the last day.

One day some one was telling about my deliverance. They then said that I was in the audience. Sister Etter called me to the platform. The Lord took all fear away, and gave me boldness to stand before the multitude, a witness for Christ. They said that it was like in the days of Christ, surely a miracle has been wrought.

Truly my heart is melted in deep gratitude to God for all he has done for me. I praise him for the joy of salvation which passes all understanding. Tongues cannot tell the joy and peace that I have in my soul. Hallelujah! Every longing of my soul is satisfied. I'm happy with Jesus alone. My life and all that I have is consecrated to Jesus for his service. My desire is to live a true devoted life to God, and let him have his way with me. Hallelujah! I earnestly solicit the prayers of all the saints, that God will keep me humble at the feet of Jesus.

This is the experience of Miss Goldie Howell, Twenty-fifth and Dearborn streets, Chicago, Illinois.[6]

---

[6] Woodworth-Etter, Maria. A Diary of Signs and Wonders. Tulsa, Harrison House, 1916

LESSON THREE:
DIVINE DELIVERANCE

The deliverance of the demon-possessed occupied an important part of the personal ministry of Jesus as he walked the length and breadth of ancient Palestine. The Lord frequently faced the challenge of Satanic power, not only against himself, but also in the lives of those whom he came to heal.

> *"...The reason the Son of God appeared was to destroy the devil's work." 1 Jn 3:8b (See also Mt 4:1-11, 23-24; 8:28-34).*

Wherever Jesus Christ healed the sick, he also cast out devils; he recognized that people could be directly afflicted by both sickness and Satan.

Accordingly, when he issued his Great Commission to the church the Lord declared, not only-

> *"...They will place their hands on sick people and they will get well."*

but also -

> *"...IN MY NAME THEY WILL DRIVE OUT DEMONS." Mk 16:15-18*

With great confidence the disciples joined with their master in this divinely appointed ministry, and abundant record of their success has been left for our encouragement.

> *"The seventy-two returned with joy and said, Lord*

> even the demons submit to us in your name.
> Lu 10:17

> "Crowds gathered also from the towns around Jerusalem bringing their sick and those tormented by evil spirits, and all of them were healed."
> Ac 5:16

If Christ loosed the demon-possessed, and if the disciples also brought liberty to those who were bound, and if the Great Commission lays the same responsibility upon the whole church, should not this ministry of deliverance be part of our service today?

WHAT ARE DEMONS?

They are the great host of militant forces which make up what the Bible calls "the kingdom of darkness". Their chief prince is Satan, and beneath him is ranked many principalities, rulers and powers.

> "...For our struggle is not against flesh and blood, but against the rulers, against the authorities against the powers of this dark world and against spiritual forces of evil in the heavenly realms."
> Ep 6:12

> "...And having disarmed the powers and authorities, he made a public spectacle of them, triumphing over them by the cross." Cl 2:15 (See also Lu 4:6; Ep 1:20-21; Re 9:11).

The Bible indicates that Satan's original name was 'Lucifer' and that he was once among the most beautiful and powerful beings in heaven.

> "...How you have fallen from heaven, O morning

> *star, son of the dawn! You have been cast down to the earth, you who once laid low the nations!"*
> Is 14:12

Despite his lofty station, he desired still greater exaltation and rebelled against the will of God. This led to his abject downfall and exclusion from heaven, along with those angels which had joined him in his revolt. (See Re 12:7-9; and compare also Is 14:12-15 and Ez 28:13-16 where the language obviously goes beyond the merely local scene and points to the pride and the downfall of the devil.)

"Devils" or "demons" or "evil spirits" are generally believed to be fallen angels, the devil's angels, which were cast out of heaven with him. If this is so then to them falls the main prosecution of the devil's work of deception, temptation, possession and destruction. It is probable that the devil himself and the princes immediately beneath him in the kingdom of darkness, are rarely engaged in the affliction of individual persons, but concern themselves more with the overthrow of nations. (See Da 10:12-13 'the prince of the Persian kingdom;' Re 12:9 "Satan, who leads the whole world astray." Mt 4:8-10, etc.) The temptation and troubling of individuals is no doubt committed largely to the multitude of devils who work in perfect accord with their master's grand design. In this sense the Bible uses the words "Satan" or "devil" in both a personal and general sense, referring either to "the prince of this world" (Jn 14:30) himself, or else to his minions, whether man or demon. (Compare Mt 16:23).

EVIDENCE OF DEMON-POSSESSION

Whatever may be the true nature of demons, it is certain that they are a spiritual forces, "the powers of this dark world"; they create "spiritual wickedness" they are armed with "flaming arrows", they are "thieves", and their one desire is to "steal, kill, and destroy" as many lives as possible, See Ep 6:12; Jn 10:10.

In this warfare against God and man they desperately desire human embodiment so that they may better work wickedness and wreak havoc in human society. To this end they strive with every means at their disposal to possess or demonize the spirit, or the mind, or the body of a person; and if possible, all three, thus gaining complete control of that personality.

Numerous passages in the four gospels, and the Book of Acts, describe the condition of men and women who were demonized. The New Testament plainly indicates that mental sickness, chronic diseases of every kind, many infirmities, and moral and physical breakdown, all frequently stem from the onslaught of these evil spirits. We read of spirits of infirmity, blindness, deafness, dumbness, uncleanness, etc.

This being so, what are we to say about present day conditions?

What lies behind the mounting tide of mental sickness, and our overcrowded hospitals and rest homes? What is the cause of raging epidemics, and new and strange diseases which wonder-drugs and over-taxed hospitals cannot combat? Despite our advanced civilization and an abundance of material wealth, crime, delinquency, religious apostasy, drunkenness, gambling, immorality, are everywhere increasing at a frightening rate.

Many modern terms - medical, psychiatric, scientific, philosophical - are used to explain these trends, but the New Testament identifies the cause in the opposing, oppressing, and possessing power of the evil spirits under Satan's command.

JESUS CHRIST'S VICTORY OVER SATAN

Faced with such dread array of spiritual powers, all ruthlessly bent on our destruction, we might feel inclined to live our days in shivering fear, were it not for three things -

It appears from life that every man and woman has an in-built natural defense against Satanic possession unless, by reason of sin or circumstances, that defense is broken.

1. When we turn to the pages of scripture we discover that everywhere the devil is spoken of only in terms of total defeat. Satan is never mentioned without his name being linked to a declaration of his utter subjugation by God, and the perfect victory which the people of God can enforce against him.

2. The armies of heaven have overwhelmingly crushed the armies of hell! Certainly in the sovereign will of God and because his purpose requires it, a time of liberty has been allowed the powers of darkness. Within this liberty the devil is able to "look for someone to devour." (1 Pe 5:8b)

And especially is this true today, when he knows that his time is short before the return of Christ and his imprisonment in the pit, the devil has come down against men with a very great wrath. (See Re 12:12; and 20:1-3.)

3. And we have the victory because Jesus Christ, in his death on the cross, routed every principality and power, inflicted terrible destruction on the devil's domain, and sweepingly overthrew his kingdom (Cl 2:15). The final consummation of this tremendous triumph awaits the end of the resurrection and the day of judgment (Re 20:10). But its promise and power are already offered to all who believe in Jesus Christ. This is because the Lord wrought the victory, not on his own behalf, for his

superiority had been demonstrated ages before with the outcasting of Lucifer, but on your behalf and mine. It was done, not to show the might of God, but to MAKE US MORE THAN CONQUERORS. (see Ro 8:37) When Jesus Christ died and rose again he defeated Satan in five realms:

a. Jesus Christ conquered him as the author of sin -

"...He who does what is sinful is of the devil, because the devil has been sinning from the beginning. The reason the Son of God appeared was to destroy the devil's work." 1 Jn 3:8

"...God made him who had no sin to be sin for us, so that in him we might become the righteousness of God." 2 Co 5:21

b. Jesus Christ conquered him as the author of sickness -

"...Surely he took up our infirmities and carried our sorrows, yet we considered him stricken by God, smitten by him, and afflicted." Is 53:4

"...how God anointed Jesus of Nazareth with the Holy Spirit and power, and how he went around doing good and healing all who were under the power of the devil, because God was with him." Ac 10:38 (See also Mt 8:16-17; 1 Pe 2:24).

c. Jesus Christ conquered him in the realm of death -

"Since the children have flesh and blood, he too shared in (our and us) humanity so that by his death he might destroy him who holds the power of death

- that is, the devil - and free (us) who all (our) lives were held in slavery by (our) fear of death." He 2:14-15

"...I am the Living One; I was dead, and behold I am alive for ever and ever! And I hold the keys of death and Hades!" Rev 1:18

d. Jesus Christ conquered him as the ruler of the kingdoms of this world -

"...The kingdom of the world has become the kingdom of our Lord and of his Christ, and he will reign for ever and ever." Re 11:15b. (See also Mt 4:8-10).

e. Jesus Christ conquered him in the realm of universal dominion - heaven, earth, and under the earth -

"...Therefore God exalted him to the highest place and gave him the name that is above every name, that at the name of Jesus every knee should bow, in heaven and on earth and under the earth, and every tongue confess that Jesus Christ is Lord, to the glory of God the Father." Ph 2:9-11. (See also Ep 4:8-10).

Thus the victory of Jesus Christ on Calvary's cross has defeated Satan in heaven, on earth, and beneath the earth, and has made Jesus Christ Lord of all. Now it can be boldly said that all who believe in him, who know the power of his blood and the authority of his word (Re 12:11) can easily overcome every devilish attack.

DELIVERANCE FROM DEMON POSSESSION

When the seventy-two disciples returned to Jesus, they rejoiced because devils were subject to them when they issued a command in his name. (Lu 10:17). The Lord immediately told them why they had been able to do this. He said -

> "...I saw Satan fall like lightning from heaven!" Lu 10:18b

It was because Jesus Christ was in the throes of defeating the devil, by his life and death on Calvary, that the servants of Jesus Christ could overthrow the servants of Satan. The destruction of the chief prince has made certain the ruin of all his lesser spirits. Having established his own authority over Satan -

> "...Now is the time for judgment on this world; now the prince of this world will be driven out." Jn 12:31 (See also Jn 16:11).

Jesus is now able to say to his disciples -

> "...I HAVE GIVEN YOU AUTHORITY TO TRAMPLE ON SNAKES AND SCORPIONS, AND TO OVERCOME ALL THE POWER OF THE ENEMY; NOTHING WILL HARM YOU." Lu 10:19

The word 'authority' is from the Greek word "*exousia*". This authority is given to the believer in Christ. The word 'power' is from the Greek word '*dunamis*' meaning strength. This strength belongs to the evil spirits. However no matter how strong they are, over all of their power the believer has AUTHORITY IN CHRIST. Before the authority of the humblest child of God even the devil himself must bow. So the Lord said again,

> *"...IN MY NAME THEY WILL DRIVE OUT DEMONS..." Mk 16:17*

Thus in the name of Jesus we are given authority over every work of the devil; and more, as we are quickened by his Spirit, and walk in his anointing, we are also given power over all the might of the devil. Christ gave, and gives, his disciples

> *"...POWER AND AUTHORITY TO DRIVE OUT ALL DEMONS AND TO CURE DISEASES." Lu 9:1b*

However to carry on such a ministry, real faith is needed, faith generated by -

1. Identification with Christ

We have to see that we are in Christ, and that in him we share in the fruits of his resurrection and ascension to heaven's glory.

> *"...and you have been given fullness in Christ, who is the head over every power and authority." Cl 2:10 (See also Ep 1:18-20; 2:4-7).*
>
> *And we have to see that Christ is in us, the hope of glory, and the assurance of victory. (See Ga 2:20, 4:6,; Cl 1:27).*

2. The Word of God

Like Paul we must be able to say -

> *"...that Satan may not outwit us. For we are not unaware of his schemes." 2 Co 2:11*

So to the Word of God we must go and from its pages familiarize ourselves with the works and power, and weakness of our foe. To know your enemy is an important step toward victory. In the scripture we can also discover God's invincible armour, and those things which enable us to -

> *"...Put on the full armour of God so that you can take your stand against the devil's schemes." Ep 6:11*

Still further, it is by the Word of God the Lord is able to give birth to faith in our hearts.

> *"...Faith comes from hearing the message, and the message is heard through the word of Christ." Ro 10:17*

This faith will help us to -

> *"...extinguish all the flaming arrows of the evil one." Ep 6:16b*

and to drive out every devil and remove every barrier.

> *"...Have faith in God," Jesus answered. "I tell you the truth, if anyone says to this mountain, Go throw yourself into the sea, and does not doubt in his heart but believes that what he says will happen, it will be done for him. Therefore I tell you, whatever you ask for in prayer, believe that you have received it, and it will be yours." Mk 11:22-24*

It is also by the Word of God we learn of the victory which has been secured for us by the Lord Jesus Christ, and of the authority and power he has given us over every devil, and of his command to us to go and cast out devils; so we become emboldened to make a stand against the oppressions of the devil, and to actively resist and destroy him wherever we are. From the Word of God we learn of our proper warfare, and we learn also of our true spiritual weapons, weapons that are:

> "...not the weapons of the world. On the contrary, THEY HAVE DIVINE POWER TO DEMOLISH STRONGHOLDS." 2 Co 10:4b

3. The Name of Jesus

Every believer has the right and privilege to use the name of the highest power and authority in the universe - JESUS. In the name of Jesus we can rebuke, command, resist, overcome, and deliver from Satan and every evil spirit. (Mk 16:17; Acts 16:18; Ph 2:9-11).

When we speak in THE NAME OF JESUS, it is as though Jesus Christ himself spoke. But we must speak with perfect confidence, being fully assured that every power of darkness must yield before the command which is given in that matchless name. Devils may often vocally defy us, and resist our right to drive them out (See Mk 5:7; Lu 4:33-34) but we must persist in faith, knowing that if we resist the devil he will be compelled to flee from us.

> "...Resist the devil, and he will flee from you."
> Ja 4:7b

4. The Blood of Jesus

Satan and all his minions hate and fear the precious blood of the Lord Jesus Christ. They know the sinless blood of Jesus Christ was shed that their right and authority over believing men and women might be utterly destroyed (He 2:14-15), and also that we who believed in the power of the blood might have perfect redemption and release from all bondage. So we should plead the efficacy of the blood of Jesus Christ against Satan; we should have absolute faith in the authority the blood gives to us.

> *"...They overcame him by the blood of the Lamb and by the word of their testimony."*   *Re 12:11a*

5. The Power of the Holy Spirit

We must be filled with the Spirit, and learn to rely on the Spirit's divine power. It was by the power of the Holy Spirit that the Lord cast out devils.

> *"But if I drive out demons by the Spirit of God, then the kingdom of God has come upon you."*   *Mt 12:28*

The Holy Spirit, by his power and gifts, can give us adequate equipment to fight against and overcome all the strength and cunning of the kingdom of darkness. One particular gift of the Holy Spirit which should be coveted in relation to this ministry of casting out devils is the gift of discerning of spirits (literally, to thoroughly assess the nature, strength, and work of a demon. 1 Co 12:10).

We are also taught -

> *"...you will receive power when the Holy Spirit comes on you."*   *Ac 1:8a*

By the Holy Spirit supernatural and invincible faith can be given to us. (1 Co 12:9).

6. Prayer and Fasting

This is an often neglected, but essential part of the preparation which is needed before anyone can properly fulfill the Lord's command to "cast out demons." Jesus indicated that certain kinds of demons would yield only before prayer and fasting. (Mt 17:19-21)

So let us do all of these things and we shall discover the joy and godly pleasure of seeing men and women loosed from the bondage of the devil, as we take our stand in the name and authority of Jesus Christ our Lord.

PROTECTION FROM DEMON POSSESSION

Three things are necessary if we are to be sure of complete protection from the attack of devils-

1. We must be born again and trust completely in the power of the blood of Christ to cleanse us from all sin. (See Jn 3:1-7).

And also -

> *" But if we walk in the light, as he is in the light, we have fellowship with one another, and the blood of Jesus, his Son, purifies us from all sin. If we claim to be without sin, we deceive ourselves and the truth is not in us. If we confess our sins, he is faithful and just and will forgive us our sins and purify us from all unrighteousness." 1 Jn 1:7-9*

The unsaved have little or no protection against the power of the enemy. They lie open to the perils of sin and circumstance. But once we accept the redemption purchased for us by the Lord Jesus Christ we become God's children, and can lay claim to his protection against the power of the enemy. We are God's redeemed property, and he will keep his own!

> *"...Do you not know that your body is a temple of the Holy Spirit, who is in you, whom you have received from God? You are not your own you were bought at a price. Therefore honour God with your body." 1 Co 6:19-20. (See also Ps 91; Ep 2:1-10).*

2. We should be filled with the Holy Spirit and KEEP FILLED with the Holy Spirit.

> *"...Do not get drunk on wine, which leads to debauchery. Instead, be filled with the Spirit." Ep 5:18 (See also Ac 1:8; 4:31).*

The translation of Ephesians "be filled with the Spirit" is literally "be being filled with the Spirit," that is a continuous experience. The Lord spoke very strongly about the person who has been delivered, cleansed, and freed, but who remains "empty" not progressing in righteousness or the fullness of God; and he issued a grave warning -

> *"When an evil spirit comes out of a man, it goes through arid places seeking rest and does not find it. Then it says, 'I will return to the house I left'. When it arrives, it finds the house unoccupied, swept clean and put in order. Then it goes and takes with it seven other spirits more wicked than itself, and they go in and live there and the final condition of that man is worse than the first. That is how it will be with this wicked generation. Mt 12:43-45.*

So we must be filled with the Spirit of God, and must live "self-controlled, upright and godly lives" every day.

> *"For the grace of God that brings salvation has appeared to all men. It teaches us to say 'No' to ungodliness and worldly passions, and to live self-controlled, upright and godly lives in this present age, while we wait for the blessed hope - the glorious appearing of our great God and Saviour, Jesus Christ, who gave himself for us to redeem us from all wickedness and to purify for himself a people that are his very own, eager to do what is good." Tit 2:11-14.*

Only thus can we remain

> *"...strong in the Lord and in his mighty power."*
> *Ep 6:10*

3. We must be fully clothed with the armor of God. (Ep 6:10-18).

We are exhorted to be ever ready to resist the devil and to live victoriously by shielding ourselves in both defense and attack with the whole armor of God. Taking hold of this passage let us grasp some of its secrets -

> *"...Finally, be strong in the Lord and in his mighty power."*

1. Be strong! Adopt an attitude of strength! Accept the strength and power of the Lord in your life! Don't confess weakness, but claim yourself to be more than a conqueror in Christ, strengthened with all power according to his glorious might, able to do all things through him who strengthens you!

> *"...No, in all these things we are more than conquerors through him who loved us." Ro 8:37 (See also Ph 4:13; Cl 1:11).*
>
> *"...Put on the full armor of God so that you can take your stand against the devil's schemes..." Ep 6:11*

2. Remember the devil has no authority over you. You have to guard, not against his power, but rather against his SCHEMES and DECEPTIONS as he tries to trick you out of your victory in Christ.

   > *"...Therefore put on the full armor of God, so that when the day of evil comes, you may be able to stand your ground, and after you have done everything, to STAND. STAND FIRM ..." Ep 6:13-14a*

3. Don't fight in your own strength, but STAND in the strength of the Lord, complete in Christ. STAND on the ground of your redemption. Refuse to believe Satan's lies!

   > *"...Put on the armor of..."*

   TRUTH...

   RIGHTEOUSNESS...

   THE GOSPEL OF PEACE...

   THE SHIELD OF FAITH...

   THE HELMET OF SALVATION...

   THE SWORD OF THE SPIRIT WHICH IS THE WORD OF GOD...

AND PRAY IN THE SPIRIT ON ALL OCCASIONS..."

The devil will always endeavour to deceive men and women out of their standing in Christ, but by grasping hold of this God-given armor we can meet all his deceptions and cast him aside. Our faith is our protection; the Word of God is our sharp sword. By these we may defend ourselves and destroy our foe. The Word of God is sure; the enemy is defeated; the victory of Christ is certain; for all who believe there can be glorious deliverance and complete freedom from all the power of Satan and his forces!

BOOK THREE: THE POWER OF PENTECOST TODAY

Introduction to Lesson One
Lesson One - **The Personality And Power Of The Holy Spirit**

Introduction to Lesson Two
Lesson Two - **The Purpose Of The Baptism In The Holy Spirit**

Introduction to Lesson Three
Lesson Three - **The Spirit Filled Life**

INTRODUCTION TO LESSON ONE

Many recent surveys have shown that the Pentecostal movement is the largest and fastest growing Protestant body in the world today.

Altogether there are approximately 250 million Pentecostal Christians. If members of the charismatic movement are added to this, the number rises to double that number.

If the present growth rate continues, Pentecostals could become the largest group of Christians, apart from the 'Roman Catholic church.

There is a dynamic in the Baptism of the Holy Spirit which is vitally needed in the church. There must be a concrete reality about our faith to combat the creeping in-roads of modernistic theologies, the New Age movement, and the hedonistic philosophies of this age.

With the Baptism of the Holy Spirit comes an experience with God which no man can deny, a living faith, a definite reality, which no one can shake or destroy.

LESSON ONE:
THE PERSONALITY AND POWER OF THE HOLY SPIRIT

The Bible gives us a thrilling picture of the mighty personality and power of the Spirit of God. Yet to most people the Holy Spirit is little more than a vague and mysterious influence of which they know practically nothing. Because of the prevailing lack of understanding of the work and ministry of the Holy Spirit in the church it is necessary for us to examine the Bible teaching in some detail. We want to discuss the vital importance of the activity of the Spirit of God in the plan of redemption. But before we consider our relation to the Holy Spirit in this regard, let us become familiar with the description of the Spirit. He is not, as some have taught, a mere influence emanating from God. In the whole universe there is no more real and warm personality than the Holy Spirit.

THE PERSONALITY OF THE HOLY SPIRIT

It is the easiest thing in the world to prove beyond any doubt the vital personality of the Spirit of God. It can be done simply by looking at the descriptive terms the Bible uses in speaking of the Holy Spirit. For example, here is a list of the various names and titles ascribed to the Holy Spirit, all of them applicable only to a living being; certainly not to an impersonal influence. His name is "Comforter, the Instructor, the Advocate, the Guide." These vividly descriptive names could not be applied to an abstract influence. They naturally refer to a warmly sympathetic, personal, and active friend and helper. And then these further titles are accorded the Holy Spirit: He is called

- Spirit of adoption.
- Spirit of counsel.
- Spirit of glory.
- Spirit of grace.
- Spirit of judgment.
- Spirit of knowledge.
- Spirit of life.
- Spirit of might.
- Spirit of understanding.
- Spirit of wisdom.

In connection with these names and titles given to the mighty Spirit of God, we have the terms used in describing his activity among men and relationships with them. Hence we read that ...

- He strives with man.
- He can be rebelled against.
- We can blaspheme the Holy Spirit.
- He gives us instruction.
- We must be born of the Spirit.
- He brings conviction of sin.
- He inspires the ministry of God's servants.
- We can lie to the Holy Spirit.
- He gives us guidance.
- He brings revelation of the scripture.
- He is able to command and to forbid.

- He gives life to our mortal bodies.
- In time of need he helps us.
- When our own praying fails the Holy Spirit intercedes for us.
- He searches out the mind and heart of man.
- According to his own will he gives gifts to men.
- He can be grieved.
- It is the Spirit of God who sanctifies us for the service of God.

All these phrases portray an immense energy and activity. These things could not be said of a lifeless influence, but are properly attributes of a vital and loving person: one who sees, hears, feels, wills, and who has a purpose to accomplish.

However, all these names and titles and expressions are quite inadequate to describe the great glory and wonderful work of the Spirit of God, so the Bible also uses various symbols to portray his divine character more vividly. The Holy Spirit is likened to ...

FIRE

John the Baptist said,

> *"...I baptize you with water for repentance. But after me will come one who is more powerful than I, whose sandals I am not fit to carry. He will baptize you with the Holy Spirit and with fire."* Mt 3:11

As fire, the Holy Spirit purges, purifies, illuminates, brings warmth and comfort.

In this there is a picture of fearsome strength, of awesome majesty. It is a picture also of one who is of infinite value and goodness to mankind.

WIND

Jesus said,

> *"...The wind blows wherever it pleases. You hear its sound, but you cannot tell where it comes from or where it is going. So it is with everyone born of the Spirit." Jn 3:8*

The wind symbolizes the work of the Spirit in bringing men to the "new birth". It also speaks of his mysterious, independent, penetrating, life-giving power, especially in regard to redemption.

WATER

> *"...whoever drinks the water I give him will never thirst. Indeed, the water I give him will become in him a spring of water welling up to eternal life." Jn 4:14 (See also Jn 7:38-39).*

The Holy Spirit is the fountain of living water, the purest and the best; the river of life washing from our lives all the dust of sin, and flooding and filling them with the fullness of God. Here too we have a picture of the Holy Spirit quenching the fires of wrongful desire, bringing refreshment to our lives and making us fruitful. And he is as "living water," not as the stagnant water of cistern or marsh, but as the fresh water of a woodland brook, springing, bubbling, crystal clear.

OIL

> *"So Samuel took the horn of oil and anointed him in the presence of his brothers, and from that day on the Spirit of the Lord came upon David in power."*
> *1 Sa 16:13*

Whenever oil was used in the Old Testament, it spoke of something eminently useful to man: it also spoke of fruitfulness and beauty, of new life, and the anointing of God. Oil was used extensively for food, for light, for lubrication, and for healing.

Lifted into the activity of the spiritual realm, this is what God has made the Holy Spirit to be to us in all of our service to him.

DOVE

> *"As soon as Jesus was baptized, he went up out of the water. At that moment heaven was opened, and he saw the Spirit of God descending like a dove and lighting on him." Mt 3:16*

Here is a sweet symbol of many delightful things: of gentle tenderness, of precious loveliness, of mildness, and of peace, purity, and patience. As the dove in the Ark brought good news to Noah of the world's salvation out of the flood so the Holy Spirit is ever the one who impresses the message of the gospel, the good news of salvation, onto our hearts.

SEAL

> *"And you also were included in Christ when you heard the word of truth, the gospel of your salvation. Having believed, you were marked in him with a seal, the promised Holy Spirit." Ep 1:13*

As a seal upon our lives the Holy spirit indicates our fixed relationship to God as Christians. We are to become children of our heavenly Father, adopted into his family, and secure as long as we walk with him.

BUT THE MOST TREMENDOUS THOUGHT OF ALL IS THAT WE ARE SAID TO BE TEMPLES OF THE HOLY SPIRIT, AND MAY BE FILLED! FILLED! FILLED! WITH ALL THE MIGHTY LIFE AND DYNAMIC POWER OF THE DIVINE SPIRIT OF GOD. WHAT DOES IT MEAN TO BE INDWELT BY THE HOLY SPIRIT?

In the Bible we read,

> *"May God himself, the God of peace, sanctify you through and through May your whole spirit, soul and body be kept blameless at the coming of our Lord Jesus Christ." 1 Th 5:23*

We find here that God wants us to be kept blameless in body, soul, and spirit, until Jesus comes again, and we are told that THIS WORK IS ACHIEVED IN OUR LIVES BY THE HOLY SPIRIT.

The Bible says that,

> *"...The spirit of man is the candle of the Lord." Pr 20:27a (KJV)*

But sin has extinguished that candle so that the light of God no longer shines in the inward part of man. The Holy Spirit re-kindles the flame and brings us again into the light and fellowship of God. The following thrilling expressions are used in the Word of God to describe the man who is filled with the Spirit and walking in the strength of the law of God, being fruitful and prosperous, delivered from all sickness, crowned with abundant blessings, contented in heart and mind, having his strength renewed, being righteous with God, at peace in the will of God, being a mighty warrior for the Lord!

THE NEW BIRTH AND THE BAPTISM OF THE HOLY SPIRIT

Many of these things the Spirit of God begins to achieve in the life of the believer from the moment of the "new birth". But the Bible clearly teaches us that there is a special infilling or Baptism of the Holy Spirit - an experience which every believer should receive - which gives us a renewed and vital opportunity to fulfill this glorious portrayal of a powerful, God-filled Christian life.

It is a fact that every Christian has received a measure of the Holy Spirit. We are "born again" by the Spirit of God. It was the moving of the Holy Spirit which first brought conviction of sin into our hearts. As the scripture says,

> "...if anyone does not have the Spirit of Christ, he does not belong to Christ." Ro 8:9b.

But it is also a fact that there is a special "infilling" or "baptism" of the Holy Spirit which every believer should experience. It is described for us in the following verses by John the Baptist,

> "I baptize you with water for repentance. But after me will come one who is more powerful than I, whose sandals I am not fit to carry. He will baptize you with the Holy Spirit and with fire." Mt 3:11

> "I am going to send you what my Father has promised; but stay in the city until you have been clothed with power from on high." Lu 24:49

On one occasion, while Jesus was eating with them, he gave them this command:

> *'Do not leave Jerusalem, but wait for the gift my Father promised, which you have heard me speak about. For John baptized with water, but in a few days you will be baptized with the Holy Spirit'* Ac 1:4-5

> *But you will receive power when the Holy Spirit comes on you: and you will be my witnesses in Jerusalem, and in all Judea and Samaria, and to the ends of the earth."* Ac 1: 8

Just after his resurrection the Lord Jesus Christ appeared to his disciples and it says that

> *"And he breathed on them and said, Receive the Holy Spirit." Jn 20:22*

It was then that the disciples were fully "born again" by the "breath" or "wind" of the Holy Spirit as in Jn 3:8.

But Jesus still gave them the command to:

> *"...wait in Jerusalem." Lu 24:49*

until they were baptized in the Holy Spirit in all his tremendous power. It is this special baptism in the Holy Spirit which now claims our attention.

THE BAPTISM OF THE HOLY SPIRIT

The Lord Jesus Christ said,

> *"If you love me, You will obey what I command. And I will ask the Father, and he will give you another counselor to be with you for ever - the spirit of truth. The world cannot accept him because it neither sees him nor knows him. But you know him, for he lives with you and will be in you."*
> *Jn 14:15-17*

The particular doctrine we are now going to study relates to the definite experience promised to all believers known as the "baptism of the Holy Spirit." It is our concern to establish first of all that this is an experience subsequent to conversion and quite separate from the new birth. We can state it clearly in this way:

THE EXAMPLE OF CHRIST

It is needful for everyone to be BORN OF THE SPIRIT and after that to be BAPTISED IN THE SPIRIT. Jesus set us an example in this. When Christ, the eternal Son of God, was born into this world as the little child of Mary, it was a miracle which sprang from the power of the Holy Spirit

> *"The angel answered, 'The Holy Spirit will come upon you, and the power of the Most high will overshadow you. So the Holy one to be born will be called the Son of God' Lu 1:35*

But 30 years later, as Jesus stood in Jordan with the water of his baptism streaming from him, the Spirit of God descended from heaven upon him again, mightily filled him and especially empowered him for his supernatural ministry.

This experience of the Lord should be duplicated in the life of all those who believe in him. We are all

> "...born of the Spirit." Jn 1:12-13; 3:6-8:

we should all be baptised in the Spirit. So it is in John 14:15-17 Jesus said to his disciples -

> "...The Holy Spirit lives WITH YOU (born of the Spirit) and will be IN YOU." (baptised in the Spirit).

Let us enlarge on this.

THE EXAMPLE OF THE DISCIPLES

The disciples had been convinced of sin, had believed in the Lord Jesus Christ, had come to love him, and desired to keep his commandments; their understanding had been opened to know the scriptures, and they believed that the Christ was bound -

> "... to suffer and rise from the dead on the third day..."

and that -

> "...repentance and forgiveness of sin will be preached in his name to all nations..." Lu 24:46-47

In other words, these men were plainly believers in the Lord Jesus Christ, they were saved, were born again, were witnesses of Christ (Lu 24:48). No difference can be found in their condition and that of people today who accept Christ as Saviour.

Now notice the command Jesus gave them:

> "...I am going to send you what my Father has promised; but stay in the city until you have been

clothed with power from on high." Lu 24:49

From the hour of their conversion, the Holy Spirit had been with the disciples, and their bodies had been his temples.

During the ten days in which they stayed in the city waiting for the promise of the Father, the same Spirit remained with them, guiding them in prayer, increasing their desire for his fullness, united them in one accord, preparing them for the promised outpouring.

Every day until the day of Pentecost, the Holy Spirit was preparing the disciples for the coming baptism; by the Spirit they had been born again; by the Spirit they were being led and influenced; and these things were all essential to their receiving the enduement of power, but it is evident that they had not yet received it. Had the disciples continued in this preparatory stage of experience, or had they gone out to preach the gospel before receiving the promise of the Father, the world would never have felt their influence, the church would never have been established, the Acts of the apostles would never have been written.

But they loved the Lord, they obeyed his command, they waited and prayed; the Holy Spirit who had been with them before Pentecost was found in them after Pentecost, and in the power of the Spirit they went out, preaching the Word everywhere with the Lord working with them, confirming the Word with signs following, and they...

"...turned the world upside down." Ac 17:6 (KJV)

THE EXAMPLE OF THE EARLY CHURCH

As with the first disciples, so it was with the whole of the early church and so it should be for every believer in this gospel age. After bringing a person to repentance and faith in the Lord Jesus

Christ, the Holy Spirit abides with the new born Christian and works in him, as he did in the disciples before Pentecost. But the Holy Spirit works in the believer for the one purpose, to perfect his love and obedience and inward preparation, so that the Holy Spirit may fall on him just as in the beginning.

If the convert falls short of this experience, in the belief that he received the fullness of the Holy Spirit at conversion, thereby reckoning that nothing remains for him but a gradual increase of what he then received, he will almost certainly suffer great lack. There will inevitably be a great difference between his experience and the experience of the apostolic church.

A person lacking the baptism of the Holy Spirit (unless by mighty faith he is able to appropriate an extraordinary measure of the grace of God) will almost unavoidably remain through life in the darkness and weakness of the old nature. Instead of going to his life's work "clothed with power," illuminated by the Spirit, bearing the rich anointing of God, and in deep fellowship with the Lord, he will suffer from daily consciousness of his shortcomings and infirmities and lack of spiritual power.

THE LORD JESUS CHRIST AND THE BAPTISM OF THE HOLY SPIRIT

Jesus was born among men, both Son of God and Son of Man. He came to show us God as he is and man as he should be.

As Son of God, the Lord secured for the whole human race an all-sufficient salvation bearing away the weight of sin and death that lay upon all men and reconciling us to God. As Son of Man, Jesus by word and action displayed a perfect life and showed an example that we are everywhere exhorted to follow. But Christ did not only show us what we should be; he also set down HOW we may become all that God requires. And reference to the scripture reveals the startling fact that Christ, in his humanity, was entirely dependent upon the baptism of the Holy Spirit to equip him for his divine service.

Isaiah records then:

> *"A shoot will come up from the stump of Jesse; from his roots a Branch will bear fruit. The Spirit of the Lord will rest on him - the Spirit of wisdom and of understanding, the Spirit of counsel and of power, the Spirit of knowledge and of the fear of the Lord - and he will delight in the fear of the Lord."*
> *Is 11:1-3a*

It is plainly stated that Christ required the fullness of the Holy Spirit to bring forth in him WISDOM, UNDERSTANDING, COUNSEL, POWER, and KNOWLEDGE.

When was this done? Without doubt at the time of his baptism by John in the river Jordan. (See Mt 3:13-17.)

It was here that the Holy Spirit descended on Christ and from this point the Lord is spoken of as being -

> *"...full of the Holy Spirit...." Lu 4:1a*

as moving in -

> *"...the power of the Spirit." Lu 4:14a*

and as having the Spirit -

> *"...without limit." Jo 3:34b*

It was only after he was filled with the Spirit that the Lord began to preach with the divine unction that caused vast multitudes to assemble for hours, enthralled beneath the sound of his voice. It was only after the glory of the Lord had so filled him, when the Holy Spirit descended on him, that

> *"...news about him spread through the whole countryside." Lu 4:14b*

The same thought is brought out in the following quotation from the great prophecy of Isaiah:

> *"Here is my servant, whom I uphold, my chosen one in whom I delight; I will put my Spirit on him and he will bring justice to the nations Is 42:1*

> *"The Spirit of the Sovereign Lord is on me, because the Lord has anointed me to preach good news to the poor. He has sent me to bind up the broken-hearted, to proclaim freedom for the captives and release from darkness for the prisoners." Is 61:1*

The wording of these texts suggest that Christ was not born with the fullness of the Spirit abiding in him. Each of the following phrases indicates a definite time when the Lord was baptised in the Spirit - a baptism which resulted in the glorious manifestations of divine power and wisdom that shone forth in his ministry:

- The Spirit of the Lord will rest on him.
- To him God gives the Spirit without limit.
- I will put my Spirit on him.
- The Spirit of the Sovereign Lord is on me.

WHY WAS CHRIST BAPTISED IN THE HOLY SPIRIT?

1. Because the Lord God anointed him to preach the Gospel, to heal the sick, to loose the captives.

> *"...how God anointed Jesus of Nazareth with the Holy Spirit and power, and how he went around doing good and healing all who were under the power of the devil, because God was with him."*
> *Ac 10:38*

2. Because Christ as man, needed the baptism of the Spirit to fill him with wisdom and understanding, power and grace.

It is certain that without the baptism of the Spirit, the Lord could not have finished the work which the Father had given him to do. However, in saying this, we must be careful to distinguish between the state of Christ when, as the eternal Word, he dwelt with the Father and when, as the same Word, he...

> *"... became flesh and made his dwelling among us."*
> *Jo 1:14a*

In the former state as the word, he had an all-sufficiency in himself: in the latter in the flesh, he was like us

> *"For this reason he was .made like his brothers in every way."* He 2:17a

For this reason, he had the same need of the baptism of the Spirit that we have, and Jesus obtained...

> *"...power from on high."* Lu 24:49b

on the same conditions on which the same blessing is promised to us.

The basic condition required to receive the gift of the Holy Spirit is to recognise the need of that baptism and to earnestly seek God for it. The baptism of the Holy Spirit is given only to those who pray for it. So it was in the example of Christ:

> *"...Jesus was baptised too. And as he was praying, heaven was opened and the Holy Spirit descended on him in bodily form like a dove." Lu 3:21b-22a*

Jesus himself taught that the Holy Spirit is given to those who "ask, seek, and knock."

> *"So I say to you: 'Ask and it will be given to you; seek and you will find; knock and the door will be opened to you. For everyone who asks receives; he who seeks finds; and to him who knocks, the door will be opened. Which of you fathers, if your son asks for a fish, will give him a snake instead? or if he asks for an egg will give him a scorpion? If you then, though you are evil, know how to give good gifts to your children, how much more will your Father in heaven give the Holy Spirit to those who ask him!' Lu 11:9-13*

This is surely one reason why Jesus frequently spent whole nights in prayer before his Father.

AN IMMEDIATE AND WONDERFUL RESULT

> *The effects of Christ's baptism in the Spirit were immediate and widespread (see Lu 4:14-22).*

The people were amazed at the gracious words that came from his lips. But why did they wonder? They had known him since childhood, had frequently spoken to him and heard him speak. Undoubtedly the Lord had publicly addressed the congregation in that synagogue on many occasions. But now they observed a remarkable change in his whole manner and bearing and authority. The Lord himself was conscious of this change; he knew the people's surprise and so explained the transformation in the words

"...The Spirit of the Lord is on me."

Now the scripture states in the most definite manner that the experience of the Lord should be the experience of his people. We find it so in the words of John the Baptist, who not only foretold Christ's baptism in the Holy Spirit, but also that Christ in turn would baptise his followers in the same Spirit:

> *"Then John gave this testimony: 'I saw the Spirit come down from heaven as a dove and remain on him. I would not have known him, except that the one who sent me to baptise with water told me, "'The man on whom you see the Spirit come down and remain is he who will baptise with the Holy Spirit.' I have seen and testify that this is the Son of God." Jo 1:32-34.*

We conclude then...

    a. It was absolutely essential that the Lord Jesus Christ be baptised in the Holy Spirit before he could properly fulfil his mission on earth;

    b. If this were true of the perfect Son of God, how much more is it true of ordinary people, who, although they are redeemed, still bear within them much infirmity?

The Baptism of the Spirit is better than the physical presence of Christ.

The Lord taught that those who were baptised in the Spirit would enjoy greater privileges and blessing than did the disciples who accompanied him during his ministry in Palestine. In the baptism of the Spirit, we are able to obtain greater benefit than the disciples could who heard Jesus, who saw him and touched him. This would be hard to believe if it were not for the fact that Jesus expressly said it would be so:

> "...But I tell you the truth: It is for your good that I am going away. Unless I go away, the Counselor will not come to you; but if I go, I will send him to you." Jo 16:7

The disciples who ministered with the Lord enjoyed great privileges, for Jesus himself said,

> "... 'Blessed are the eyes that see what you see. For I tell you that many prophets and kings wanted to see what you see but did not see it, and to hear what you hear but did not hear it'." Luke 10:23-24

But this was small, compared with the higher light and glory they were to receive after Christ was raised to his Father's right hand and the comforter was given. So Jesus confirmed in another place:

> "Whoever believes in me, as the scripture has said, streams of living water will flow from within him.' By this he meant the Spirit, whom those who believed in him were later to receive. Up to that time the Spirit had not been given, since Jesus had not yet been glorified." Jo 7:38-39

The privileges enjoyed by even the most humble believer who is baptised in the Holy Spirit surpass anything ever known by the prophets or kings of the past!

INTRODUCTION TO LESSON TWO

Why should we pray for the Holy Spirit baptism? There are many good reasons. The Holy Spirit is called the "Comforter", a word that goes back took the time of Wycliff, and is taken from the Latin word "fortis", which means "brave". Comforter then has the meaning of courage or strength. The Holy Spirit is our courage, he is our strength.[7]

We need the Baptism in the Holy Spirit to give us a "holy boldness", not only to be a witness for Christ but also for courage in the face of Satan and all of his demonic hosts. This "holy boldness" was evident in the life of the early church. What a change was wrought in the attitude of the apostles once they had received the Baptism! Over and over again they triumphed in Christ and overcame the enemy.

But there are other reasons for the Baptism. By it we are brought into perfect union with Christ, we have access to the throne of grace, and power in prayer. The Spirit quickens us, not only spiritually, but mentally, physically, and morally. Through him we bear fruit and are changed into the image of Jesus our Saviour.

What about tongues? Why is it necessary for all to speak in tongues? Howard M. Ervin in his book "These are not Drunken as ye Suppose", writes:

---

[7] "The Daily Study Bible" William Barclay, 17 vols. St. Andrew Press, Edinburgh. 1964 ed. This ref. from "The Acts of the Apostles", pg.2.

"This is unquestionably the thorniest question in any discussion of the Pentecostal experience. Sooner or later it evokes the question: Must everyone speak in tongues to be filled with the Holy Spirit?

"Perhaps an understanding of the rationale of tongues would obviate the objections to it. Speech is a unique manifestation of personality. It is, in fact, one of the most distinctly personal things men do. It is rightly regarded as evidence of personality. It is not accidental to personality. It is rather indispensable to human personality. The perceptive comment of Eduard Thurneysen is a welcome emphasis of this very fact: 'Only the fact that man can speak and does speak makes him man...In the last analysis, the mystery of speech is identical with the mystery of personality, with the image of God in man.'

"God is also created personal, and as a person manifests himself in speech...It was by speech that God created the world." [8]

In this lesson we learn more about this purpose of the Baptism in the Holy Spirit and how to receive it.

---

[8] These Are Not Drunk As Ye Suppose; Howard M Ervin; Published by Logos, Plainfield N.J. 1968. This ref. from pg. 52.

LESSON TWO:
THE PURPOSE OF THE BAPTISM IN THE HOLY SPIRIT

The immense importance of the ministry of the Spirit of God in the church is seen in the tremendous events that surrounded the initial outpouring of the Holy Spirit on the day of Pentecost.

Let us examine these events...

THE DAY OF PENTECOST

All history records no more tremendous occurrence than the ascension of the Lord Jesus Christ into heaven. Forty days after his mighty resurrection, Jesus ascended to his Father's right hand and sat down on the throne of his glory utterly victorious over every work of evil. From this exalted seat the Lord Jesus Christ began the work and ministry toward which the course of the history of the whole world had been directed. All heaven waited with enthralled interest to witness the first act of the ascended Christ.

For ten days they waited and watched; then suddenly, with a surge of mighty power, Christ poured forth his Spirit upon the little company of disciples and set in motion his redeemed church. Heaven shook and trembled and the echo reached the earth, the scripture says, with "a sound like the blowing of a violent wind." The sound of it filled the house where the disciples were praying; and with the wind came tongues of fire which darted from one to the other and settled upon them. Every fibre of their being thrilled with the awesome wonder of God as they were filled with the Holy Spirit and quickly, forcibly, passionately, they began to speak in other tongues.

In his great sermon on the day of Pentecost, with the power of God coursing through him, Peter caught a vision of the heavenly drama. With his voice swelling under the impulse of God's love, he declared:

> *"God has raised this Jesus to life, and we are all witness of the fact. Exalted to the right hand of God, he has received from the Father the promised Holy Spirit and has poured out what you now see and hear." Ac 2:32-33*

THE FIRST ACT OF THE CHRIST OF GLORY WAS TO GIVE THE GIFT OF THE HOLY SPIRIT. THIS STUPENDOUS WORK WAS THE CULMINATION OF THE THREE PERFECT YEARS OF JESUS' MINISTRY.

Why did the lord put such importance on the work of the Holy Spirit that he made it the first gift he sought of the Father and gave to the church?

1. Because Jesus himself in his own ministry among men had conclusively proved the value and need of the Spirit filled life.

Christ was born without sin; we were born with sin. Jesus had every natural advantage; his physical and mental strength were not dulled by inward corruption.

> *"...The holy one to be born will be called the Son of God." Lu 1:35b. See also Lu 2:40-52.*

Yet still he had need of the baptism of the Holy Spirit. How much more then do we?

The greater need we have of the strength and influence of the Holy Spirit is indicated by a comparison between the descent of the Spirit upon Christ and the experience of the day of Pentecost.

The Holy Spirit came to the Lord Jesus Christ as a dove, the symbol of peace and purity, tender and gentle. In contrast with this, listen to the stern word of John the Baptist when addressing men:

> *"But after me will come one who is more powerful than I. He will baptise you with the Holy Spirit and with fire. His winnowing fork is in his hand, and he will clear his threshing floor, gathering his wheat into the barn and burning up the chaff with unquenchable fire." Mt 3:11b-12*

Hence the characteristic of the day of Pentecost were great noise, strong wind, tongues of fire, speaking in tongues, confusion, fear, mockery and astonishment. It is exactly the same today - all because the Spirit of God comes into direct conflict with the corrupted spirit of men.

2. The second purpose of the Lord was to fulfill the promise of scripture.

> *"For I will pour water on the thirsty land, and streams on the dry ground; I will pour out my Spirit on your offspring, and my blessing on your descendants. They will spring up like grass in a meadow, like poplar trees by flowing streams. One will say, "I belong to the Lord;" another will call himself by the name of Jacob; still another will write on his hand, "The Lord's," and will take the name Israel." Is 44:3-5*

> *"I will bless them and the places surrounding my hill. I will send down showers in season; there will be showers of blessing." Ez 34:26*
>
> *And afterward, I will pour out my Spirit on all people. Your sons and daughters will prophesy, your old men will dream dreams, your young men will see visions. Even on my servants, both men and women, I will pour out my spirit in those days and they will prophecy." Acts 2:17-18 (See also Is 32:15, 59:19-21, 60:1, Ho 6:3, Ze 10:1.)*

Encompassed in the many marvelous prophecies concerning the expected outpouring of the Spirit there are promises of rest, peace, beauty and refreshing; and promises of power and of supernatural utterance and of divine equipment. All of this was to be given to men and women abundantly as God poured out his Spirit on all people. In his own ministry on earth the Lord Jesus Christ frequently spoke of his Father's promise to give the Holy Spirit to the disciples.

> *"but whoever drinks the water I give him will never thirst. Indeed, the water I give him will become in him a spring of water welling up to eternal life." Jo 4:14*
>
> *"...On the last and greatest day of the Feast, Jesus stood and said in a loud voice, 'If anyone is thirsty, let him come to me and drink, whoever believes in me, as the scripture has said, streams of living water will flow from within him. By this he meant the Spirit, whom those who believed in him were later to receive. Up to that time the Spirit had not been given, since Jesus had not yet been glorified" Jo 7:37-39*

> *"And I will ask the Father and he will give you another Counselor to be with you forever the Spirit of Truth." Jn 14:16,17 (See also Lu 11:13; Lu 24:49; Ac 1:5-8)*

To fulfill his own words it was necessary for him to quickly send the Spirit.

3. The third purpose of the Lord is found in the fact that the ministry of the Holy Spirit is essential to our redemption and our eventual glory in Christ.

A great number of Bible references could be mentioned here, but the whole matter is charmingly illustrated by the lovely story of Isaac and Rebekah (Ge 24:1-67). In this story Abraham (who typifies the Father) sent his servant (the Holy Spirit) into a far country (the world) to find a bride (the church) for his son Isaac (Christ). Please read the story yourself and rejoice as you see in this delightful story a wonderful picture of our own way.

> As the servant wooed and won Rebekah for Isaac, so does the Holy Spirit reveal Christ to us and plants within us a godly love. As the servant heaped precious gifts upon Rebekah, so are the rich graces and supernatural gifts of Christ given to us by the Holy Spirit. As the servant took Rebekah and guided her safely over the long and dangerous journey from her parents home to the far distant home of Isaac, so the Spirit of Go4 guides us safely through the journey of life until we reach the splendid mansion of heaven. But except the Holy Spirit had been sent, how could we ever have been wooed and won for the heavenly bridegroom? How could we have responded to his gracious invitation? Except we are baptized in the Spirit how can we

properly receive the splendid gifts he desires to heap on us, and how can we know his full protection and guidance until we reach our heavenly home?

4. Fourthly, the Lord Jesus Christ has absolutely promised us many high and wonderful privileges providing we receive the Holy Spirit after we believe.

Here are some of those privileges (all spoken of in close connection with the Baptism of the Holy Spirit).

    a. To know that we are thereby brought into a perfect union with Christ and God -

"...that all of them may be one, Father just as you are in me and I am in you. May they also be in us so that the world may believe that you have sent me. I have given them the glory that you gave me, that they may be one as we are one. I in them and you in me. May they be brought to complete unity to let the world know that you sent me and have loved them even as you have loved me. Father I want those you have given me to be with me where I am, and to see my glory, the glory you have given me because you loved me before the creation of the world" Jn 17:21-24. (See Jn 14:15- 20.)

    b. We are to enjoy a similar access to the throne of grace, and have the same power in prayer, that Christ possessed -

"In that day you will no longer ask me anything. I tell you the truth, my Father will give you whatever you ask in my name. Until now you have not asked for anything in my name. Ask and you will receive,

and your joy will be complete. Jn 16:23-24. (See also vs 7)

c. The baptism of the "rivers of living water."

"... But the Counselor, the Holy Spirit, whom the Father will send in my name, will teach you all things and will remind you of everything I have said to you. Peace I leave with you; my peace I give you. I do not give to you as the world gives. Do not let your hearts be troubled and do not be afraid." Jn 14:26 - 27

d. Ability to work the works of God, divine strength, supernatural power, are all part of the harvest which results from this mighty baptism -

"I tell you the truth, anyone who has faith in me will do what I have been doing. He will do even greater things than these, because I am going to the Father" Jn 14:12

"You may ask me for anything in my name, and I will do it." Jn 14:14

GOD'S GREAT PURPOSE

The "clothing with power from on high" quickens our physical, mental, moral and praying power beyond measure. It must be true of us, as of our Lord,

The Spirit of the Lord will rest on him - the Spirit of wisdom and of understanding and the Spirit of counsel and of power the Spirit of knowledge and of the fear of the Lord - and he will delight in the fear of the Lord" Is 11:2-3a

Only thus will the perfect plan of the lord for his church be accomplished; to organize the entire membership into one harmonious body; to impart to every member, through the Spirit, such a full and special baptism of power as will perfectly qualify and equip them for their proper work within the body; to so strengthen every member that there shall be no infirmity, or weakness, or disunity in the church; through the abiding presence of the Spirit to unite every member in such love and fellowship with each other and with God, that the whole world will know them to be disciples of Christ; and to secure in all such peace, assurance and joy that people everywhere will be willingly brought to the same salvation.

Thus it was in the early church: thus it may be again today.

YESTERDAY AND TODAY

Just before his ascension the Lord Jesus Christ led his disciples outside the city of Jerusalem as far as Bethany. There he delivered to them his FINAL COMMISSION to -

> "...go into all the world and preach the good news to all creation." Mk 16:15 And also his FINAL COMMAND -

> " ...stay in the city until you have been clothed with power from on high." Lu 24:49b

These two commands are still vital for us today. . "Go!" But first, "Stay!"

Wrath will be incurred if we disobey the first: barrenness will blight us if we disregard the second. May all who read these lines, having believed, receive the Holy Spirit, and then go, bringing forth much fruit.

HOW TO RECEIVE THE HOLY SPIRIT

The manner of receiving both the initial baptism of the Holy Spirit and then further infillings of power can be set out quite simply.

1. A right attitude is essential. The first group who experienced the Baptism of the Holy Spirit

   "joined together constantly in prayer." Ac 1:14a

And again, we read of

   ".. the Holy Spirit, whom God has given to those who obey him." Ac 5:32b

Saul fasted and prayed for three days before being filled with the Spirit. (Ac 9:9)

2. The receiving of the gift of the Holy Spirit following conversion is connected with the prayers of Christian workers, and the laying on of hands.

   "When they arrived they prayed for them that they might receive the Holy Spirit. Then Peter and John placed their hands on them, and they received the Holy Spirit Ac 8:15 &17 (See also Ac 9:17 and 19:6)

3. The receiving of spiritual power is also connected with the united prayers of the church. After the Christians of the church at Jerusalem had prayed for boldness to preach the Word,

   "...the place where they were meeting was shaken. And they were all filled with the Holy Spirit and spoke the Word of God boldly." Ac 4:31b

4. A spontaneous outpouring may, in some cases, make prayer or effort unnecessary as was the case with those in the house of Cornelius, whose hearts had already been purified by faith. (Ac 10:44; and 15:9)

5. Since the baptism of power is described as a gift (Ac 10:45) the believer may plead before the throne of grace the promise of Jesus.

> *"If you then, though you are evil know how to give good gifts to your children, how much more will your Father in heaven give the Holy Spirit to those who ask him!" Lu 11:13*

6. The fullness of the Holy Spirit is a freely given gift but it is still essential for every individual to actively ask for and appropriate this gift by faith. The same principle holds as with salvation. God gave his Son (Jn 3:16) but we must receive the Son.

> *"Yet to all who received him, to those who believed in his name, he gave the right to become children of God" Jn 1:12*

As sinners we accept Christ: as saints, we accept the Holy Spirit. As there is a faith toward Christ for salvation, so there is a faith toward the Spirit for power and consecration.

The day of Pentecost was once for all; the baptism of believers is ever for all.

THE TRUE EVIDENCE OF THE BAPTISM OF THE HOLY SPIRIT.

While freely admitting that all true believers have been born of the Spirit, and all have a measure of the anointing of the Spirit, we maintain that not all Christians have experienced the special baptism of the Holy Spirit with its attendant power and divine operation.

How do we know when a person receives the baptism of the Holy Spirit? What is the evidence that one has received this baptism?

These questions cannot be decided from the four Gospels, because they contain prophecies of the then future outpouring of the Spirit, and a prophecy is only made perfectly clear in its fulfillment. (The same holds true of the Old Testament prophecies.) Neither can the matter be settled from the epistles, for they are largely pastoral instructions, addressed to established churches where the power of the Spirit, with outward manifestations, was considered the normal experience of every Christian. It is therefore evident that the matter must be settled by the book of Acts which records many instances of people receiving the baptism of the Spirit, and describes the results that followed.

In every case in the book of Acts where the results of this baptism are described, there is always an immediate, supernatural, outward expression, convincing not only the receiver, but also providing startling evidence to the people nearby that a divine power was blessing and anointing the person.

THE APOSTLES BEFORE AND AFTER PENTECOST

We may take the apostles as examples, and contrasting their intellectual, moral, and spiritual state before and after Pentecost, we are staggered to find a transformation that was scarcely ever paralleled in the experience of men.

How many times Jesus had sorrowed at their dullness, how many times the Lord had expressed amazement at their lack of faith, how often he had rebuked them for their limited and obscure vision;

what a great love they had still shown for the world, how little real courage, how small their love for each other, and how like ropes of sand were all their strong resolutions.

But then came Pentecost! The Holy Spirit came upon them! In a moment they became truly crucified to the world and the world to them; their weak hearts became strong in the glorious beauty and perfection and might of the risen Christ, so that they became a spectacle of wonder to the world, and to angels, and to men.

From that day on, they had a clear vision of the kingdom of God; the truth of the Gospel blazed in their hearts; with a splendid unction they gave witness to the resurrection in great power. Their preaching brought the world to its knees before God.

Peter, the reed, became a rock of faith and courage and strength. James and John vindicated their right to be called "sons of thunder." In all things they all became truly more than conquerors through him that loved them. No power in heaven or in earth could induce them to deny the Lord who died for them. They witnessed for the Lord Jesus everywhere, nothing could trouble their peace in God, nothing could move their assurance of hope, their everlasting consolations, their triumphs of faith, their fullness of joy. This same result should be seen today.

THE SPECIFIC BIBLE EVIDENCE

If you have read all the scripture references mentioned in this study, you will have fully realized by now that there is nothing merely theological about this experience of being filled with the Spirit. It is indeed an EXPERIENCE! A definite, powerful, purging, dynamic, vital, spiritual experience! It is a baptism of fire, rivers of living water, of power. These expressions vividly describe a marvelous outpouring from heaven and something of each of them must be present in the Christian's life before one can honestly claim to be FILLED with the Spirit of God.

However, there is one distinctive universal evidence of receiving the Holy Spirit recorded in the Bible. In each of the five historical accounts of people receiving the gift of the Holy Spirit, there is one visible evidence: they ". . .spoke in other tongues:"

> *"While Peter was still speaking these words, the Holy Spirit came on all who heard the message. The circumcised believers who had come with Peter were astonished that the gift of the Holy Spirit had been poured out even on the Gentiles. For they heard them speaking in tongues and praising God". Acts 10:44-46. (See also Ac 2:1-18; 8:1~25; 9:17; and compare 1 Co 14:18; Ac 19:1-7; compare also Mk 16:17.)*

(The only exception is the description of the Samaritans; but even here something extraordinary and visible must have happened to have brought forth Simon's offer. This could not have been miracles of healing, nor casting out devils, for Phillip had wrought these signs among the people without Simon offering him money. It is reasonable to assume that the phenomenon which staggered Simon and captured his whole interest was the unique sign of speaking in other tongues.)

So we have at least four clear cut examples before us, and probably five. It is therefore our conviction that this is the Bible evidence that a man or woman has been filled with the Holy Spirit. We know they are filled with the Spirit because we hear them speaking in tongues and praising God. (Ac 10:46)

WHY SPEAK IN OTHER TONGUES?

God has made this *"speaking in other tongues"* the necessary and universal evidence of the initial baptism of the Holy Spirit because.

1. It is the only unique and distinctly New Testament experience. The baptism of the Holy Spirit in the New Testament sense is vastly different from the anointing of the Spirit the saints of God knew in Old Testament days. This is decisively proved by the words of John 7:39b;

   " *Up to that time the Spirit had not been given, since Jesus had not yet been glorified"*

2. It was therefore necessary that a distinctive witness to this new experience be given. In Old Testament days people witnessed every other manifestation of the Holy Spirit but this. They prophesied, they saw visions, they felt the power of God, they wrought miracles, they had knowledge, wisdom, grace, and power, but not once did they speak in tongues. So today people may do mighty exploits under the influence of the Holy Spirit; but the evidence that they have received the distinctive New Testament experience, the complete fullness of the Spirit of God, is the unique sign of speaking in other tongues.

3. Across the world today there are more than 100 million people who are rejoicing in the rich infilling of the Holy Spirit and the wonderful evidence of speaking" in other tongues as the Spirit enables them." (Ac 2:4b)

4. Speaking in other tongues is an entirely supernatural gift and so demands full consecration of the whole body, mind and spirit. All of these must be absolutely yielded to God before the Holy Spirit can move upon the believer and impel him to speak in

another tongue. This thought is consistent with the clear New Testament teaching that our bodies are the temples of the Holy Spirit.

5. One of the primary purposes of the baptism in the Holy Spirit is to empower the Christian's witness.

   "But you will receive power when the Holy Spirit comes on you; and you will be my witnesses. . ."
   Ac 1:8a

6. It is therefore proper that the tongue which causes so much strife and speaks so much evil (Ja 3:1-13) should be purged by this marvelous operation of the Holy Spirit, and given over entirely to speak the language of heaven under the inspiration of God.

Wait therefore! Until you are clothed with power from on high!

INTRODUCTION TO LESSON THREE

"It is not hard to walk in the Spirit. You can do that while you drive the car, do housework, teach a class, or run a business. Walking in the Spirit is not a mystical exercise in which a person falls into some kind of trance. Nor is it a feeling. Walking in the Spirit is simply walking in constant fellowship and communion with the Spirit of God resident within us; it is walking in line with God, moment by moment." (Bob Yandian)

The most important part of walking in the Spirit is to keep a balance, to use common sense. Not falling behind God through disobedience, nor going ahead of God with reckless disregard for the consequences.

Michael Harper in his book "Walk in the Spirit", says:

"We should beware of sudden impulses to do anything, especially those which appear unreasonable or even ridiculous. Guidance usually comes when we have had time to wait on God, and test the leadings which we may have had. The more important the action or decision the more surely he prepares us for its consequences. It is a mark, though, of Satan's tactics that he seeks to catch us unawares and trick us into thinking we have discerned God's voice when in reality we have done nothing of the kind. Recklessness is a mark of spiritual immaturity... True balance springs from humility - and the ability to learn and take correction from others. And this will need to be more and more treasured as time goes on - for in the last days, we are warned, false prophets and teachers will abound, deceiving if possible even the elect[9]

In this lesson we learn how to walk in the Spirit, and how to be rid of the old self and to put on the new self, which is righteous in God's sight and made into his image.

---

[9] Walk In The Spirit; Michael Harper; Published by Hodder and Stoughton, London. 1968. These ref. pg. 31&33

LESSON THREE:
THE SPIRIT FILLED LIFE

TRUE CHRISTIAN CHARACTER

The Bible gives us a beautiful picture of the loveliness of a perfect Christian life. This ideal and gracious character is the perfect pattern to which every believer is expected to conform.

This perfection of character is described to us as being our "new self", in opposition to the "old self.

The "old self" is our previous unrenewed, corrupted, sin-darkened moral and spiritual nature.

The "new self" is the new creation we have become in the Lord Jesus Christ.

> *"....Therefore, if anyone is in Christ he is a new creation; the old has gone, the new has come!"* 2 Co 5:17

> *"Do not lie to each other since you have taken off your old self with its practices and have put on the new self which is being renewed in knowledge in the image of its Creator."* Cl 3:9-10

> *"and put on the new self, created to be like God in true righteousness and holiness."* Ep 4:24

Here we see.

1. We are told to PUT OFF the "old self" and to PUT ON the "new *self.*"

2. This "new self" brings us KNOWLEDGE, shapes us to the IMAGE OF GOD, produces RIGHTEOUSNESS, and TRUE HOLINESS within us, gives us VICTORY over all old things, and makes us NEW in every way.

If we have failed to realize in our daily walk ALL OF THESE CHARACTERISTICS of the " new self," it is because of one or both of the following reasons:

1. We have not attempted true obedience to the command to "take off the old self and put on the new self:" that is we have been indifferent to God's challenge to live a life centered in Christ.

2. We have attempted to obey this command in ways differing from God's revealed method.

IT IS TOO LITTLE REALIZED THAT, WHEN GOD GIVES A WARNING OR A PROMISE, HE ALWAYS TELLS MEN HOW TO AVOID THE ONE AND APPROPRIATE THE OTHER. For example. . When Noah was warned of the flood, he was also given complete instructions as to how to build the ark.

When Sodom was about to be destroyed, Lot was told exactly how to escape.

When it was time to deliver the Israelites from Egypt, Moses was given precise directions on how to perform the mighty miracles needed to accomplish this deliverance.

There is a Bible way to find healing of body - by the laying on of hands and the prayer of faith.

There is a Bible way to experience remission of sins, and the burying of our "old self" - by baptism.

SO ALSO THERE IS A BIBLE WAY TO PUT ON THE "NEW SELF."

This brings us to two questions: What is this "new self"? What is the Bible method by which we put on the "new self"?

In the Bible the "new self" is described as being cleansed from all sin and idolatry, as having a new heart, as keeping the law of God, being abundantly fruitful and prosperous.

> *I will sprinkle clean water on you, and you will be clean; I will cleanse you from all your impurities and from all your idols. I will give you a new heart and put a new spirit in you; I will remove from you your heart of stone and give you a heart of flesh. And I will put my Spirit in you and move you to follow my decrees and be careful to keep my laws. You will live in the land I gave your forefathers; you will be my people, and I will be your God. I will save you from all your uncleanness. I will call for the grain and make it plentiful and will not bring famine upon you. I will increase the fruit of the trees and the crops of the field, so that you will no longer suffer disgrace among the nations because of famine." Ez 36:25-30*

The man who is made new in the blessing of God is also shown to be cleansed of sin, healed of all sickness, crowned with abundant blessings, contented in heart and mind, and renewed in strength and victory. (Ps 103:1-5)

Such will be the blessing of God upon the "new self" that in his weakness he will yet be as the Angel of the Lord.

> *"On that day the Lord will shield those who live in*

> *Jerusalem, so that the feeblest among them will be like David, and the house of David will be like God, like the Angel of the Lord going before them."*
> *Zc 12:8*

So we find it also in the New Testament. The new self is spoken of as being:

Righteous In God's Sight And Made Into His Image.

> *"And we, who with unveiled faces all reflect the Lord's glory, are being transformed into his likeness with ever increasing glory, which comes from the Lord, who is the Spirit." 2 Co 3:18 (See also Ep 4:22-23; Cl 2:9-10; and 3:10.)*

As Indwelt By Christ.

> *"I have been crucified with Christ and I no longer live, but Christ lives in me. The life I live in the body, I live by faith in the Son of God, who loved me and gave himself for me." Ga 2:20 (See also Cl 1:27; 1 Jn 3:24)*

As Being At Peace In The Will Of God.

> *"Therefore, since we have been justified through faith, we have peace with God through our Lord Jesus Christ through whom we have gained access by faith into this grace in which we now stand. And we rejoice in the hope of the glory of God." Ro 5:1-2 (See also Romans 8:28; 8:38-39; Ph 4:12-13.)*

And Finally He Is Spoken Of As A Mighty Warrior

In the strength of the Lord overcoming every enemy, triumphing in every difficulty.

> *"I have given you authority to trample on snakes and scorpions and to overcome all the power of the enemy; nothing will harm you." Lu 10:19 (See also Ep 6:1-11)*

HOW TO PUT ON THE NEW SELF

Whenever the leading characteristics of the new self are mentioned, they are specifically represented as being produced by the INDWELLING PRESENCE AND INFLUENCE OF THE HOLY SPIRIT.

> *"Now the Lord is the Spirit and where the Spirit of the Lord is, there is freedom. And we, who with unveiled faces all reflect the Lord's glory, are being transformed into his likeness with ever-increasing glory, which comes from the Lord, who is the Spirit." 2 Co 3:17-18*

(See also Ez 36:27, Ro 5:3-5; 8:1-26; 15:13,and 19; Ga 5:22; Ep 3:16-19; 6:17-18; and many other references could be quoted.)

The Holy Spirit begins to achieve many of the characteristics of Christ in the life of the believer from the moment of the new birth. But there is no doubt that the special baptism of the Holy Spirit greatly accelerates the influence of God upon the life, and gives the believer a renewed and vital opportunity to fulfill the Bible pattern for the "new self" in the Lord Jesus Christ.

To realize completely in our experience God's revealed pattern for Christian living we must be clothed with power from on high by the mighty infilling of the Holy Spirit.

HOWEVER, IT IS VITAL THAT WE RECOGNIZE A FURTHER FACT. THE BAPTISM OF THE HOLY SPIRIT WILL NOT AUTOMATICALLY CLOTHE US WITH ALL THE BEAUTY OF CHRISTIAN CHARACTER.

> *"Since we live by the Spirit let us keep in step with the Spirit." Ga 5:25*

The command to "put on the new self" was given to men and women who were already filled with the Holy Spirit, e.g. the Ephesians.

In Acts 19:6 and Ephesians 1:13 we have it recorded that the Ephesians had very definitely experienced the supernatural baptism of the Holy Spirit. Yet the command is strongly given to them that they should now, in the strength of the Spirit of God, "put off the old self and put on the new self."

> *"You were taught, with regard to your former way of life, to put off your old self which is being corrupted by its deceitful desires; to be made new in the attitude of your minds; and to put on the new self created to be like God in true righteousness and holiness." Ep 4:22-24*

The apostle urged them to continue being filled with the Spirit for they would then find much praise in God, would have a song in their hearts, would be in unity with one another, and would walk in the fear of God, knowing the full riches of the blessing of God.

> *"Therefore do not be foolish, but understand what the Lord's will is. Do not get drunk on wine, which leads to debauchery. Instead, be filled with the Spirit speak to one another with psalms, hymns and spiritual songs. Sing and make music in your heart*

> *to the Lor4 always giving thanks to God the Father for everything in the name of our Lord Jesus Christ" Ep 5:17-20*

So we are told again,

> *"Since we live by the Spirit (that is, are made alive by the Spirit and have been baptized in the Spirit, our bodies becoming the living temples of the Holy Spirit) LET US KEEP IN STEP WITH THE SPIRIT." Ga 5:25*

And again,

> *".. live by the Spirit and you will not gratify' the desires of the sinful nature." Ga 5:16*

Arising from this, we see that it is essential for every person.

- to be born of the Spirit, and so receive eternal life;
- to be baptized in the Spirit, and thus receive all the potential of the new life in Christ;
- to then walk in the Spirit, and thus release all of that divine potential into effective activity in daily living.

HOW TO WALK IN THE SPIRIT

THE FOUNDATION FOR A SUCCESSFUL WALK IN THE SPIRIT IS LAID IN THE FOLLOWING THINGS. . Firstly, constantly applying ourselves to every means used by the Spirit of God to produce Christian character; that is, the Word of God, prayer, worship, fellowship with God's people, and so on.

Secondly, having greater care for our souls than for our bodies: by loving heaven more than earth, and the reward of God more than the reward of men.

Thirdly, in everything yielding instant obedience to the promptings of the Spirit when he speaks to us through preaching, through the scripture, through the operation of spiritual gifts, or through the advice or admonition of spiritual persons.

Fourthly, by the laying hold in faith of the fact that we have been filled with the Spirit. Having once received the anointing of God, that anointing abides, unless we willfully grieve the Holy Spirit.

> *"As for you, the anointing you have received from him remains in you, and you do not need anyone to teach you. But as his anointing teaches you about all things and as that anointing is real not counterfeit - just as it has taught you, remain in him." 1 Jn 2:27*

We are not concerned as to whether we can FEEL the anointing or the presence of the Spirit, or whether we FEEL strong in the Lord and able to overcome all things. It is enough that, having been baptized in the Holy Spirit, we should BELIEVE in the promise of that baptism. Having once been baptized in the Holy Spirit, and continuing to love God, we must accept the declaration of God's Word that the anointing of that baptism is still with us. We may at any time lay hold of it and claim the support and strength of the Holy Spirit in any time of trial.

THE VALUE OF SPEAKING IN TONGUES

In this regard the singular evidence of the Baptism of the Holy Spirit, speaking in other tongues, is of great value. Peter knew that Cornelius had received the gift of the Holy Spirit when he heard him speak with tongues and magnify God.

> *"While Peter was still speaking these words, the Holy Spirit came on all who heard the message. The*

> *circumcised believers who had come with Peter were astonished that the gift of the Holy Spirit had been poured out even on the Gentiles. For they heard them speaking in tongues and praising God."*
> *Ac 10:44-46*

So with us; let us in time of great need, when the grace and help of the Holy Spirit seem far removed from us, kneel before God, and with our hearts thrilling with love and faith toward God, magnify him in the supernatural language of the Spirit.

To do this is to renew our consciousness of the abiding anointing, so that we may rise and boldly claim the might of the Holy Spirit in every conflict against evil.

It was for this reason that Paul, said,

> *"...I would like everyone of you to speak in tongues." 1 Co 14:5a. and*
>
> *"...He who speaks in a tongue edifies himself..." 1 Co 14:4a*

and

> *"...I thank God that I speak in tongues more than all of you." 1 Co 14:18*

BUT NOTE: it is our faith in the operation of God that will make us victorious. To merely speak in tongues is of no value unless we boldly claim the promise of God. The speaking in tongues is simply the outward evidence of the indwelling Spirit, and as we speak in tongues we must allow the witness to rise in our hearts that the mighty Spirit of God is resting upon us. We must arise from the time of prayer with full assurance of faith and walk in the knowledge that we are indwelt by the Holy Spirit.

We must resist the onslaught of evil, and yield to the guidance and persuasion of the Holy Spirit of God in our lives, knowing that the Holy Spirit will surely lead us in the way we ought to go. So shall we be victorious over all the works of the flesh.

THE FRUIT OF THE SPIRIT

To do these things - to walk in love toward one another, and to war against the flesh by walking in the Spirit-will produce in our lives the nine-fold fruit of the Spirit:

> *"...But the fruit of the Spirit is love, joy, peace, patience, kindness, goodness, faithfulness, gentleness and self control" Ga 5:22-23*

As with Aaron's rod that budded overnight, so the moment we begin to walk in the Spirit the fruit of the Spirit will become more prominent in us; and, as we continue to so walk, that fruit will increase in ever richer power and beauty, until every work of the flesh is entirely subdued.

Two great promises are given to those who walk in the Spirit.

Firstly -

> *Against such things there is no law." Ga 5:23*

That is, they will be dead to sin (which stands only because of the law), and triumphant over the works of the flesh. They will also stand pure and justified before God. Those whose lives are dominated in any respect by the works of the flesh will never inherit the kingdom of God.

But the person whose life is dominated by the fruit of the Spirit, even though there may be failure and weakness found, will be free of accusation before God. There is no law connected with the fruit of the Spirit, because there is no need of law

These wonderful graces embody their own law which is entirely righteous and acceptable. There is no law and therefore those whose lives are characterized by this fruit are free of any barrier between them and God: they will stand high in the favor of God. The Lord will have no restraint in his dealings with them, but being made full of fidelity and faith by that blessed fruit, the Lord will be able to heap on them his abundant blessings and every spiritual gift, and they will truly have power and authority in Christ.

Secondly -

> *Those who belong to Christ Jesus have crucified the sinful nature its passions and desires." Ga 5:24*

Those who bring forth the fruit of the Spirit will have in their hands the mightiest weapon for righteousness they could ever hold. As the works of the flesh are as poison to the influence of the Spirit, so is the fruit of the Spirit the most deadly poison to the works of the flesh.

The lusts of the flesh are the 'works' of unrighteousness which the apostle Paul listed before in detail.

> *"...The acts of the sinful nature are obvious: sexual immorality, impurity, and debauchery; idolatry and witchcraft; hatred, discord, jealousy, fits of rage, selfish ambition, dissentions, factions and envy; drunkenness, orgies, and the like. I warn you, as I did before, that those who live like this will not inherit the kingdom of God" Ga 5:19-21*

So in the fruit of the Spirit we find the fountain of victory over all sin, and sickness, and failure, and suffering, and infirmity, and temptation.

THEREFORE

> *"...IF WE LIVE IN THE SPIRIT (that is have been made vitally alive by the Spirit and baptised in the Spirit) LET US KEEP IN STEP WITH THE SPIRITI" Ga 5:25*

Here is an Outline Study on the Bible Teaching Concerning the Baptism of the Holy Spirit.

1. It is not the New Birth.

Compare Ac 8:12 (salvation) with Ac 8:14-17. Ac 9:3-6 (salvation) with Ac 9:17, Ac 19:1-2 & 5 (salvation) with Ac 19:6.

2. It is not Sanctification.

Compare John 15:3 (and see Jn 17:17) (sanctification) with Acts 1:5. Sanctification is an operation of the Holy Spirit (1 Pe 1:2), but the baptism is the reception of the Spirit. (Ac 8:15; 10:47; 19:2.)

3. The Baptism in the Holy Spirit is:
- Being baptized in the Holy Spirit by Jesus Christ. (Mt 3:11-12; Ac 1:5; 11:16)
- Being filled with the Holy Spirit (Ac 2:4; Ac 9:17; Ep 5:18).
- The Holy Spirit falling on one (Ac 8:16; 10:44; 11:15).
- The Holy Spirit coming on one (Ac 19:6)
- Receiving the Holy Spirit (Ac 8:15,17; 10:47; 19:2).

- Receiving the gift of the Holy Spirit (Ac 2:38).
- The gift of the Holy Spirit poured out (Ac 10:45).
- God giving the Holy Spirit (Ac 5:32; 8:18; 15:8; Jn 7:39).

4. **The conditions for receiving the Holy Spirit are:**
   - Regeneration (Ac 2:38). (See also Section 1 above)
   - Baptism in water (Ac 2:38; 8:12; 19:5). In exceptional cases immersion follows the receiving of the Spirit (Ac 9:17-18; 10:47-48).
   - Obedience to God's will (Ac 5:32)
   - Faith (Ga 3:2 & 14; Jn 7:39).
   - Thirst (Jn 7:37; Is 44:3).
   - Prayer (Lu 11:13)

5. **The methods of receiving the Holy Spirit are:**
   - Suddenly, while waiting (Ac 2:1-4).
   - Suddenly, while hearing the Word (Ac 10:44; 11:15).
   - Through prayer, followed by the laying on of hands (Ac 8:15-17; 9:17; 19:6).
   - Through prayer and earnest desire (Lu 11:11-13; Jn 7:37-39; 1 Co 12:13; Ep 5:18).
   - Tarrying sometimes necessary (Lu 24:49; Acts 8:16) (waiting inferred) It is through faith and patience we inherit the promises (He 6:12).

6. **Some results are:**

Immediate.

- Speaking in an unknown tongue (Ac 2:4; 8:18, with 2:33; 10:46; 11:17; 19:6; 1 Co 12:7).
- Often other manifestations also- praise (Ac 2:11; 10:46); prophecy (Ac 2:13-18) various (Ac 2:17,18; 19:6)

Permanent.

- Jesus Christ glorified and revealed (Jn 15:26; 16:14-15).
- Power in witnessing (Ac 1:8; 2:41; 4:8, 4:31; 5:32; Jn 15:26, 27; 16:8; 1 Co 2:4-5).
- Miracles and gifts (Ac 7:55; 13:9-11; Ro 15:19; 1 Co 12:13-14; Ga 3:5; 1 Ti 4:14; 2 Ti 1:6-7).
- Other revelations (Jn 16:13; Ac 11:28; 13:2-4; 16:6-7; 1 Ti 4:1; 1 Co 2:9-11).
- Better understanding of God's ways (Jn 14:26; 16:13; 1 Co 2:12-13; 1 Jn 2:20 & 27).
- Mortal bodies quickened (Ro 8:11; 1 Th 5:23-24).
- Assurance (Ac 5:8, 1 Jn 3:24; 4:13).
- Help (Jn 14:16; 16:7; Ro 8:26-27; Ju 20).

7. **The Necessity:**
   - It is God's will (Ac 2:39; Lu 11:11-13; Mt 3:11-12; Mk 1:8; Lu 3:16-17; Jn 1:32-34).
   - It is God's command (Ep 5:18).
   - It is for your and your fellowman's present and eternal good (See -references in Section 6 above.) Zechariah 4:6.

HAVE YE RECEIVED THE HOLY GHOST SINCE YE BELIEVED? Ac19:2. (KJV)

BOOK FOUR: SIGNS WONDERS AND GIFTS

Introduction To Lesson One

Lesson One - **Concerning Spiritual Gifts**

Introduction To Lesson Two

Lesson Two - **More About The Gifts**

INTRODUCTION TO LESSON ONE

Every person born into this world is unique in some way. We are born with certain gifts and abilities that we can, by education and application, develop for the good of ourselves and others.

When we are born again and filled with the Holy Spirit of God we are graced with more gifts from the Father. Gifts that can be used for the edification and instruction of the body of Christ.

When we use these gifts, the Holy Spirit works in us to the extent that we make room for him. It is our task to seek earnestly the best gifts, making sure that we live in purity before the Lord; not in any way grieving the Holy Spirit or hindering his work in us. Do not forget that they are gifts:

"You cannot earn any gift or obtain it by labouring for it; it is only received by him who comes before God in his helplessness and grasps hold of the grace of God in simple trust. God places his gifts into our unholy hands and takes the risk of our misusing them. It is, therefore, of greatest importance that everyone who reaches out for these gifts of divine grace, should, at the same time, observe carefully the help and instruction then offered to protect against misuse."[10]

In your next lesson we will begin the study of Spiritual Gifts and their place in the body of Christ.

---

[10] "Gifts and Graces" a commentary on 1 Cor 12-14. Arnold Bittlinger. Hodder and Stoughton, London. This ref. pg. 26.

LESSON ONE:
CONCERNING SPIRITUAL GIFTS

In his letter to the church at Corinth Paul wrote three remarkable chapters on the supernatural Gifts of the Holy Spirit. However to many Christians there are no other places in the Bible more hard to understand than these discussions on the miraculous activities of the Holy Spirit in the worship of the church. It is not possible for us to consider in detail in this lesson the whole passage in question, but we can pick out the particular gifts the great apostle mentioned, and consider his teaching concerning their proper place in the church.

The three chapters we are talking about are the twelfth, thirteenth, and fourteenth chapters of Paul's first letter to the Corinthians. Paul begins his argument with these words...

> "Now about spiritual gifts, brothers, I do not want you to be ignorant." 1 Co 12:1.

At the outset this text tells us three things...

- There are certain 'spiritual gifts.'
- There is Bible teaching concerning these gifts.
- There are many who are ignorant of these gifts.

1. The ignorance of the Corinthian Christians.

These early believers were certainly not ignorant of the existence of the availability of the spiritual gifts. Earlier Paul had said:

> "I always thank God for you because of his grace

> *given you in Christ Jesus. For in him you have been enriched in every way" 1 Co 1:4-5a*
>
> *"Therefore you do not lack in any spiritual gift....."*
> *1 Co 1: 7a*

The Corinthian church was replete with every Gift of the Spirit, but they were greatly deficient in their understanding of the proper purpose and functioning of these gifts. Hence the urgent instruction of the apostle on the true exercise and co-ordination of these gifts. He wanted them to keep the gifts and their spiritual experience, but to add to those gifts knowledge, and love, and due regard for the glory of God and the comfort of the church.

2. The ignorance of present-day Christians.

Today we are faced with a more serious and challenging ignorance concerning spiritual gifts. Many Christians are almost completely unaware of these gifts and their purpose in the church today. Even those who do know about them rarely have any experience of them in their own worship. This absence of the distinctive Gifts of the Holy Spirit from many churches today occasions many embarrassing inquiries, and so the leaders of the church are compelled to resort to many excuses to remove the challenge and significance of the three chapters under consideration.

Before going any further it may be wise for us to list these gifts, and mention briefly some of the objections to them.

1. WHAT ARE THE GIFTS OF THE SPIRIT?

When Jesus lived in Palestine, his disciples leaned heavily upon him day by day. They were greatly distressed when they learned that he would soon leave them. It was when the Master told them that if he went away, he would sent ANOTHER COMFORTER TO

THEM. This Comforter was the Holy Spirit who would be the agent of Christ in every believer. In the strength of the Holy Spirit and his divine gifts the church would fulfil the words of the Lord when he said,

> *"I tell you the truth, anyone who has faith in me will do what I have been doing. He will do even greater things than these, because I am going to the Father." Jn 14:12*

It was the purpose of the Lord to ascend into heaven, and, taking hold of the promise of his Father, to pour out the Holy Spirit upon his church. Through this outpouring of his Spirit, the disciples would be empowered to continue his ministry on earth.

Accordingly the New Testament pattern of receiving Christ is always REPENT, then BELIEVE ON THE LORD JESUS CHRIST AS SAVIOUR, after that be BAPTISED and then RECEIVE THE FULLNESS OF THE HOLY SPIRIT. (Ac 2:38-39; 19:1-7)

It was to people thus filled with the Holy Spirit that Paul wrote the three chapters we are studying. He was explaining how the Holy Spirit had come to bring various GIFTS so that the miraculous ministry of the Lord Jesus Christ might be continued unabated through the members of his body here on earth.

Here then is God's SUPERNATURAL EQUIPMENT for the ministry of the church: equipment especially designed to bring deliverance to those who are captives of sin and sickness and to make the proclamation of the gospel most effective.

The apostle Paul lists nine of these gifts, and for the sake of convenience, we shall divide these nine gifts into three sets of three as follows (See 1 Co 12:7-11)

GIFTS OF REVELATION
- Word of Wisdom
- Word of Knowledge
- Discerning of Spirits.

GIFTS OF POWER
- Gift of Faith
- Gift of Healing
- Working of Miracles.

GIFTS OF INSPIRED UTTERANCE
- Gift of Tongues
- Gift of Interpretation of Tongues
- Gift of Prophecy.

We want to examine each of these gifts individually, but before doing so, let us consider some of the objections which are raised against the use of these gifts today...

WHAT ARE THE OBJECTIONS TO THE GIFTS OF THE SPIRIT?

1. Spiritual gifts are no longer needed now that we have a completed New Testament.

Answer: Spiritual gifts were never intended to be a substitute for the written Word of God, and the early church at no time accorded these gifts such authority. The early believers always referred back to their Old Testament scriptures for doctrinal authority. (Acts 2:16-21; 15:15-18; 28:23) not once do we hear of anyone appealing to the Gifts of the Spirit to establish a particular doctrine. Rather,

Paul taught that these gifts are not infallible, and are subject to judgment.

> *"Two or three prophets should speak, and the others should weigh carefully what is said."*
> *1 Co 14:29*

Moreover we cannot believe that God would provide us with a New Testament containing so much detailed instruction concerning the use and purpose of spiritual gifts if those gifts were to pass away as soon as the New Testament was completed!

2. The Gifts of the Spirit were special signs for Jewish Christians only, and ceased when the Jews were scattered from Jerusalem in 70 AD.

Answer: Nowhere in the New Testament is it indicated that spiritual gifts were only for Jewish believers. The Corinthians, for example, were mostly NON-Jewish people, and to them the apostle taught that -

> *"Now you are the body of Christ, and each one of you is a part of it. And in the church God has appointed first of all apostles, second prophets, third teachers, then workers of miracles, also those having gifts of healing, those able to help others, those with gifts of administration, and those speaking in different kinds of tongues."* *1 Co 12:27-28*

Thus it is seen that these gifts were not to be regarded as temporary signs to the Jewish people, but rather as being permanently set in the church which is the body of Christ.

3. The Gifts of the Spirit ceased at the close of the apostolic age.

Answer: There is not one scripture which says these supernatural manifestations of the Holy Spirit were to continue for such a limited duration, but we are left with the logical conclusion that they are a vital part of the ministry of the Holy Spirit throughout this entire dispensation of the Holy Spirit - i.e. from Pentecost to the Second Advent.

Jesus said supernatural signs were to follow the preaching of the Gospel

>*"...into all the world."*

>*"...to all creation." Mk 16:15.*

>*and this was to continue*

>*"...to the very end of the age." Mt 28:20*

>*So we read also*

>*"...God's gifts and his call are irrevocable." Ro 11:29*

>*and that*

>*"...Jesus Christ is the same yesterday and today and forever." He 13:8*

4. History proves that the Gifts of the Spirit ceased with the apostolic age.

Answer: This statement is true that the Gifts of the Spirit became less and less common with the passage of years. But for all that, even a slight examination of history will show that in every age of the church these gifts have been in evidence, and especially in times of revival. It is true that the exercise of spiritual gifts became a rare thing in the worship of the church, but certainly not because God had withdrawn them, but rather because of the apathy and unbelief of the church with regard to these gifts.

5. If these gifts were available today, the great church leaders would have them.

Answer: The basic principle in spiritual things is always this -

> *"...without faith it is impossible to please God."*
> *He 11:6a*

God gives nothing to unbelief. It is therefore possible for men and women to be very clear in their understanding and appropriation of many of the good things of the gospel and yet to be entirely ignorant of, and lacking in, other parts of the same gospel. These gifts could be had by all, if all would seek them in full fervency and faith.

WHY WE BELIEVE IN THE GIFTS OF THE SPIRIT

1. **Because the Bible declares they are `appointed in the church. This word is used in a two-fold connection with the Gifts of the Spirit, each time conveying the thought of permanency and continuity.**

    a. Firstly, then, Paul speaks of the Gifts of the Spirit as being `appointed' in the church (1 Co 12:28). The Greek word so translated means `to put, to place, to establish, to institute, to ordain.' Each of these expressions carry in them a sense of finality, of continuity, and if the word had no further meaning than contained in these terms we would be justified in counting the Gifts of the Spirit to be still appointed in the church today.

However, there is another graphic meaning of the word 'appointed'. It was used in a special sense by the early Greek world to describe something which was 'set up in a temple' - and specifically an idol.

Paul evidently had this sense in mind when he used the word in connection with the Gifts of the Spirit. You will notice that he contrasted the dumb idols of the heathen with the living manifestations of the Holy Spirit (vs 2). Now, unquestionably, an idol was set up in a temple to become a permanent part of that temple. In fact the temple was built for the sole purpose of sheltering the idol. The idol was essential to proper worship in the temple. Without the idol the temple would have been an empty shell, and the worship of the people valueless husks.

Now Paul says that one time these people had worshipped the idol that was set up in their heathen temple, the idol was dumb - dumb because it could not hear, neither could it heal, neither could it speak. However by way of supreme contrast, he reminds them that now they were to come to the true temple of the God of heaven, the temple that was the church of the Lord Jesus Christ, the church that was the body of Christ, made up of all its members (vs 12 & 27); appointed in this church, were the manifestations of the Spirit that was not dumb. They spoke, they wrought deliverance, they brought revelation, they revealed the reality of God in the midst of his people. And these gifts are essential to the worship of the people: remove them from the temple of God and worship became a thing lifeless, voiceless, a matter of form and dulling tradition.

    b. Secondly, Paul uses the same Greek word for 'appointed' (here translated 'arranged') in connection with the members of the body of Christ. He said,

> *"But in fact God has arranged the parts in the body, every one of them, just as he wanted them to be." 1 Co 12:18*

This setting also is spoken of in connection with the manifestations of the Spirit. Men and women are arranged in the church as members of the body of Christ, and into this living church are set the manifestations and ministries of the Holy Spirit, all designed to enable the church to carry on the work of Christ on earth, and to make the worship and witness of its people fully effective.

The apostle uses the analogy of the human body to describe the formation of the church. It cannot be disputed that our bodies are the same in construction now as they were in Bible days, neither can it be disputed that the church of the Lord Jesus Christ is still spoken of as the body of Christ, and that the `members' are still `arranged' in that body.

The only conclusion which remains reasonable is that the Gifts of the Holy Spirit are also still appointed in this same manner and for the same purpose in which they were appointed in Bible days.

2. Because there is immense profit in the gifts.

The apostle said,

> *"Now to each one the manifestation of the Spirit is given for the common good." 1 Co 12:7*

We find it difficult to understand the incredible folly of those who feel they can dispense with that which God says is for their good.

The apostle said that the Gifts of the Spirit were for EVERY man; not just to some men, nor to some churches, but to all men everywhere who would receive them.

This word translated `good' is used infrequently in the New Testament, but it has very great meaning. It is used in connection with the vast good given to the church through the ascension of the Lord Jesus Christ to his Father's right hand: the Lord said,

> *"But I tell you the truth: It is for your good that I am going away. Unless I go away, the Counsellor will not come to you; but if I go, I will send him to you." Jn 16:7*

It is used in connection with us becoming sharers in the holiness of God -

> *"...but God disciplines us for our good, that we may share in his holiness." He 12:10b*

When the apostle says that the Gifts of the Spirit are "given for the common good," he uses a term of great magnitude, an expression rich with vivid meaning and one which strongly excludes all thought of these Gifts of the Spirit being one of little value. No man can afford to despise the wonderful profit given to the church in the Gifts of the Holy Spirit.

Paul brings the matter closer to home when he says that these gifts are given to use for the purpose of `edification' (strengthening) exhortation (encouragement) and comfort:' and again `for the edification that excels'; and again, that all may learn and all may be comforted. (1 Co 14:3; 12, *& 31. KJV)

Believing the Bible statement that the Gifts of the Spirit are valuable and coveting these gifts earnestly, we have found that they are exactly as the scripture says, `GOOD!'

3. Because they are commanded by the Lord.

Toward the end of his instruction concerning the Gifts of the Spirit, Paul spoke these blunt words

> *"If anybody thinks he is a prophet or spiritually gifted, let him acknowledge that what I am writing to you is the Lord's command. If he ignores this, he himself will be ignored."* 1 Co 14:37-38

If we were to gather some of the preachers of our community together, and set them before the apostle Paul, and have them express to him their opinion concerning themselves and the Gifts of the Spirit, we would perhaps hear them say something like this - "we are spiritual men, we are preachers and prophets, but we do not consider that the Gifts of the Holy Spirit are to be found in the church today, nor do we feel that they have any usefulness for our times. We can well dispense with those supernatural gifts."

If this were to happen do you think Paul's answer to them would differ in any way from his answer to the Corinthians? Do you not think he would scoff at their spirituality? Do you not think that he would be appalled at their ignorance? Do you not think that he would thunder back at them - "If anybody thinks he is a prophet or spiritually gifted, let him acknowledge that what I am writing to you is the Lord's command?"

It is our prayer that preachers everywhere may tremble before these strong words of the scripture, and may search their Bible anew, yielding themselves to the commandment of the Lord, setting themselves to "eagerly desire the greater gifts." (1 Co 12:31)

And, becoming zealous for spiritual gifts, that they -

> *"...try to excel in gifts that build up the church."*
> *1 Co 14:12b*

DIVERSITIES OF GIFTS

There is a great variety of way in which the Holy Spirit will work in and through men and women. There are many extraordinary powers which the Spirit is able to bestow on the servants of God to equip them for service and for every emergency. But there are certain outstanding endowments - nine in number - which are common to the whole body of Christ and which are especially manifestations of the Spirit. These are listed by the scripture in this manner...

> *"Now to each one the manifestation of the Spirit is given for the common good. To one there is given through the Spirit the message of wisdom, to another the message of knowledge by means of the same Spirit, to another faith by the same Spirit, to another gifts of healing by that one Spirit, to another miraculous powers, to another prophecy, to another distinguishing between spirits, to another speaking in different kinds of tongues, and to still another they interpretation of tongues. All these are the works of one and the same Spirit, and he gives them to each one, just as he determines."*
> *1 Co 12:7-11*

It is the desire of the Holy Spirit to manifest the ministry of Christ through the believers; but so marvellous is the superb character and rich ministry of the Lord Jesus Christ that different kinds of gifts are needed to reveal that complete ministry through many people to the whole world.

These marvellous workings of the Holy Spirit are called gifts; that is, they are gifts in that they are given freely, without charge, as unmerited favours of God. However, the scripture clearly indicates that they are not gifts in the sense of being given to a believer as a conscious possession to be exercised at will. These are not gifts given to believers so much as manifestations of the Holy Spirit THROUGH believers. The scripture does not show that one or another special gifts is given to this man or that man, but rather that various manifestations of the Holy Spirit are given "for the common good."

These gifts then are 'appointed in the church' (1 Co 12:28) and should be evident in the worship and activity of every local company of God's people. In the course of our ministry and service for the Lord, as the need arises and as we have a clear understanding of the Word of God and by faith yield ourselves to become channels of the divine favour these gifts will be revealed in us.

Every spirit filled believer has the potential capacity for every manifestation of the Holy Spirit, but always subject to the will of God in the prevailing circumstances. It must be evident though that before any person can receive spiritual gifts he or she must first receive the Gift of the Spirit himself. (Ac 2:38)

SUPERNATURAL GIFTS

Still further concerning these spiritual gifts, we may note that they stem from the Holy Spirit and are hence ENTIRELY SUPER-NATURAL as far as their source is concerned. The apostle is not speaking of natural qualities of wisdom or knowledge or faith, etc.

It is gross error to claim for example, that the "gifts of healing" or "the working of miracles" are now fulfilled through the skill of modern medical science. To make such a claim is to blatantly ignore everything the Bible has to say concerning the supernatural endowments of the Holy Spirit. People who are out rightly atheistic and ungodly may be brilliant medical practitioners but they most certainly cannot claim to have received one of the precious Gifts of the Spirit of God. These are holy gifts, centered in the Spirit who is holy, and they are only given to holy men and women who wholeheartedly believe their God.

I am not decrying the wonderful work of modern medical missionaries, nor Christian doctors in our communities. They have dedicated their talents and skill to the service of the Lord and undoubtedly the hand of the Lord is upon them. None the less it is folly to say that such people in their natural skill are displaying the supernatural Gift of the Holy Spirit.

So it is also with the gift of "speaking in other tongues." It is sometimes said that this gift is now fulfilled in the Lord enabling missionaries to readily learn foreign languages. But such a claim makes nonsense out of every Bible reference to speaking in other tongues. The Bible plainly indicates that this is an entirely supernatural Gift of the Holy Spirit given absolutely apart from any natural ability.

More of these thoughts when we come to consider each of the gifts individually. It is enough now to repeat again that these gifts must be imparted by the Holy Spirit in answer to faith or they will not be known at all. Notice also that they are each a manifestation of the Spirit and as such these gifts are designed to work in harmony with the activity of the Father and of the Son and in the church. No manifestation of the Spirit will appear in opposition to the ministry and function of the other members of the body of Christ, but every diverse Gift of the Spirit will work harmoniously to the benefit of the whole church.

The scripture says that these gifts are given for the COMMON GOOD therefore this test should be applied to every exercise of the Gifts of the Holy Spirit - namely, "Is it good and profitable for all concerned?" If it is not, then the manifestation is either not genuine, or it is out of order. The Gifts of the Spirit in the scriptural order will always be good and profitable for all concerned, and will serve to produce greater unity and richer worship in the church.

In the next lesson we will consider the gifts individually...

INTRODUCTION TO LESSON TWO

Have you noticed the occasions in the New Testament when our Lord Jesus used the gifts of the Holy Spirit?

Many times in the gospels Jesus used a word of Wisdom, confounding his enemies, who were seeking to trap him into making a serious mistake; for example, when the woman was taken in adultery (Jn 8:1-11); on the giving of tribute to Caesar (Lu 20:20-26). There were times when Jesus had a Word of Knowledge; that is, he knew things that normally he could not know: with the woman at the well (Jn 4:4-22); in the calling of Nathanael (Jn 1:44-50).

Jesus had discerning of Spirits; he knew when a person was being troubled by evil spirits, and he had the authority to cast them out. The demon possessed man in the region of the Gerasenes was delivered by Jesus (Lu 8:26-38); as was the man in the Synagogue (Lu 4:31-36).

He manifested the gifts of Faith, Healing, and the Working of Miracles. In Acts 10:38 we read:

> *"how God anointed Jesus of Nazareth with the Holy Spirit and power, and how he went around doing good things and healing all who were under the power of the devil, because God was with him."*

Did Jesus pray in the Spirit (that is, in other tongues)? This cannot be proved from the gospels; but it is true that Jesus did pray with "sighings and groanings" too deep for words (Mk 7:34; 8:12; He 5:7).

Then of course, Jesus used the Gift of Prophecy in many remarkable ways, both in forth-telling and in fore-telling; both in preaching to strengthen, encourage, and comfort, and in prophesying things that were to come. We see in him our wonderful example, our Lord and our God.

LESSON TWO:
MORE ABOUT THE GIFTS

GIFTS OF REVELATION

1. THE WORD OF WISDOM

This Word of Wisdom and the associated gift of the Word of Knowledge are Spirit-imparted fragments of the measureless resources of the wisdom and knowledge that are in Christ. You will notice that this is not the gift of Wisdom, but a manifestation of a WORD OF WISDOM. That is, a small portion of God's wisdom revealed under the inspiration of the Holy Spirit to meet a specific need.

Some may have this gift operating more frequently or more constantly than others; but each time it is manifested, it is a new flash of divine wisdom, a quick revelation of the Spirit given in response to faith, for the benefit or profit of some member of the church of the Lord Jesus Christ.

The gift of the Word of Wisdom is of immeasurable benefit in...

Preaching ministry: Inspired wisdom, showing what to preach and how to preach, directing and anointing the servant of God even while he is proclaiming the message of God to the people.

Pastoral ministry: There is scarcely any gift more precious than this to a faithful pastor as under the anointing of the Spirit he cares for the personal needs and problems of the flock.

Business matters: Those who are chosen to guide the business affairs of the church must realise their need for the operation of this

Gift of the Holy Spirit. One of the qualifications for the first seven chosen for such work was that they be -

> "...full of the Spirit and wisdom." Ac 6:3b

Emergencies: In any sphere of activity in which the believer finds himself engaged how wonderful it is to know that there is always the possibility of receiving from God this "Word of Wisdom" that will dispel the confusion, resolve the uncertainty and reveal the method of solution.

2. THE WORD OF KNOWLEDGE

This second gift of revelation is closely related to the gift of the Word of Wisdom. God is all-knowing, as he is all-wise, and in Christ are hid all the treasures of wisdom and knowledge. It is the ministry of the Holy Spirit to take a fragment of that all-knowingness and impart it to a member of the body of Christ as the occasion requires. This is not knowledge gained by learning, or by information received from any human source. It is a supernatural manifestation of the Holy Spirit, imparting knowledge of things, or people, or the scripture, or devils, which would not be gained any other way.

When faced with an obscure passage of the scripture, sincere prayer and expectant faith will frequently bring the illumination of the Holy Spirit - a fragment of divine knowledge that will unfold the treasure of his own Word. Many times while preaching under the anointing of the Spirit, a flood of knowledge will pour into the preacher's mind and be given to his hearers for their edification, and exhortation, and comfort.

But this gift is not confined to preaching; it operates also in relation to persons, places, and incidents. It is often manifested in the ministry of healing, giving knowledge of diseases of which sometimes even the sufferers were unaware. It is knowledge flashed into the consciousness of the person concerned so that, without inquiry or reasoning, that person simply KNOWS the matter the HOLY SPIRIT desires him to know.

Jesus spoke of both these gifts in Luke 21:14-15.

> *"But make up your mind not to worry beforehand how you will defend yourselves. For I will give you WORDS and WISDOM that none of your adversaries will be able to resist or contradict."*

3. THE DISCERNING OF SPIRITS

The word translated "discerning" means literally "a thorough judging" or "summing up" or "assessing." This Gift of the Holy Spirit enables one to completely sum up the position in the case of demon possession, revealing the name, the nature, and the strength of the demon, thus making it possible for the servant of God to cast out the evil spirit. This gift will also frequently reveal whether a person is being activated by the Spirit of God or by Satan.

The apostle Paul strongly indicated the need for this gift when he spoke of those who come into the church who are -

> *"...false apostles, deceitful workmen, masquerading as apostles of Christ. And no wonder, for Satan himself masquerades as an angel of light. It is not surprising then, if his servants masquerade as servants of righteousness. Their end will be what their actions deserve." 2 Co 11:13-15*

The apostle John also indicated the need to test the spirits.

> *"Dear friends, do not believe every spirit, but test*

> *the spirits to see whether they are from God, because many false prophets have gone out into the world. This is how you can recognise the spirit of God: Every spirit that acknowledges that Jesus Christ has come in the flesh is from God, but every spirit that does not acknowledge Jesus is not from God..." 1 Jn 4:1-3a*

We also read of a time when a young girl came to Paul and cried out that he was a servant of the most high God (Ac 16:16-18)

What she said was true, but Paul discerned the presence of a demon spirit in her which was hindering his ministry and bringing wrongful reproach onto the gospel. In great indignation he cast the devil out of the girl and won a striking victory for the Lord.

These then are the three gifts of Revelation; they are definitely specific, supernatural, manifestations of the Holy Spirit given to any Spirit-filled believer who has need of them and only as the Spirit wills. Let no one then claim to have a gift of Wisdom, or a gift of Discernment. Rather let every believer humbly and earnestly seek God that, as the need arises, their ministry might be graciously enriched by these precious manifestations of the Holy Spirit's indwelling fullness and power.

GIFTS OF POWER

1. FAITH

The "faith" here considered as a Gift of the Holy Spirit must not be confused with the more general kind of faith that is frequently referred to in scripture.

The gift of faith is not saving faith.

The gift of faith is not merely faith in God's word.

The gift of faith is a special manifestation of the Holy Spirit which is as entirely supernatural as the other manifestations of the Spirit referred to in this lesson.

This gift is the divine implanting of the irresistible, all powerful, "faith of God" into the heart of a believer to meet a special need. Something of the nature of this faith appears in the Old Testament stories of Joshua commanding the sun to stand still, of Elijah binding and loosing the waters of heaven, of Isaiah moving the shadow back ten degrees; and in the statement of Jesus that, if any man had "the faith of God" (Mk 11:22 lit.) he could move a mountain with a word of command.

This faith is given to the trusting child of God to meet a deep crisis, or to enable him to take advantage of a rich opportunity: it brings him to a triumphant certainty which brooks no barrier, demolishes every difficulty, and makes the impossible almost absurdly easy.

2. GIFTS OF HEALING

It is to be noted that this gift is referred to in the plural - GIFTS of healing. There are two probable explanations: Firstly that every time a person is healed in answer to prayer, this is a gift in itself, a specific manifestation of the Holy Spirit.

Secondly, that there are different forms of the gift of healing: various believers being especially used of God in praying for specific afflictions, e.g., demon possession, cancer, deafness, etc.

More than likely, both these explanations contain an element of truth. Certainly we know that the person through whom the gift operates is merely an agent, and each particular work of healing is a manifestation of the Holy Spirit.

Concerning the gifts of healing, though, note...

They are not medical science, for they are an entirely supernatural manifestation of the Holy Spirit.

They are not mind-over-matter, or auto-suggestion, but are wholly dependent upon simple faith in God.

They are not a permanent power given to any one person to heal all sick people.

They are set in the true church by the Lord Jesus Christ, hence there is potential healing for every sick person who will properly enter into the fellowship of that church.

They are gifts of the Holy Spirit and will therefore be manifested only as the circumstances are pleasing to God.

They were very prominent in New Testament evangelism,

> *"When the crowds heard Phillip and saw the miraculous signs he did, they all paid close attention to what he said. With shrieks, evil spirits came out of many, and many paralytics and cripples were healed. So there was great joy in that city."* Ac 8:6-8 (see also Ac 28:8-9 etc)

As far as the scripture is concerned they should be no less prominent in the evangelism of the church today. We do not see these gifts as much as we ought to, not because God has withdrawn them, or hidden them, but because there are not many who are bold enough to believe for them. Despite the tragic need of men and women today there are very few who are willing to covet earnestly these gifts which are meant to enable the church to carry on the healing ministry of the Lord Jesus Christ.

3. THE WORKING OF MIRACLES

The word "working" is from the Greek "*energeema*" meaning OPERATION or ACT.

"Miracles" is from the Greek "*dunamis*", meaning POWER, DIVINE ABILITY, etc. Thus the "working of miracles" is literally "ACTS OF DIVINE POWER".

a. Miracles include physical healing.

There are some healings which are obviously within the scope of this spectacular Gift of the Holy Spirit. This is particularly so of a healing of an outstanding nature, such as a CREATIVE MIRACLE when a missing organ is replaced in the body. Hence this gift would include the re-creation of an eardrum, growth of a withered hand, restoring sight to a person born blind, and other physical manifestations which are contrary to the process of nature. "Healing" in the ordinary sense, means a CURE or RECOVERY, brought about by the power of God.

b. This gift is not confined to healing.

The working of miracles covers a much wider field of manifestation than mere physical healing. It may embrace healing, but also go far behind it. For example, Jesus healed the demoniac when the devils were cast out of him, but the Lord wrought a mighty miracle in the man himself to so transform him that all the years of insanity were washed away from his memory and he was found in his right mind, clothed, fully intelligent, drinking in the words of Jesus (Mk 5:15). The work of healing, and the working of a miracle, are also suggested in the account of the ten lepers (Lu 17:12-19)

All the ten lepers were CLEANSED, (or healed of the disease), but the one who returned and worshipped Christ was MADE WHOLE; that is fully restored, so that he was left without a trace of leprosy or its scars anywhere in his body.

    c. Miracles other than physical healing.

Some of the miracles, other than miracles of healing, as demonstrated in the ministry of Jesus and of the early church, are as follows...

- Miraculous catch of fish. (Lu 5:4-9; Jn 21:4-6)
- Water turned to wine. (Jn 2:1-11)
- Withering of the fig tree. (Mt 21:18-22)
- Raising the dead. (Jn 11:43-44; Ac 9:36-41, Lu 7:12-19)
- Acts of judgment. (Ac 5:1-11; and 13:6-11)

These three gifts of power - FAITH, HEALING and MIRACLES - may at times overlap, or dovetail, but they remain three distinct manifestations of the Holy Spirit which have been set in the church.

GIFTS OF UTTERANCE

These three gifts of inspired utterance (and to a large extent the ministry of healing) are regarded as the distinguishing feature of the worship and ministry of the churches which have accepted the Baptism of the Holy Spirit. It would be wrong to say that these churches consider the gifts of utterance and healing to be the most important of the Gifts of the Spirit - but it is probably right to say that these gifts are those which most catch the eye and attention of the public. This is so mainly because the three vocal Gifts of the Spirit, and the gifts of healing, are the more obvious and spectacular manifestations of the Spirit in the church. However, for that very reason it is vitally important that we be scrupulously correct in our understanding and use of these gifts. So we have firstly...

1. DIFFERENT KINDS OF TONGUES

What are these tongues? The historical passages in the Bible referring to tongues (Ac 2:1-11; 10:44-48; 19:1-6) show them to be a powerful, fervent utterance in a foreign tongue which is actually unknown to the speaker. It is the miraculous work of the Holy Spirit enabling a man or woman to speak in a language of which they have no natural knowledge. As such, it is an absolutely supernatural gift.

The New Testament indicates a three-fold purpose in speaking in tongues.

>   a. The sign of the Baptism of the Holy Spirit. (A full study of this is set forward in Section Three, Lesson One.)
>
>   b. As a personal edification of private devotion.

> *"For anyone who speaks in a tongue does not speak to men but to God. Indeed no one understands him; he utters mysteries with his spirit"..."He who speaks in a tongue edifies himself, but he who prophesies edifies the church"..."I thank God that I speak in tongues more than you all." 1 Co 14:2, 4, 18*

These references are evidently not to the initial sign of the baptism of the Holy Spirit (they are spoken in connection with people who had already experiences that baptism), but to the continuation of this supernatural exercise in private devotions as distinct and inspired communion with God (1 Co 14:2), which he frequently enjoyed (verse 18).

    c. As a means of addressing the church when associated with the gift of interpretation.

> *"What then we shall we say, brothers? When you come together, everyone has a hymn, or a word of instruction, a revelation, a tongue or an interpretation. All of these must be done for the strengthening of the church. If anyone speaks in a tongue, two - or at the most three - should speak, one at a time, and someone must interpret. If there is no interpreter, the speaker should keep quiet in the church and speak to himself and to God." 1 Co 14:26-28 (See also 1 Co 12:10 & 30; 14:5 & 13*

When the gift is used to address the church it is to be interpreted, that the church may receive "edification (strengthening), exhortation (encouragement) and comfort."

2. INTERPRETATION OF TONGUES

This is the second of the three gifts of utterance, and is a "twin gift" to that of tongues. This gift is indispensable for the profitable use of tongues in a meeting of believers. It conveys the message from the exercise of the human spirit in speaking in tongues to the understanding of the mind of the hearer. But though the gift of interpretation is channelled through the native language of the speaker, it is nevertheless a supernatural gift, equally as miraculous as tongues.

One does not learn the language, but the same Holy Spirit that inspires the message in tongues inspires the interpretation of it. Nor is this a "translation" of the "other tongues." Translation is virtually a word for word rendering of the unknown tongue; but this gift of interpretation is intended to give only the meaning of the message in tongues, to press home to the hearers the burden of the word of the Holy Spirit to the church. The main connection between the one who speaks in tongues and the one who interprets, is the Holy Spirit who gives inspiration and utterance to both.

3. THE GIFT OF PROPHECY

Prophecy means forth-telling and fore-telling. It is not ordinary teaching, but speaking forth from sudden inspiration. It is a message given by revelation from God, spoken under the divine anointing, unpremeditated, unprepared. It is an activity of the human spirit, under the moving of the Holy Spirit, and not a function of the human mind. The gift of prophecy seems to have been quite common in the early church, but there were only a limited number of PROPHETS in the sense of a clearly defined and officially regarded class. Paul indicates that ALL MAY PROPHECY (that is, use the gift of prophecy - 1 Co 14:24 &31) but not all are PROPHETS (1 Co 12:29).

The gift of prophecy is rarely for the purpose of fore-telling the future, and in cases where predictions of the future are given, they are subject to the acid test...do they come to pass? If they do not, then that "prophecy" was not from the Holy Spirit, but from either one of two sources - the human mind, or demonic power. The latter would no doubt be in rare and (to spiritual minds) obvious cases. As a general rule, if a prophecy (or interpretation of tongues) is not fully inspired by the Holy Spirit then it is from the natural mind.

No gift of prophecy, therefore, is to be regarded as infallible, but is always subject to judgment.

> *"Two or three prophets should speak, and the*

others should weigh carefully what is said."
1 Co 14:29

The purpose of the gift of prophecy is "edification (strengthening) exhortation (encouragement) and comfort". The supreme test of the orderliness of the operation of this, as other gifts, is whether it edifies or builds up the church.

THE MORE EXCELLENT WAY

The fourteenth chapter of the first epistle to the Corinthians contains a large body of teaching on the relative value and proper use of the supernatural gifts of "tongues", "interpretation of tongues" and prophecy". These gifts, being channelled through human vessels, can be subject to misuse. They may be exercising the anointing of the Spirit, or they may be manifested carnally, by the will of man. For these reasons, Paul sets down very carefully the specific attributes of these gifts, where and when they should be exercised, and other connected matters. It is not our purpose to study this chapter at this time, but you are earnestly requested to carefully read the Bible teaching on this subject in your own Bible.

You will see that the apostle Paul is quick to correct wrongful use of these gifts, but at the same time is equally quick to commend their very real value when properly used. They serve to bring strengthening, encouragement and comfort to the people of God. When put into proper operation in the worship of the church, and when they stem truly from the anointing of the Holy Spirit, these three wonderful gifts of inspired utterance do indeed bring abundant profit to the church.

THE WAY OF LOVE

Nine powerful spiritual gifts are set before us. These supernatural operations of the Holy Spirit should be evident in every properly constituted and fully equipped assembly of spirit-filled Christians. They are a distinctive characteristic of a true New Testament church. But when presented with the challenge of spiritual gifts today many resort to a misapplied text saying - *"I prefer the more excellent way."*

> *"And now I will show you the most excellent way."*
> *1 Co 12:31b (see also 1 Co 13).*

It is claimed without warrant that the "most excellent way" is a way of LOVE instead of GIFTS. But are we to believe that in spite of two long chapters setting forth the correct use, and outlining the great value of these spiritual gifts, the apostle Paul now destroys it all by saying that we should have LOVE instead of the GIFTS OF THE SPIRIT? Far from it! Paul's wonderful hymn on love is wisely placed between the two chapters on the Gifts of the Spirit in order to provide a beautiful balance, a proper harmony of Christian behaviour.

The "most excellent way" of which the apostle speaks is not to emphasise love at the expense of the Gifts of the Holy Spirit, nor to emphasise the Gifts of the Spirit at the expense of love. No, obviously the "most excellent way" is -

THE GIFTS OF THE SPIRIT HARMONIOUSLY JOINED WITH GODLY LOVE.

We do not want to see the Gifts of the Spirit exercised in clanging discord because they are void of Christian love. Neither do we wish to see a church replete with love, but powerless through lack of Gifts of the Spirit. Jesus emphatically said that we should love one another; but Jesus also said -

> *"You will receive power when the Holy Spirit comes on you." Ac 1:8*

The true Bible pattern is to establish a godly balance: the Gifts of the Spirit equipping us for service, coupled with the delightful Fruit of the Holy Spirit producing in us the character of Christ.

The "most excellent way" then, is obviously what Paul himself expresses in the verse which immediately follows his chapter on love -

> "FOLLOW THE WAY OF LOVE AND EAGERLY DESIRE SPIRITUAL GIFTS." 1 Co 14:1a

It is clear that we are to desire and seek after the Gifts of the Spirit; but we must be very sure to always walk in the way of love. Paul is not striking a damaging comparison between love and spiritual gifts, but he desires rather to show the vivid contrast between spiritual gifts exercised WITH LOVE, and spiritual gifts exercised WITHOUT LOVE.

It is plain then, that the "most excellent way" is certainly not claiming love at the expense of spiritual gifts and good works. Some people say "Love is the most important gift," but nowhere is love called a gift. Others say, "We need a baptism of love," but love is never called a baptism. It is incorrect to compare love with the baptism of the Holy Spirit. Love is complementary to these things, not antagonistic to them.

Hence it is clear that the "most excellent way" is firstly, to walk in love so that God may see in us fit vessels through which to manifest the Gifts of the Holy Spirit; and secondly that love should be the motivating force behind all seeking for spiritual gifts and thirdly, that love should clothe with beauty every exercise of spiritual gifts. May God grant that we may all seek to excel in the exercise of spiritual gifts, to the edification of the church (1 Co 14:12).

BOOK FIVE:
LAW AND GRACE

Introduction to Lesson One

Lesson One - **The Law Of The Lord**

Introduction to Lesson Two

Lesson Two - **The New Glory**

INTRODUCTION LESSON ONE

> *"I will sprinkle clean water on you, and you will be clean; I will cleanse you from all your impurities and from all your idols. I will give you a new heart and put a new spirit in you; I will remove from you your heart of stone and give you a heart of flesh. And I will put my Spirit in you and move you to follow my decrees and be careful to keep my laws"* (Ez 36:25-27).

Thank God for his promise to make it possible for his children to live a holy life, not through self effort, but through his power!

It is extremely difficult for us to comprehend the grace of God.

We continually feel obliged to do something to earn our salvation, or even just to assist God a little by keeping some rules. This stems from pride.

However we must realise that there is nothing we can do to please God, except to throw ourselves on his mercy and claim as our own the sacrifice of Jesus Christ our Saviour. Once we have done that then good works can be built on the foundation of our salvation by grace. We must not boast in ourselves but only in God. He is the Lord who exercises kindness, justice, and righteousness in the earth. He is the Lord who has made a way for us to be righteous.

In this lesson we learn about the Law in all of its aspects. We learn what is meant by the Law, why it was given and how it affects us as Christians.

LESSON ONE:
THE LAW OF THE LORD

The Bible abounds with references to the "Law of the Lord", and this law is spoken of as holy, just, good and eternal. In many places people are solemnly told to keep God's law; but in other places, in the Old Testament, and more especially in the New Testament, the law is spoken of as being ineffective, and dead, and done away, and supplanted by God's grace. Many people find difficulty in reconciling these two differing lines of instruction. Shall we keep the law? All of it? Or just part of it? Or none of it?

For those whose deepest desire is to please God, these are vital questions, and this lesson will attempt an answer to them.

WHAT IS MEANT BY THE LAW?

When the New Testament writers use the term "law", they are referring to the Law of Moses, given at the time of Israel's exodus from Egypt.

> *"For the law is generally divided into three major groups..."*

1. THE COMMANDMENTS

These are the famous Ten Commandments (Ex 20:1-17)

2. THE JUDGMENTS

or Statutes relating to Israel's social life (Ex 21:1-23; De 12:1-26)

3. THE ORDINANCES

directing Israel's worship and service in the sanctuary. (Ex 25:1-31)

These divisions are not absolute. There are exceptions. But they are helpful and broadly true.

THE JUDGMENTS

There is little difficulty in deciding the New Testament attitude to the judgments. Christ himself absolutely overruled some of them.

For example, we find that the "eye for an eye" of Moses becomes the "turn the other cheek" of Christ (Ex 21:24 and Mt 5:38-42).

As a rule of life for the Christian the Judgments have been totally abolished.

However, arguments have arisen particularly in regard to the Christian's attitude to the food laws contained within these ancient Judgments (De 14:3-21). Many Christians keep these food laws rigidly, and feel themselves under an obligation before God to do so.

It is usually assumed by these people that the foods forbidden in the laws must be of themselves bad and unhealthy, but there does not appear to be any proven reason for making such a sweeping assertion. Nor does it seem reasonable to invest the food laws with a special value, and yet ignore all the other prohibitions concerning household duties, cooking, clothing, etc. which no one considers binding on our community today.

It seems illogical to separate only the food laws and credit them with a particular obligation. If we are debtors to part of the law, then we are bound to it all!

The apostles were well aware of this, and in the plainest possible terms, released Christians for all times from the necessity of keeping these laws.

> *"As one who is in the Lord Jesus I am fully convinced that no food is unclean in itself. But if anyone regards something as unclean, then for him it is unclean"..."For the kingdom of God is not a matter of eating and drinking, but of righteousness, peace and joy in the Holy Spirit..." Ro 14:14 & 17 (See also Ac 10:9-16; 15:5-29; 1 Co 8:6-8; 1 Ti 4:1-5; He 9:10).*

Whether or not certain of the forbidden foods do not make for good health is of little value as far as the Bible is concerned; that is a matter for dieticians to decide, not theologians. The Bible is concerned with moral issues, not merely physical. Note Jesus' pungent words:

> *"Are you so dull? he asked. Don't you see that nothing that enters a man from the outside can make him `unclean'? For it doesn't go into his heart but into his stomach, and then out of his body." (In saying this, Jesus declared all foods `clean') Mk 7:18-19 (See also Mt 15:17-18)*

But the great harm observed in many who keep these food laws, even if for reasons of health alone, is that adhering to these laws has become with them a moral issue, a matter of righteousness or unrighteousness. They now consider it a sin to eat certain things, and a sign of grace or purity not to eat them. Such an attitude is directly opposed to the forthright teaching of Jesus and the apostles.

If any person feels God cannot answer their prayers because they have eaten a plateful of pork, that person has most certainly moved away from the freedom of the Gospel of grace into the fetters of the old law and its pitiful bondage!

THE ORDINANCES

The letter to the Hebrews makes it abundantly clear that the ordinances relating to the sanctuary and its sacrifices and services have no demands to make on Christians.

The ordinances dealt with the different sacrifices and offerings to be presented by Israel, the appointment of priests, and so on. In Hebrews however, we read that we have in Christ a high priest whose ministry does not cease (thus doing away with the old priesthood), whose sacrifice of himself is once and for all sufficient (thus doing away with the former repetitive sacrifices and offerings), and that his temple is of God's building and not man's (thus doing away with the need for a temple as possessed by Israel).

> *"but because Jesus lives forever, he has a permanent priest-hood. Therefore he is able to save completely those who come to God through him, because he always lives to intercede for them."* He 7:24-25

> *"...We do have such a high priest, who sat down at the right hand of the throne of the majesty in heaven, and who serves in the sanctuary, the true tabernacle, set up by the Lord, not by man."* He 8:1b-2.

THE COMMANDMENTS

There remains only to consider the commandments:

In Exodus Chapter 20 we find statements of obvious relevance to our time - *"You shall have no other god's before me"*, *"You shall not murder"*, *"You shall not steal"*, *"honour your father and your mother"* etc...

Are these to be ignored in the same way as the Judgments and Ordinances? The answer to this question depends on where you find these injunctions. If you are thinking of them only as the Ten Commandments, engraved on Mt Sinai, then the Bible calls them irrevocably a "ministry of death" and they have been forever cancelled out as far as the Christian is concerned.

> *"Now if the ministry that brought death, which was engraved in letters on stone, came with glory, so that the Israelites could not look steadily at the face of Moses because of its glory, fading though it was, will not the ministry of the Spirit be even more glorious?" 2 Co 3:7-8.*

But if you are thinking of them as they have been re-written into the New Covenant made for us by Christ on Mt. Calvary, then we are most certainly bound to obey them and to guide our living by them!

Keep the Ten Commandments in the Old Testament, and they have absolutely nothing to say to us. But read them as they are found in the New Testament, and they are of infinite value!

Understanding of this basic fact refutes conclusively once and for all those who endeavour to enforce the keeping of Israel's ancient

Sabbath. As this is a point of controversy, let us examine it more closely.

THE FOURTH COMMANDMENT

Shall we keep the Sabbath?

Or, for that matter, shall we keep any of the Ten Commandments as they are written in the Old Testament, keeping to the terms and provisions that surround them there?

If we can solve the problem with regard to the Sabbath, it is solved for them all.

Now, those who claim that we must observe the old Sabbath put forward scores of scriptures which urge the solemnity, and sacredness, and vast importance of keeping the Sabbath day holy unto the Lord. But out of all their proof texts, the foundational one is,

> *"Remember the Sabbath day by keeping it holy. Six days you shall labour and do all your work, but the seventh day is a Sabbath to the Lord your God. On it you shall not do any work, neither you, nor your son or daughter, nor your manservant or maidservant, nor your animals, nor the alien within your gates. For in six days the Lord made the heavens and the earth, the sea, and all that is in them, but he rested on the seventh day. Therefore the Lord blessed the Sabbath day and made it holy." Ex 20:8-11 (See also Ge 2:1-3 and compare).*

To keep the "moral law" as a CONDITION OF SALVATION, is evident from: Examining these scripture for ourselves we see...

1. The Sabbath has its roots in remotest antiquity. Nevertheless, until the giving of the Law of Moses the Bible does not record any command given to any man to keep the Sabbath. Indications are that the original custom was built simply on the basis of resting one day in seven. No doubt this is still wise; it is certainly pleasant; but, as we shall see, it is by no means morally binding on Christians.

2. A command was given in the days of Moses, the Sabbath was legalised, and was incorporated into the statutes that governed Israel's national, moral, and religious life.

Now, the custom observed by ancient peoples before the time of Moses, in keeping one day in seven, and even the example of the Lord God who rested on the seventh day, do not in themselves establish for us a law we must keep. But are we placed under obedience by the fact of the Sabbath law being inluded in the Ten Commandments?

We maintain that these commandments are abolished, all of them, and we adhere only to those which have been re-written into the New Covenant. Others claim that we are solemnly bound by God to keep them, as much as Israel of old ever was. They try to prove their case this way.

They divide the Law of Moses into two groups, "ceremonial" and "moral"; the "moral law" is the Ten Commandments; all that remains is classed as "ceremonial law." They then claim that Christ, at Calvary, abolished the "ceremonial law" but insist that our ultimate salvation is totally dependent on us keeping this "moral law", notably the law pertaining to the Sabbath!

1. The "ceremonial law"

was given for one reason only, to atone for transgressions of the Ten Commandments. Men could fully keep the "ceremonial law" and be blameless in its observance (as Saul was before he became Paul, (Ph 3:6) but no man save Christ has ever yet succeeded in keeping the "moral law".

2. This "moral law"

or the Ten Commandments, which Christ has perfectly fulfilled on our behalf (thereby removing the need for us to fulfil it) is evident in the following passages...

> *"...I would not have known what sin was except through the law. For I would not have known what coveting really was if the law had not said, do not covet"..."For apart from law, sin is dead. Once I was alive apart from law; but when the commandment came, sin sprang to life and I died. I found that the very commandment that was intended to bring life actually brought death." Ro 7:7b; 8b-10*

Here we discover that the commandment of God, far from bringing forth salvation or making us acceptable to God, served only to bring us under condemnation of sin, with its penalty of death. If we are to keep the law, then, and escape its punishment, we must keep it in the person of another, and that one is Christ.

> *"For what the law was powerless to do in that it was weakened by the sinful nature, God did by sending his own Son in the likeness of sinful man to be a sin offering. And so he condemned sin in sinful*

> *man, in order, that the righteous requirements of the law might be fully met in us, who do not live according to the sinful nature but according to the Spirit" Rom 8:3-4*
>
> *"But now righteousness from God, apart from the law, has been made known, to which the Law and the Prophets testify. This righteousness from God comes through faith in Jesus Christ to all who believe. There is no difference, for all have sinned and fall short of the glory of God" Rom 3:21-23*
>
> *"For we maintain that a man is justified by faith apart from observing the law" Rom 3:28*
>
> *"Through him everyone who believes is justified from everything you could not be justified from by the law of Moses" Ac 13:39*
>
> (FOR THE LAW MADE NOTHING PERFECT), AND A BETTER HOPE IS INTRODUCED, BY WHICH WE DRAW NEAR TO GOD!" He 7:19

It is therefore impossible to draw any nearer to God by the keeping of any law, including the Ten Commandments; to attempt to do so is to insult the full sufficiency of Christ's sacrifice and perfect obedience on our behalf. The scriptures clearly declare that, in our name and in our stead, Christ kept every provision of the law, so that we, in his name, may count ourselves to have fulfilled already its every requirement.

> *"For just as through the disobedience of the one man the many were made sinners, so also through the obedience of the one man the many will be made righteous." Ro 5;19*

FROM THE OLD SABBATH REST TO THE NEW

That the necessity to keep the Sabbath, in particular, is done away with, may be seen at once by reference to the following scriptures:

> *"Therefore do not let anyone judge you by what you eat or drink, or with regard to a religious festival, a New Moon celebration or a Sabbath day. These are a shadow of the things that were to come; the reality, however is found in Christ.' Cl 2:16-17*

> *"You are observing special days and months and seasons and years! I fear for you, that somehow I have wasted my efforts on you." Ga 4:10-11*

> *"One man considers one day more sacred than other; another man considers every day alike. Each one should be fully convinced in his own mind." Ro 14:5*

There are some who say that the "Sabbath days" mentioned in these passages are special days of celebration, and quite distinct from the weekly seventh day Sabbath.

By way of proof they mention this verse of Scripture!

> *"These offerings are in addition to the Lord's Sabbaths and in addition to your gifts and whatever you have vowed and all the free will offerings you give to the Lord. So beginning with the fifteenth day of the seventh month, after you have gathered the crops of the land, celebrated the festival to the Lord for seven days; the first day is a day of rest, and the eighth day also is a day of rest." Le 23:38-39*

But while various other days, apart from the regular seventh day, were designated as Sabbaths in the Old Testament, there is not the slightest indication that the New Testament writers made any difference between them. They were all part of those ancient ordinances which Christ removed on the cross.

It is claimed also that worship on days other than the Sabbath (which is said to be Saturday) was instituted by pagan leaders of the church after it had fallen into corruption and worldliness.

However, the following church fathers and leaders, along with many others from the earliest times until now, strongly refuted the need to keep Israel's Sabbath and, in fact, mostly worshipped on Sunday, the Lord's day - Barnabus (100 AD), Ignatius (107 AD); Martyr (145 AD); Irenaeus(155 AD); Tertullian (200 AD); Eusebius 315 AD); Luther, Calvin, Knox, etc...

In fact one scripture actually foretold the advent of a new day of worship and praise:

> *"The stone the builders rejected has become the capstone; the Lord has done this, and it is marvellous in our eyes. This is the day the Lord has made; let us rejoice and be glad in it."* Ps 118:22-24

Also compare:

> *"On the Lord's day I was in the Spirit, and I heard behind me a loud voice like a trumpet,..."* Re 1:10

This day, as the psalm shows, was to be the day of Christ's resurrection, namely the first day of the week.

But the final truth of the position is that, as far as the New Testament is concerned:

1. Here is no special sanctity attached to any day whatsoever; we are under no obligation to keep any holy day in any way at all.

2. Whatever day we choose to worship is very acceptable to God, whether it is Saturday, or Sunday, or any other day.

> *"Who are you to judge someone else's servant? To his own master he stands or falls. And he will stand, for the Lord is able to make him stand. One man considers one day more sacred than another; another man considers every day alike. Each one should be fully convinced in his own mind. He who regards one day as special, does so to the Lord."*
> *Ro 14:4-6a*

It depends only on whether the observance of a particular day is honouring to God and carried out in love for one's fellow man. In other words it depends on our ability to do what we do in faith towards God.

> *"So whatever you believe about these things keep between yourself and God. Blessed is the man who does not condemn himself by what he approves."*
> *Ro 14;22*

To clarify this Paul uses the example of eating different foods. He says that he will eat only those foods which will not cause harm to a weaker brother.

> *"One man's faith allows him to eat everything but another man, whose faith is weak, eats only*

vegetables." Ro 14:2 (See also verses 3, 6, 15 & 21)

In another place, he discusses the question of meat offered to idols which was afterwards sold in the markets for human consumption. Paul clearly states that there is NO HARM in eating such meat.

> *"But not everyone knows this. Some people are still so accustomed to idols that when they eat such food they think of it as having been sacrificed to an idol, and since their conscience is weak, it is defiled. But food does not bring us near to God; we are no worse if we do not eat; and no better if we do." 1 Co 8:7-8*

But if it should be that a weaker brother seeing him eat thus would be drawn into idolatry, he would eat no such meat as long as he lived.

> *"...Therefore if what I eat causes my brother to fall into sin, I will never eat meat again, so that I will not cause him to fall." 1 Co 8:13*

Love for a weaker brother decided the issue.

And this is a pattern laid down in the New Testament. If an action can be done in love, it is good. If not, it is sin.

In fact, the New Testament states that those who completely FORBID the eating of certain foods are DEPARTING from the faith, giving heed to seducing spirits and doctrines of DEVILS, and speaking LIES in HYPOCRISY.

> *"...The Spirit clearly says that in later times some will abandon the faith and follow deceiving spirits and things taught by demons. Such teachings come*

> *through hypocritical liars, whose consciences have been seared as with a hot iron. They forbid people to marry and order them to abstain from certain foods, which God created to be received with thanksgiving by those who believe and who know the truth. For everything God created is good, and nothing is to be rejected if it is received with thanksgiving, because it is consecrated by the word of God and prayer." 1 Ti 4:1-5*

No need for further warning!

Let us simply live as Jesus said:

> *"So in everything do to others what you would have them do to you, for this sums up the Law and the Prophets." Mt 7:12*

3. Nevertheless, it appears that the first disciples and the bulk of the church from their day onward have, by common consent, set aside Sunday, the first day of the week, the day on which Christ rose from the dead, as a proper day for worship and praise (see again Ps 118:22-24) and its obvious connection with the day of Christ's resurrection.

4. It is incumbent upon every believer to join with all other saints in worship, and to prepare themselves for true spiritual worship it is certainly wise to devote the whole day to Godly pursuits - hence we advocate the sanctity of Sunday, the day commonly chosen for worship; yet not as a binding law, but as an expression of love to God and true devotion. For Scriptures which advise us to come together for worship on a commonly appointed day (See Ps 26:8; 27:4; 84:4 & 10; 122:1; Je 3:15, Ep 4:11-13; He 3:13; 10:25).

INTRODUCTION TO LESSON TWO

The Law was given for two reasons: first to reveal what sin is; and second, to point us to Christ. Now that you have Christ (assuming that you are a born again Christian) you naturally desire to live a holy life.

If you examine the New Testament you will come across passages such as Ephesians 4:17-32; 5:1-33, which give many instructions to young Christians:

> *"Put off your old self, which is being corrupted by its deceitful desires; ...put on the new self, created to be like God in true righteousness and holiness... put off falsehood and speak truthfully... Do not let the sun go down while you are still angry, and do not give the devil a foothold. He who has been stealing must steal no longer, but must work...that he may have something to share with those in need...Do not let any unwholesome talk come out of your mouths...and do not grieve the Holy Spirit of God...Get rid of all bitterness, rage and anger, brawling and slander, along with every form of malice. Be kind and compassionate to one another, forgiving each other, just as in Christ God forgave you...Live a life of love...there must not be even a hint of sexual immorality, or of any kind of impurity, or of greed...Nor should there be obscenity foolish talk, or coarse joking...but rather thanksgiving...find out what pleases the Lord... submit to one another...love one another."*

You may feel it is impossible to keep all of these instructions; and if you try to do them in your own strength, of course it will be impossible. What you must do is yield yourselves to God, claim the righteousness promised you in Christ, and trust God to begin to change you (2 Cor 3:17-18). In this lesson we learn of the new law, the law of love, and how we can claim freedom from sin and gain power to serve God; not trusting in our own strength but in the strength of the Holy Spirit.

LESSON TWO:
THE NEW GLORY

FROM THE OLD GLORY TO THE NEW GLORY

Here is what Paul has to say about the contrast between the old way and the new. It is found in 2 Co 3:3-18 (Phillips)

> *Our message has been engraved not in stone."...(as were the Ten Commandments) "...but in living men and women...we deal not in the letter but in the Spirit. The letter of the law leads to death of the soul; the Spirit of God alone can give life to the soul."*

(And again when he speaks of the "letter", he does not mean the letter of the Law as against the spirit of the Law; he means simply that the Law itself, however it is observed, leads to death, while the Spirit of God alone brings life; it is a plain contrast between the Law of Moses and the gospel of Christ).

> *"...The administration of the Law which was engraved in stone,...(and only the Ten Commandments were so written)..."and which led in fact to spiritual death, was so magnificent that the Israelites were unable to look unflinchingly at Moses' face, for it was alight with heavenly splendour. Now if the old administration held such heavenly, even though transitory splendour, can we not see what a much more glorious thing is the new administration of the Spirit of life? If to administer a system which is to end in condemning men had its*

> *glory, how infinitely more splendid is it to administer a system which ends in making men good! And while it is true that the former temporary glory has been completely eclipsed by the latter, we do well to remember that it is eclipsed simply because the present permanent plan is such a very much more glorious thing than the old." 2 Co 3;3-12, (Phillips Translation)*

With this passage the apostle answers the question, "Why do people still keep the Law if it has been replaced by the gospel?" There are two reasons.

1. Because there was and still is, great glory in the Law. There was a glory in its giving, and a glory in its keeping. People are conscious of this. They still find a kind of satisfaction and spiritual pleasure in adhering to a list of prescribed rules; or in adding to the gospel a rigid adherence to, say, the food laws, or the Sabbath. People still like to regulate their lives by rules, rather than by simple faith and the guidance of the Spirit.

   > *"Since you died with Christ to the basic principles of this world, why, as though you still belong to it, do you submit to these rules; Do not handle! Do not taste! Do not touch!? These are all destined to perish with use, because they are based on human commands and teachings. Such regulations indeed have an appearance of wisdom, with their self-imposed worship, their false humility and their harsh treatment of the body, but they lack any value in restraining sensual indulgence." Cl 2:20-23*

Even Christians who begin well in the Spirit seem all too readily inclined to fall back on laws of doing, and to think they are spiritual if they successfully keep their rules, or carnal if they fail to.

> *"It is for freedom that Christ has set us free. Stand firm, then, and do not let yourselves be burdened again by a yoke of slavery. Mark my words! I, Paul, tell you that if you let yourselves be circumcised, Christ will be of no value to you at all. Again I declare to every man who lets himself be circumcised that he is obligated to obey the whole law. You who are trying to be justified by law have been alienated from Christ; you have fallen away from grace. But by faith we eagerly await through the Spirit the righteousness for which we hope. For in Christ Jesus neither circumcision nor uncircumcision has any value. The only thing that counts is faith expressing itself through love. You were running a good race. Who cut in on you and kept you from obeying the truth?" Ga 5:1-7*

2. People are caught up in the inferior glory of law, and find advantage in living by letter, only because they have not truly discovered the infinitely greater glory of the Spirit. This factor the apostle Paul goes on to explain further in 2 Co 3:13-18. Phillips Translation.

> *"...We are not like Moses, who veiled his face to prevent the Israelites from seeing its fading glory. But it was their minds really which were blinded, for even today when the old agreement is read to them there is still a veil over their minds. Though the veil has actually been lifted by Christ. Yes, even to this day there is still a veil over their hearts when the writings of Moses are read."*

(That is, just as Moses hid his face, that people might not see the glory fading from it and so think God had departed from him, so today people have a veil, as it were, between them and the Law, and they cannot see that the glory has passed away from all such "dealing in letters" and has passed to Christ. They still think the Law is honoured by God, and this is confirmed to them by the sense of satisfaction they gain from keeping it. But this is only because they have not fully partaken of Christ!)

So he says...

> "...Yet if they turned to the Lord the veil would disappear. For the Lord to whom they could turn is the Spirit of the new agreement, and wherever the Spirit of the Lord is men's souls are set free...We are transfigured in every increasing splendour into his own image, and the transformation comes form the Lord who is the Spirit."

THE TEN COMMANDMENTS IN THE NEW TESTAMENT

We have been emphasising the vanishing away of the old covenant and all its law, and the establishment of a new covenant and its abundant grace. And it is perfectly true that if we attempt to strive after commandments and law, "the letter that kills, the death of Christ for us becomes vain, and of no benefit whatever.

So we find it:

> "...know that a man is not justified by observing the law, but by faith in Jesus Christ...by observing the law no one will be justified...if righteousness could be gained through the law have been alienated from Christ; you have fallen away from grace." Ga 5:4

> *"Therefore, brothers, we have an obligation - but it is not to the sinful nature, to live according to it."* (i.e. after the law) Ro 8:12

Does the law then have no value? Most certainly it does!

> *"Do we, then, nullify the law by this faith? Not at all! Rather we uphold the law."* Ro 3:31

> *"So then the law is holy, and the commandment is holy, righteous and good."* Ro 7:12

What then is the purpose of the Law?

Its purpose is two fold. Firstly to reveal sin; secondly to point to Christ.

THE TWOFOLD PURPOSE OF THE LAW

1. TO REVEAL SIN

When man was created, he was made in the image of God (Ge 1:26). He was also made sinless and thus with the ability to face God fearlessly, and to commune with him. Hence we read that God issued specific commands to Adam (Ge 2:16-17) and in the cool of the evening, God called to Adam to commune with him. (Ge 2:8-9)

However, sin had entered the scene, and Adam was ashamed to face his creator. So he and Eve hid. Their direct fellowship with God was marred for the first time. As a result they were banished from the place of the high calling given them, and the gulf between Man and God widened. It was not so wide that God could not still speak to Man. Even Cain could talk with the Lord (Ge 4:9-15). But as generations passed, so the gulf widened more.

Not only did it mean less fellowship, it meant less knowledge of the WILL OF GOD (Ge 6:5, 11-12). Nor could the fresh start in the time of Noah bridge the gulf, and the time came when there was a need for a complete RESTATEMENT of God's laws in written form, so that all might know the will of God. This was the Law of Moses.

In other words, the Law was written to show the world again the standard of God, and to show HOW FAR SHORT MAN HAD FALLEN from the standard. This is what Paul meant when he said that through the commandment:

> "...sin might become utterly sinful." Ro 7:13b

And again:

> "...By the law is the KNOWLEDGE OF SIN." Ro 3:20b (KJV)

> "...sin is NOT IMPUTED when there is NO LAW." Ro 5:13; 3:19-20. (See also Ro 7:7-14 KJV)

Some people say that to know what a house is like we must live in it; to know what love is like, we must love. But not to with sin; the person who is MOST in sin knows LEAST about it! (Is not the dirty person less aware of the need for cleanliness?) Without some standard, some measure of comparison, sin's power and vileness is unknown to men.

It may be objected that it is promised even of the statutes that

> "The man who does these things will live by them" Ga 3:12b (See also Le 18:5).

Precisely. That is the standard. If we can do all these things, we can live by them. But the fact is that no man has ever succeeded in being completely obedient, and thus, through the standard of the law, all the world has become guilty before God. (Ro 3:19 & 23)

2. TO POINT TO CHRIST

Four hundred and thirty years before the Law was given, a promise was made to Abraham and his "Seed". This "Seed" refers to Christ. (Ga 3:16)

Thus before the Law was given in written form, there was a promise made - a promise that embraced the whole world. "All nations will be blessed through you." (Ga 3:8b) This means that God would justify (that is, make righteous) the Gentiles THROUGH FAITH. (Ga 3;8)

Why, then, was the Law given 430 years later? It cannot, as Paul correctly says, disannul (cancel) the promise or agreement made with Abraham (Ga 3:17).

It was given to EMPHASISE the promise of FAITH by showing man's inability to save himself, and that in CHRIST ALONE is there salvation. It was a temporary measure, pending the arrival of the "issue" to whom the promise was made (Ga 3:19).

It was a kind of tutor, to reveal God's standards, and to show us our desperate need of Christ, UNTIL HE CAME (Ga 3:24).

Thus the second purpose of the Law is closely related to the first. Because it shows sin to be what it is and because it reveals human weakness so clearly, men are forced to realise the need of faith in Christ, Abraham's seed. Thus the Law simply supports Faith.

This is summed up in the words of Paul:

> *Is the law, therefore, opposed to the promises of God? Absolutely not! For if a law had been given that could impart life, then righteousness would certainly have came by the law. But the Scripture declares that the whole world is a prisoner of sin, so that what was promised, being given through faith in Jesus Christ, might be given to those who believe (Ga 3:21-22).*

CHRISTIANS AND THE LAW

Does the law now have no relevance for a Christian?

Let us go back to the illustration of Adam and Eve. Men had lost their fellowship with God. Thus they needed a written Law to show them the way to live: a Law going into minute details because of human weakness.

The New Testament teaches, however, that man can be restored to fellowship with God, and can know the will of God for his own life through his OWN PERSONAL experience and knowledge of God.

> *"because those who are led by the Spirit of God are sons of God." Ro 8:14*

> *"...the anointing you received from him remains in you, and you do not need anyone to teach you..." 1 Jn 2:27b*

> *"...we have not stopped praying for you and asking God to fill you with the knowledge of his will through all spiritual wisdom and understanding." Cl. 1:9b (see also Cl 1:17; and Ja 1:5)*

Thus by faith we can know once again the position that Adam once knew, of personal fellowship and communion with God, and of deep knowledge of his will. Far from being a life lived on a lower plain than that lived according to the Law, this life is lived on a far higher plane. There is no need of the Law because this life is lived in the realm of such sweet fellowship with God that he himself speaks to us and guides us.

Thus it is obvious that to say a Christian can live as he will because he is not under the Law is completely false.

NEW BIRTH

Furthermore, a Christian is a person who has experienced a new birth.

> *"For we know that our old self (old life) was crucified with him so that the body of sin might be done away with, that we should no longer be slaves to sin." Ro 6:6*

In this verse is embraced the essence of the meaning of new birth. Sin and disobedience are the works of the unregenerate life. But that life is dead; the "body of sin" is destroyed; therefore the works of the life are dead also.

Now we are new creatures, alive to God in Jesus Christ (Ro 6:11). We are indwelt by Christ (Cl 1:27) and the life we now live is by faith in him. Consequently, Christ now guides us, and provides strength to follow his guidance. He forgives sin and gives strength to overcome sin. He sets a standard of holiness, and gives ability to live up to it.

What a change from the old weak striving after the written standard of the Law! Now Christ within guides us, helps us, and restores the fellowship that Adam lost!

The blessing of this is expressed in the words...

> *"I have been crucified with Christ and I no longer live, but Christ lives in me..."* Ga 2:20a

LAW OF LOVE

The high plane of life experienced by a Christian is a life lived in love. Love for God and for one's neighbour. This new relationship with God means that a Christian is dead to the Law (the Law has no power over a dead man!) and, as it were, MARRIED to Christ. Just as a woman is bound to her husband while he lives, but is free to "marry" Christ now that he is dead to the Law. Because of this "marriage" he now lives motivated by love (Read Romans 7:1-6).

Moreover this new life of LOVE actually FULFILS the Law. Paul says:

> *"...Let no debt remain outstanding, except the continuing debt to love one another, for he who loves his fellow man has fulfilled the Law... whatever other commandments there may be, are summed up in this one rule: "love your neighbour as yourself." Love does no harm to its neighbour. Therefore love is the fulfilment of the law."*
> Ro 13:8-10

Therefore a Christian's motive for conduct is now the "Law of love". All that he does is now done in a spirit of love to his neighbour. He refuses to steal, not just because it is said to be wrong, but because it is not a fruit of love. So with murder, hatred, disobedience to parents, coveting, adultery, bearing false witness, and so on.

These things are not acts of love, so they are not part of a Christian's conduct.

So for the Christian, the Old Law in all its aspects is completely done away, and we have come under a new commandment.

> *"Jesus replied, `Love the Lord your God with all your heart and with all your soul and with all your mind. This is the first and greatest commandment. And the second is like it; Love your neighbour as yourself. All the Law and the Prophets hang on these two commandments.'" Mt 22:37-40 (See also Ro 5:5; 13:8-10; Ga 5:14).*

FROM BONDAGE TO LIBERTY

The Bible says that the Law means bondage, while faith means liberty.

> *"...It is for freedom that Christ has set us free. Stand firm, then, and do not let yourselves be burdened again by a yoke of slavery." Ga 5:1*

Abraham had two sons. One was born by his wife's slave, Hagar. Her son, Ishmael, was therefore a slave. The other son was born by his wife, Sarah. He, Isaac, was a son indeed. Moreover Isaac was born when Sarah was well past the age of childbearing, as a result of a PROMISE given BEFORE the birth of Ishmael (Gen 15:18, 21:1-21).

Soon after the birth of Isaac, Ishmael was cast out, so that he might not share the privileges of a true son.

In the New Testament, Hagar, the bondwoman, is said to represent Mount Sinai, from which came the Law. Sarah represents Mount Calvary, from which came grace (Ga 4:22-31).

We too are told to CAST OUT the bondwoman and her son, and to STAND FAST in the LIBERTY wherewith Christ has made us FREE, and not to be entangled again in the yoke of bondage (Ga 5:1). This yoke of bondage is as miserable as the yoke of any slaving, burden bearing bullock.

Grace, however, is free. Unlike the Law which demands obedience and bondage, grace is the goodness of God toward us when we least deserve it. It means freedom from the power of sin, and from death, the penalty of the Law.

FROM SLAVERY TO SONSHIP

Moreover we are told that like Isaac, we are sons (and daughters) of God, not slaves.

> "...God sent the Spirit of his Son into our hearts, the Spirit who calls out, "Abba, Father." Ga 4:6b

The word "Abba" was the Aramaic word used by a young child for "father". It corresponds to our word "daddy". It is a simple expression of faith and trust, and conveys in the deepest sense, obedience through sonship and love, not the rod of the Law.

FROM FLESH LIFE TO SPIRIT LIFE

We are told also that through grace we now walk in the Spirit, not in the flesh. The flesh, in the New Testament, stands for self-effort. To walk in the flesh means to walk in our own strength, trusting in OUR OWN ability to live rightly. To walk in the Spirit means to walk in the strength of the Holy Spirit, trusting in his ability to live rightly (Ro 8:3-4).

This is the greatest blessing of the Gospel. As well as being born again by the power of God, a Christian can now also know the glory of the blessing of the Spirit-filled life. It means power (Ac 1:8), overflowing joy (Jn 7:37), love (Ro 5:5), freedom (Ro 8:2). It is a new realm of life that is thrilling and challenging, far above the dull monotony of a lifeless routine of regulations.

It is a life filled with the supernatural power of God. It brings healing (1 Co 12:9), deliverance in time of distress (Ac 27), and spiritual power (Ac 4).

Let a man who is unsure of his spiritual position become filled with the Spirit of God, with evidence of speaking in new tongues (Ac 10:46), and he will know his God as never before, and will realise that Christ is an anchor for his soul.

The fruit of the Spirit is love: the fruit of self-righteousness through the Law brings despair and dejection.

For walking in the Spirit depends on GOD'S righteousness - which NEVER fails. Walking in the flesh depends on MAN'S righteousness - which ALWAYS fails.

> *"...do not get drunk on wine, which leads to debauchery. Instead, be filled with the Spirit. Speak to one another with psalms, hymns and spiritual songs. Sing and make music in your heart to the Lord, always giving thanks to God the Father for everything in the Name of our Lord Jesus Christ." (Ep 5:18-20*

BOOK SIX: HOW TO PRAY SUCCESSFULLY

Introduction to Lesson One
Lesson One - **The Unique Witness Of Prayer**

Introduction to Lesson Two
Lesson Two - **The Secrets Of Successfull Prayer**

INTRODUCTION TO LESSON ONE

R.A. Torrey declares in his book, "How to Pray":

"One of the most significant verses in the Bible on prayer is 1 John 3:22. John says, in so many words, that everything he asked for he got. How many of us can say this: 'Whatsoever I ask I receive'? But John explains why this was so, 'Because we keep his commandments and do those things that are pleasing in his sight.' In other words, the one who expects God to do as he asks him, must on his part do whatever God bids him." [11]

How true that is. We cannot expect God to answer our prayers if we are doing things that are contrary to his revealed will found in his Word. If we are keeping his commands, then we have a wonderful confidence in him and we will see some dramatic answers to prayer.

Study this lesson on prayer, and then see if God will not begin to answer your prayers, giving you great miracles in the name of Jesus, to whom God has given all authority in heaven and on earth.

---

[11] How to Pray; R. A. Torrey; Published by Moody Press, Chicargo. This ref pg. 35

LESSON ONE:
THE UNIQUE WITNESS OF PRAYER

There is one respect in which Christianity stands completely alone; it claims answered prayer! Nobody really expects Mohammed, or Buddha, or Confucius, to answer prayer. But the Christian claim is emphatic and bold:

> *"O you who hear prayer, to you all men will come."*
> *Ps 65:2*

The Christian declares that the true God is and must be a prayer answering God. We maintain that Prayer, when it is presented before God properly, is always properly answered.

Unanswered prayer is the brand of a false religion.

Christianity alone is able to prove the existence of God - Who sees, knows, and hears - by the simple and plain fact that he answers prayer.

MUTE IDOL VERSUS THE LIVING GOD

The prophet Elijah recognised that answered prayer gave proof of the existence of God. He challenged the prophets of Baal to show by answered prayer that their god lived! The Bible says these priests,

> *"...called on the name of Baal from morning until noon. " O Baal answer us!" they shouted. But there was no response; no one answered."*
> *1 Kg 18:26*

Throughout the weary hours they screamed and begged and tormented themselves, until with Elijah's taunts singing in their ears, they dropped to the ground exhausted. Then Elijah spoke. For a few minutes he addressed himself to the God of heaven. Suddenly! With a crackling roar, fire flamed down from the skies and the sacrifice was cremated, leaving a million smoking ashes. Elijah said no more; no more was needed; the demonstration was complete; none could gainsay the evidence of his own eyes, ears and nostrils! And the people all thundered, "The Lord, He is God! The Lord, He is God!"

Truly the distinguishing feature of our faith is its testimony of answered prayer. But how tragic is the multitude of Christian people who have no more experience of answered prayer than those who worship dumb idols! What is wrong?

OUR DEPENDENCE ON PRAYER

This instinct to pray is something that God has built into every man and woman. For this reason all men are familiar with the idea of prayer.

No doubt you have prayed sometime in your life. You have probably had some answers to your prayers: but I wonder if you are really satisfied with the effectiveness of your prayer life? It is not enough to receive a few answers to a few of your prayers. You want to know the thrill of praying and every time having that prayer answered. It is possible for you to pray and always to receive an answer to your prayer.

Learn this: we are utterly dependent upon prayer. It is the only direct link we have with God. All we are to receive from God and all we desire to receive will only become ours as we ask.

But, you say, "I do ask; I often pray. But there is no answer. How do you explain that?" Let the Bible speak:

> *"...You do not have, because you do not ask God. When you ask, you do not receive, because you ask with wrong motives, that you may spend what you get on your pleasures." Ja 4:2b-3*

There are people who do not pray at all, and so have never known the special excitement of getting an answer from heaven.

Then there are people who pray, but still there is no response from the realm of God, because they ask in the wrong spirit, "with wrong motives", in the wrong way, and for the wrong things.

Yet Jesus said,

> *"...ASK AND YOU WILL RECEIVE, AND YOUR JOY WILL BE COMPLETE." Jn 16:24b*

So there is definitely a requesting and a receiving that is ours if we will.

Here in the following pages, are some of the secrets of this successful asking; asking that brings abundant joy along with heaven's answer!

PRAYER IS MADE INEFFECTUAL BY LACK OF A FIXED DESIRE

A prayer that is no more than a half-hearted wish has little chance of reaching the ear of God. More than a vague hope for something because "it might be nice to have" is necessary to gain heaven's response. To answer prayer and "minister to those who will inherit salvation" God is pleased to dispatch his holy angels, those mighty messengers of power and plenty (He 1:14).

But it is not likely that God will disturb the angels from their glad work of rejoicing around the throne of heaven's glory (Re 5:11-12) unless we really need and deeply want the object of our prayer!

So, before you pray, establish the fact that you are asking for a good thing, and that you do indeed fervently desire it.

Yet we must go still further, for we need more than just mere longing to have our request granted; we must have a FIXED DETERMINATION to have the thing we desire!

Mark these scriptures: Jesus said,

> *"...Ask and it will be given you; seek and you will find; knock and the door will be opened to you. For everyone who asks receives; he who seeks finds; and to him who knocks, the door will be opened."*
> *Mt 7:7-8*

This is a glorious promise but it only holds true for those who diligently ask and seek and knock. What Jesus really said was,

> *"Ask and keep on asking...seek and keep on seeking...knock and keep on knocking...!*

And again

> *"...always pray and (do) not give up."*

Then elsewhere in scripture we are exhorted to "pray continually" to be faithful in prayer" and not to "give the devil a foothold" (Lu 11:9-10; 18:1; 1 Th 5:17; Ro 12:12; Ep 4:27).

So, if you want to be sure that your request will be granted, then make a definite covenant of prayer before God - and his promise will hold true: "Everyone who asks (and keeps on asking) receives!"

ACTION MUST FOLLOW ASKING

We have seen that a prayer which is not the real wish of the heart is not a prayer, but just hollow-sounding, lifeless words. But if you really desire something, you will not only pray for it with all fervency, but you will also do all you can yourself to bring it to pass.

In other words, it is a cardinal rule of prayer, that, having made our request to God, all our activities from that time must be directed towards putting ourselves in a place to have that prayer answered. If YOU do nothing to help answer your own prayer, God cannot answer it, for it is plain that you have no real desire for his gift (Ja 2:14-26).

You are praying for victory over some powerful temptation or binding sin. But are you also using every endeavour to avoid being in circumstances where the devil can present that temptation or incite you to that sin? You can claim grace and extra help from the Lord if you are unable to avoid the place of temptation, but, remember,

> "...Do not put the Lord your God to the test"
> (Mt 4:7b).

You are praying for your children. But are you doing all in your power to answer that prayer by example and teaching?

You are praying for healing of your body. But are you doing everything to facilitate healing by taking every care of yourself physically? And are you preparing yourself spiritually by worship, and by meditation in the healing promises of scripture? Cleanse your heart and life of unworthy attitudes and actions, and they you may be sure God will deliver you by his mighty power.

So - ASK - then ACT!

GOD ANSWERS THE PRAYERS OF FAITH

Jesus said,

> "...If you believe, you will receive whatever you ask for in prayer" (Mt 21:22).

Prayer alone is not sufficient; we must pray the prayer of faith.

What is the prayer of faith?

How can we ask in prayer, believing?

To pray the prayer of faith, four things are essential.

1. YOU MUST BELIEVE THAT GOD IS ABLE

Deep in your heart there must be an unwavering conviction that God is easily able to answer your prayer. And this conviction must be alive and vibrant! Many people say, "God can do anything," but their words are cold and dispassionate, there is no responding tingle of faith in their innermost soul, no thrill of joy at the immense ability of our mighty God.

When the saints of old spoke about the ability of God there was a note of exultant joy, of swelling awe, of expanding faith, of breath-catching excitement, in their fervent praise.

Detect it in these few passages from scripture:

> *"...but because Jesus lives forever, he has a permanent priest-hood. Therefore he is able to save completely those who come to God through him, because he always lives to intercede for them" (He 7:24-25).*
>
> *"...(He) is able to do immeasurably more than all we ask or imagine..." (Ep 3:20)*
>
> *"...the God we serve is able to save us...and he will rescue us..." (Da 3:17)*
>
> *"...and God is able to make all grace abound to you, so that in all things at all times, having all that you need, you will abound in every good work" (2 Co 9:8).*

A graphic example of the Lord's requirement of faith in his ability to answer our prayer is seen in his words to the two blind men:

> *"...Do you believe that I am able to do this? "Yes Lord", they replied. Then he touched their eyes and said, "According to your faith will it be done to you." and their sight was restored" (Mt 9:28b-30a).*

Notice also that Jesus was very particular in his question to the blind men. He said not just, "do you believe that I am able," but, "Do you believe that I am able to DO THIS?" "This!" This particular thing! So many say "all things are possible." But that is a very broad statement. What is important is the more personal challenge, "Is this thing possible?" This particular miracle that you need right now?

We often find that people in times of abundance will easily say that God can do anything; but when faced with a sudden great need, their certainty begins to waver, the problem looms like a massive mountain, and they are not so sure that God can really help them.

Our faith in God's ability must be a particular and personal faith. We must have an absolute certainty that God is able to do exactly what we require. Every time we pray, the Lord in effect challenges us as he did the blind men, and says, "Before we go any further, do you believe that I am able to do this?" If we can instantly and confidently respond, "Yes, Lord!" then he will certainly say to us, as he did them, "According to your faith it will be done to you!"

2. YOU MUST BELIEVE THAT GOD WILL

To be successful, all prayer must be made on the basis of God's absolute trustworthiness. It is useless for you to pray if you are in two minds as to the desire of the Lord to answer you. The psalmist recognised this need for a united heart and an unwavering confidence in God's trustworthiness, when he cried:

> *"Teach me your way, O Lord, and I will walk in your truth; give me an undivided heart, that I may fear your name." Ps 86:11*

And again, we are exhorted to ask, and in asking to believe and not doubt:

> *"...because he who doubts is like a wave of the sea, blown and tossed by the wind. That man should not think he will receive anything from the Lord, he is a double minded man unstable in all he does." Ja 1:6b-8*

Again we are told plainly, and bluntly:

> *"...without faith it is impossible to please God,*

> *because anyone who comes to him must believe that he exists and that he rewards those who earnestly seek him." He 11:6*

Lying, deceit, dishonesty, trickery, unreliability - these are the trade-marks of the world. Unhappily we have breathed this atmosphere all our lives, and distrust toward others has been deeply ingrained in us. We carry much of this when we come before the Lord and so often we have reserve in our hearts toward God.

Faith in God is simply absolute trust or confidence in God, and the scripture says that without faith it is impossible for us to please God. This is quite reasonable. As a father, it would hurt me deeply if my son showed that he did not trust me and had no confidence in my word. Yet God is vastly more reliable than we are. So Jesus said,

> *"...If you, then, though you are evil, know how to give good gifts to your children, how much more will your Father in heaven give good gifts to those who ask him!" Mt 7:11*

So we must break through our inward distrust if we would successfully pray. We can do this by remembering such promises as:

> *"...God is not a man, that he should lie, nor a son of man, that he should change his mind. Does he speak and then not act? Does he promise and not fulfill?" Nu 23:19*

Believe it then - GOD WILL ANSWER YOUR PRAYER.

3. BELIEVE THAT NOW IS GOD'S TIME TO ANSWER PRAYER

Frequently people pray just on the off chance that God might hear them, and perhaps answer. Others are not quite so casual, but they still pray without any real expectancy that God will answer them. They scarcely dare hope for any more than an approximate answer some time in the indefinite future. But we must learn that immediate expectation is just as important as prayer. A settled belief that God heard and granted our request the moment we prayed is a vital requirement of successful prayer.

Two scriptures press this truth upon us very firmly. Jesus said,

> *"...whatever you ask for in prayer, believe that you have received it, and it will be yours." Mk 11:24b*

Phillips translates it this way,

> *"...Whatever you pray about and ask for, believe that you have received it and it will be yours."*

Then the beloved disciple, John, who knew the heart of the Master so well, expanded Jesus' words and wrote:

> *"...God has give us the privilege of coming to him boldly in prayer, having perfect confidence and assurance that if we ask him for anything according to his will, he will listen to us. God invariably hears us when we pray in his will. And since we know positively that he takes notice of us in whatever we ask, we also know beyond any doubt that God has granted us the things we asked him for and we already have them as our present posses-*

sions!" 1 Jn 5:14-15 paraphrased

So, we must ask; then...

- we must believe that God listened to us; then...
- we must believe that God has granted our request; then...
- we must count ourselves as already being the owners of the thing we asked for;

then...

- we shall certainly receive it!

A graphic example of praying with this kind of expectation is given in the Bible account of the prophet Elijah.

Elijah had prophesied drought and the country had dried to a crisp during nearly forty months without rain or dew. Now the time had come for the drought to be broken, and it was to be broken by his prayer. Elijah took his servant to the top of the mountain and there bowed himself before the Lord and prayed earnestly for rain. He prayed for rain and he expected rain. So he sent his servant to the top of the hill to look for rain clouds. The servant came back and said, "I see nothing." Six times Elijah sent him to look and six times he returned with a negative report, the observations of his natural senses. But Elijah, who spoke from his faith and his knowledge of the power of God, told his servant to go back the seventh time and look again. Six times the servant said, "There is no rain." Six times Elijah retorted, "There IS rain!" And the seventh time the man came running back, shouting that a tiny cloud had just formed above the horizon. RAIN WAS COMING! Before the day was through a great deluge drenched the land. (1 Ki 18:41-45)

No matter how impossible it may seem, IF YOU HAVE GOD'S PROMISE ON IT, THEN PRAY WITH ABSOLUTE ASSURANCE, BELIVE WITH SIMPLE, UNSHAKABLE TRUST, AND KNOW THAT GOD HAS ANSWERED YOUR PRAYER. DON'T ACCEPT ANOTHER PERSON'S NEGATIVE REPORT. BELIEVE GOD'S REPORT! HE IS NOT A MAN; HE CANNOT LIE. WHAT HE HAS PROMISED, HE WILL PERFORM!

So Elijah found it. He prayed with expectation. His expectation did not waver. No opposition, no outward evidence, could destroy his inward certainty that God had heard and answered his prayer.

In those far distant days the scale of the earth's need was great. But one man was sufficient for it. The need was great, and Elijah prayed for great rain. And God gave it to him. Your need may be great also. But your prayer, coupled with the expectation of an immediate answer, is sufficient for it. Pray for great things; believe that your request is promptly granted; stand your ground without hesitating; and God will do great things for you.

4. BELIEVE IN THE POWER OF YOUR OWN PRAYER

A great number of people satisfactorily observe all the principles that we have mentioned; their faith in God, to all outward appearances, is sure and confident; yet still they fail. Why? It is often because their faith in God is not linked with faith in themselves. Let me explain that.

What is faith?

Faith is that unwavering confidence in God which is built upon absolute trust in the integrity of his Word. We read that:

> *"...faith comes from hearing the message, and the*

> *message is heard through the Word of Christ."*
> *Ro 10:17*

So faith is based on the truth of the scripture. We accept the reliability of the Word of God, and from that we have faith in God.

But it is not possible to effectively claim faith in one part of scripture while rejecting another. Or, to be more precise, you cannot successfully claim to believe what the Bible says about God and his promises unless you also believe what it says about you and your prayer.

Now we often hear the complaint, "I am not worthy", "God won't listen to my prayer", "I have no faith", "I am too weak", "My need is too great", "I am too miserable to pray", "The devil stops me from praying", "Satan stops me from believing", "I am still in darkness", and a host of other such-like negative, defeated, fearful, scripture-denying sobbings.

But into the teeth of these complaints and murmurings is hurled the emphatic declaration of God saying what you really are, in Christ. The Bible urges us to stop seeing ourselves as we may be in the flesh, but to compel our attention upon what we are in Christ. We must fasten our thoughts onto our new life in Christ, and believe with all our heart that what God says we are and have in the heavenly realm is more real and more powerful than what our natural senses tell us we are and have in the earthly realm.

We have a two fold choice - to close our natural eyes and open the spiritual eyes of faith; or to close our spiritual eyes, and look only with the natural eyes of our senses.

If our vision is wholly caught up with natural evidences, then the things of earth and the flesh will dominate and ultimately destroy us. Our prayers will remain unanswered. But if we resolutely turn away from purely natural considerations and fasten our gaze on the heavenly realm and on Christ, and on what we are and have in Christ, then the splendour of these spiritual realities will dominate and ultimately revive us. Our prayers will be abundantly answered.

The Bible says that Christ is risen from the dead: but it also says we are risen with him, and have been raised with him, and are (already) seated with him in heavenly places. The Bible says that nothing is impossible with God: but it also says that nothing shall be impossible to you.

The Bible says that Christ is stupendously wealthy: but it also says that we are co-heirs with Christ, and that the riches of his glory belong to us too.

And so on we could go, with scores of similar statements.

What the Bible says of the Lord Jesus Christ is gloriously true. We believe implicitly the record of Christ and his glory. But when the Bible, just as emphatically, just as definitely, just as factually, ascribes the same glories and honour and victory and wealth to us, by virtue of our union with Christ in the new birth, we hesitate to accept the record. We either frankly don't believe it, or else we take refuge behind the false assumption that these things cannot be fulfilled until the day of resurrection. Yet the Bible declares that whatever God has already accomplished in Christ is already accomplished in us. We only need to believe it:

> *"...count yourselves dead to sin but alive to God in Christ Jesus." Ro 6:11*

> *"...stand fast in the liberty wherewith Christ has set us free." Ga 5:1 (KJV)*

And the fruits of Jesus' immense victory will begin to manifest themselves in us.

You dare not claim to have faith in God and to believe his Word unless, along with your acceptance of the Bible revelation of Christ and his victory, you accept the revelation that is given of what you are in Christ. But to help you further in this, here is a list of relevant Bible passages. Read them, meditate on them, eagerly accept them as absolutely true. Here is the truth as heaven sees it, the truth that Jesus said, if we would learn it would set us free! (Jn 8:32 & 36)

Read: Mt 17:20; Mk 11:23-24; Lu 10:19-20; Ro 6:11; 8:31-32; 37-39; 2 Co 2:14; 9:8; Ga 5:1; Ep 1:19-20; 2:1, 5-6; 3:20; 6:10; Ph 4:13-19; Cl 1:11 & 27; 2:10 & 13; He 10:19-23; etc.

And having read those passages, meditate on them; then it will be true of you as it was of the psalmist, "whatever you do will prosper" (Ps 1:2-3; see also Jsh 1:8-9; Ps 63:5-6; 77:12-14; 104:33-34; 1 Ti 4:15).

And you may pray as David:

> *"May the words of my mouth and the meditation of my heart be pleasing in your sight, O Lord, my Rock and my Redeemer." Ps 19:14*

So the, knowing what you are in Christ, be rid of all hesitancy and the reluctance that comes from a false humility: do what God tells you to do; take your stand in the heavenly realms in Christ, far above all principality and power, and come boldly into God's presence with full assurance of faith. Remember Elijah: "(He) was a man just like us." (Ja 5:17), yet he prayed with confidence in his own words, and harnessed the whole heaven to his faith! (1 Kg 17:1; 18:1-2, 36-38, 41 & 45).

Your prayer has power if you will only believe in the power of prayer!

5. MAKE YOUR PRAYER AN ACTIVE ONE

We have already spoken of the general activity that must precede and follow prayer. Now I want to mention activity in prayer itself. Many prayers fail because they are too passive, they lack aggression and the bold actions that result from real faith. Jesus said,

> "...the kingdom of heaven has been forcefully advancing, and forceful men lay hold of it." Mt 11:12b

Then again Jesus placed the emphasis on human COMMAND and ACTION, when he said,

> "...SAY to this mountain, Move from here to there and it will move. Nothing will be impossible for you." Mt 17:20-21

> "...SAY to this mountain, Go, throw yourself into the sea, and it will be done." Mt 21:21b; Mk 11:23

> "...SAY to this mulberry tree, Be uprooted and planted in the sea, and it will obey you." Lu 17:6b

References like these indicate that it is not sufficient to pray only. It is by prayer that faith is given birth in our hearts and we gain confidence in knowing that our request is granted. But having received that full assurance, it is then necessary to rise up in vigorous faith and claim the answer from heaven.

In fact we should go even further, and take hold of our God-given authority, and stand before the mountain that hinders us and in complete confidence, knowing that we have the right to do so, COMMAND it to be removed. You can boldly and forcefully charge the "mulberry tree" of sin and sickness to be uprooted from your life, and cast into the ocean depths of God's deliverance.

Prayer gives you strength, courage, and determination, so that your faith will become immovable. When such an immovable, irresistible faith strikes against the mountain of sickness or sin, of debt or of bondage, that mountain must disintegrate. Prayer will graft into your life the strong arm of faith. But then you must act and use that arm of strength in authoritative command, maintaining a steadfast confidence that what you speak in faith will come to pass.

Moses prayed, laid hold of the faith of God, then arose from his knees, struck the Red Sea with his rod, and watched while the waters rolled back. (ref. Ex 14:15-16, 21-22).

Joshua, in the fury of a great battle, saw the sun descending and night fast approaching. He knew if the battle were to be won, the day had to be extended. He fell on his knees and prayed. Faith dawned. Then he arose, and in a voice of thunder, commanded the sun to stand still, and it obeyed him. Israel won a great victory that day (ref. Jsh 10:12-13).

The sick king, Hezekiah, earnestly sought God for healing. In another place in the city the prophet Isaiah was also praying. The faith of God flashed into the hearts of both men. Isaiah stood up and hurried to where the king lay and told Hezekiah that God would heal him. To prove it, Isaiah spoke to the sun and commanded it to recede ten degrees. It obeyed him, and the king's life was spared (ref. Is 38:1-8).

Jesus spent a night in prayer, and then commanded the winds and the waves, and they were instantly quieted at the sound of his voice (ref. Mk 4:39).

If you have a great need in your life that towers like a mountain, then learn this secret. *Jesus said, men should pray and not give up. (Lu 18:1)*

Rather, faith will be given to them so that they may speak and remove every difficulty.

Have faith in God and it will be done!

INTRODUCTION TO LESSON TWO

The great secret of successful prayer involves a daily, consistent, prayer life. We can not hope to have answers to prayer if we are sluggish in coming before the Lord. Some Christians ask for something and then forget they ever asked for it. How can God consider these to be earnest prayers, worthy of an answer?

Some pray for a time, sometimes for years, and then, just as the answer is on the way, they give up! We must persevere in our prayers. Listen to the words of Gordon Lindsay, in his book "Prayer that Moves Mountains": "This great lesson of daily dependence on God was taught in the giving of manna to the children of Israel. They were to receive only enough for a day's supply. No man could gather a supply for several days and hoard it for future use. Those who did, found that it bred worms and was unfit for human consumption.

"There is a common mistake that is made by many Christians. They would have healing that they can't "lose", rather than the health that comes from a daily dependence on the quickening power of the Spirit of God. They would rather have financial security that does not compel them daily to go to the secret chamber and ask God to meet their needs. They would have a Baptism of the Holy Ghost that does not require a daily waiting on God for a fresh anointing. But such desires are not in accord with God's purpose.

"God's plan involves a daily dependence on him."[12]

In this lesson we will study the secrets of successful prayer.

---

[12] Prayer That Moves Mountains; Gordon Lindsay; The Voice of Healing Publishing Company, Dallas, Texas. 1955. This ref. pg. 44.

LESSON TWO: THE SECRETS OF SUCCESSFUL PRAYER

YOUR REQUEST MUST BE REASONABLE

We cannot have faith for the unreasonable. We are so built that we can believe only for those things that seem to us to be reasonable.

I do not mean that we have to fully understand a thing before we can believe it, or that it has to be reasonable from an ordinary person's point of view. But we do have to be convinced of the truth and possibility of the object of our belief.

In prayer this means that we must be convinced that we are asking for something which is correct, that it is possible to receive it, and that it is probable that God will grant our request.

For example, if it is healing you stand in need of, you must know that healing has been promised in the Bible, that God is able to heal, and that God will heal you in particular. If you are convinced of these things, then your request for healing will appear reasonable to you, and you will have little difficulty in praying the prayer of faith.

Now, there are two things that prevent people from feeling that it is reasonable for God to answer their prayer...

1. BECAUSE THEY THINK THEY ARE UNWORTHY

As long as we feel unworthy to pray, or undeserving of an answer, it will appear unreasonable for God to hear us and grant our request, and so we shall be unable to pray the prayer of faith.

Two things arise here...

FIRSTLY, this feeling of unworthiness is often warranted, and stems from the conviction of the Holy Spirit. As long as we pay no heed to the divine voice there is no possibility of God allowing us to pray the payer of faith. Hence we read:

> *"If I had cherished sin in my heart, the Lord would not have listened." Ps 66:18*

> *"The Lord is far from the wicked but he hears the prayers of the righteous." Pr 15:29*

If we are deliberately harbouring sin and wilfully and continually giving place to temptation, it is impossible for God to accept our prayer. Jesus said that we could ask what we will and it would be given to us, but this would be true only as we remain in him and his words remain in us. Jn 15;7

And wise Solomon said:

> *"If anyone turns a deaf ear to the law, even his prayers are detestable." Pr 28:9*

However, there is a remedy for this:

> *"If you put away the sin that is in your hand and allow no evil to dwell in your tent, then you will lift up your face without shame; you will stand firm and without fear." Jo 11:14-15*

> *"Come near to God and he will come near to you. Wash your hands, you sinners, and purify your hearts, you double minded." Ja 4:8*

SECONDLY, this feeling of unworthiness is often quite unwarranted, and stems, not from the conviction of the Holy Spirit, but from the false condemnation of Satan. It is the voice of the devil trying to bring our past sins between us and God, accusing us, and seeking to undo the work of God's grace by casting us into guilt and despair. You and I are endowed with an inward prompting we call our conscience. But conscience does not always guide us rightly, the direction it gives us depends largely on our faith and attitude toward God. Sometimes conscience can be stirred up, not by the Lord, but by the devil. It then brings us into a false sense of condemnation. Recognising this, the apostle spoke of a "guilty conscience", that is, a conscience that is wrongfully making people feel guilty, and so preventing them from coming into God's presence.

> *"let us draw near to God with a sincere heart in full assurance of faith, having our hearts sprinkled to cleanse us from a GUILTY conscience and having our bodies washed with pure water." He 10:22*

How shall we do this? How can we shake ourselves free from an accusing and condemning conscience, a conscience that is thrusting at us with bitter pangs of guilt even though we have turned from sin?

The secret is in the word "sprinkled". It cannot be done by any effort or merit of ours, but solely by reliance on the shed blood of Jesus. So John said:

> *"If we confess our sins, he is faithful and just and will forgive us our sins and purify us from all unrighteousness." 1 Jn 1:9*

And again, if our heart persists in condemning us, despite every effort to secure rest by believing in Jesus, John adds:

> *"This then is how we know that we belong to the truth, and how we set our hearts at rest in his presence whenever our hearts condemn us. For God is greater than our hearts, and he knows everything. Dear friends, if our hearts do not condemn us, we have confidence before God and RECEIVE FROM HIM ANYTHING WE ASK, because we obey his commands and do what pleases him." 1 Jn 3:19-22*

2. BECAUSE THEY ARE NOT SURE OF THE WILL OF GOD

This is perhaps the most common reason of all why people do not feel it is reasonable to have deep assurance that God will answer their prayers.

The Bible says emphatically that we can have confidence in prayer, and be assured that we have the things we ask for as soon as we ask, only when we know that we are asking according to God's will (1 Jn 5:14-15).

Being uncertain of God's will, people are not sure that God wants to give them their desire, and therefore they cannot possibly pray the prayer of faith. The focal point of their prayer is not, "I believe!" but "If...!" This is hope not faith. And while it is possible that God in his mercy and kindness may be pleased to answer such a prayer, there is no guarantee that he will do so. If you want to be positively sure that your prayer has been heard and your request granted, you must first discover God's will, then you can pray with total confidence and the knowledge that you must receive the thing you asked for.

But so many people are far from sure of God's will when they pray, and quite often, scarcely bother to inquire as to what is the true will of God in the matter.

This is inexcusable, for with a little effort and patience and trust, the will of God can always be discovered.

How can we learn the will of God? How can we discover what God himself wants to do, and what he wants us to have?

As his children and as his servants we have an inviolable right to know the will of God; and he will reveal his will by the following means...

    a. Obedience -   Is 32:17; Jn 14:21; Cl 1:10.
    b. His Word -   Ps 119:105, 130, 133.
    c. Prayer -   Acts 1:23-24, Ja 1:5.
    d. Circumstances - 1 Co 16:9; 2 Co 2:12, Re 3:8.
    e. Godly counsel -   Pr 15:22; Acts 19:30-31.
    f. The Holy Spirit - Ro 8:26-27.

In matters of comparatively small importance, or where the scripture expressly states God's will, only one or two of those indications will be needed to give you confidence in prayer.

But when the answer to your prayers may determine the course of your whole life, or may affect the lives of many people, then it would be wise to ask for a positive witness from all of those means before proceeding any further.

WHEN GOD SAYS "NO"!

Sometimes God says "No!" - What shall we do then?

It is true that God ignores unrepentant sinners; but he always listens to the prayers of the righteous, and always answers their prayer. But it is also true that there are occasions when the Lord refuses some requests. This was once the experience of the apostle Paul. It arose when "a thorn in his flesh, a tormenting messenger of Satan," pressed hard upon him. It brought Paul much infirmity and he earnestly "pleaded with the Lord to take it away." But God's answer to the apostle was:

> *"My grace is sufficient for you, for my power is made perfect in weakness." 2 Co 12:9a*

God said "No!" to Paul's actual request, but he gave Paul a better answer, a better promise. Paul heard the answer of the Lord, accepted it, and said,

> *"...Therefore I will boast all the more gladly about my weaknesses, so that Christ's power may rest on me." 2 Co 12;9b*

And I think you know how mightily God's power did rest upon the great apostle.

So there may be some problem or burden in your life which is not God's immediate desire to remove. But, even though the Lord should refuse your initial request, he certainly will not leave you to struggle on alone, but he will surely give you abundant grace, and the power of Christ to give you victory.

To give us this confidence, we have this wonderful promise:

> *"For we do not have a high priest who is unable to sympathise with our weaknesses, but we have one who has been tempted in every way just as we are - yet was without sin. Let us then approach the*

> *throne of grace with confidence, so that we may receive mercy and find grace to help in our time of need. He 4:15-16*

SUMMARY OF SECRETS OF SUCCESSFUL PRAYER

So then in answer to the question, "How can I pray successfully?" we must adhere to the following pattern...

1. CONFESS ALL KNOWN SIN

If we hold sin in our hearts God will not hear us (Ps 66:18; Is 59:1-2).

But God will hear the prayer of a righteous man (Ja 5:16; 1 Pe 3:12). If we cover our sins, God cannot forgive them (Pr 28:13) and in any case it is really impossible to hide anything from God (He 4:13). But if we confess our sins, the Lord will readily forgive them, and make us clean before him (1 Jn 1:9).

Sometimes we must go even further than mere confession to God. James said,

> *"Therefore, confess your sins to each other and pray for each other so that you may be healed." Ja 5:16a*

And Jesus said:

> *"...if you forgive men when they sin against you, your heavenly Father will also forgive you." Mt 6:14-15 (See also Mk 11:25-26)*

And again the Lord emphasised:

> *"Therefore if you are offering your gift at the altar*

> *and there remember that you brother has something against you, leave your gift there in front of the altar. First go and be reconciled to your brother, then come and offer your gift." Mt 5:23-24*

So the Lord may require of you that you make confession or reconciliation or forgiveness or restoration to others, before your prayer can be answered.

> *"Husbands, in the same way be considerate as you live with your wives, and treat them with respect as the weaker partner and as heirs with you of the gracious gift of life, so that nothing will hinder your prayers." 1 Pe 3:7 (See also 1 Jn 3:18-21)*

2. COME HUMBLY BEFORE GOD

The Lord will resist the proud.

> *"...God opposes the proud but gives grace to the humble." 1 Pe 5:5b (See also Ja 4:6)*

But he will hear those who humble themselves, and are lowly of heart.

> *"Though the Lord is on high, he looks upon the lowly, but the proud he knows from afar." Ps 138:6*

> *"For this is what the high and lofty One says - he who lives forever, whose name is holy: I live in a high and holy place, but also with him who is contrite and lowly in spirit, to revive the spirit of the lowly and to revive the heart of the contrite." Is 57:15 (See also 2 Ch 7:14.)*

And in this respect, too, we should learn to wait upon God. The Bible says,

> "But .those who hope in the Lord will renew their strength." Is 40:31a

And again, the Psalmist said,

> "I am still confident of this: I will see the goodness of the Lord in the land of the living. Wait for the Lord; be strong and take heart and wait for the Lord." Ps 27:13-14

He believed that he would see God's hand outstretched to give him good things. Because he believed he had no fear. Because he believed, he also strengthened his courage and increased his confidence by waiting on the Lord.

You will receive no answer from the Lord if you rush pell-mell into his presence, rattle off a few words of prayer and then rush out again. Remember that you are coming into the presence of the King of heaven and the Lord of all the earth. So we read:

> "As the eyes of slaves look to the hand of their master, as the eyes of a maid look to the hand of her mistress, so our eyes look to the Lord our God, till he shows us his mercy." Ps 123:2

So we need to learn not only to wait upon the Lord in lingering communion, but also to have PATIENCE. The scripture says:

> "You need to persevere so that when you have done the will of God, you will receive what he has promised." He 10:36

Many people are denied an answer to their prayer simply because they do not wait to discover the will of God, or having discovered his will, do not allow time for the answer to come. After a few days, or even a few hours, they lose hope and consider that God did not hear them, or has perhaps forgotten them. Remember Daniel. He prayed, and the Bible says that God heard him on the first day, and dispatched an angel with heaven's reply. But the powers of darkness opposed the angel of the Lord, and it was a full three weeks before the answer finally reached Daniel. But during that time Daniel continued in prayer day by day. He did not yield to his feelings and exclaim (as so many do) "What's the use of praying anyway!" Daniel persisted in his prayer, so the angel was able to minister to him and give him God's blessing.

> *"Therefore turn thou to thy God, keep mercy and judgement and wait on thy God continually."*
> *Ho 12:6 (KJV)*

3. COME CONFIDENTLY BEFORE GOD

Proper humility must be coupled with godly boldness. You should not creep into God's throne room; if you are sincere in your heart you may have perfect boldness in your approach to the Lord.

> *"...Therefore, brothers, since we have confidence to enter the Most Holy Place by the blood of Jesus, by a new and living way opened for us through the curtain, that is, his body, and since we have a great priest over the house of God, let us draw near to God with a sincere heart in full assurance and faith, having our hearts sprinkled to cleanse us from a guilty conscience and having our bodies washed with pure water." He 10:19-22*

4. COME BELIEVING HIS PROMISE

If we would please God it is essential that we have faith; believing is the Bible condition for receiving:

> *"...without faith it is impossible to please God, because anyone who comes to him must believe that he exists and that he rewards those who earnestly seek him." He 11:6 (See also Mk 11:24)*

A person who continually wavers in his trust in God can expect no answer to his prayer (Ja 1:6-7). The antidote to a weak faith is the Word of God. It is by "drinking the Water of Life" and "eating the Bread of Life" - by constantly absorbing God's Word - that our faith is established:

> *"...faith comes by hearing the message, and the message is heard through the word of Christ.' Ro 10:17 (See also Ro 4:20-21; Ac 27:25)*

God has given us;

> *"...his very great and precious promises, so that through them you may participate in the divine nature." 2 Pe 1:4a*

5. CONSTANTLY SEEK TO KNOW GOD'S WILL

This was the foundation of the Master's prayer life (Mt 26:39 & 42), and it must also be the foundation of our prayer life (1 Jn 5:14). If there is no answer to your prayer, it is simply because you have asked with a wrong motive, or contrary to God's will (Ja 4:3). If you want to be sure of getting an answer, take time to discover the will of the Lord, before you pray, and then ask in perfect confidence!

For your interest, here are some Bible examples of God refusing to answer prayers because they were contrary to his will - Ex 33:18-20; De 3:23-26; 2 Sa 12:15-23; and because of sin - Ez 20:1-3; Pr 1:24-26.

6. CALL UPON GOD WITH ALL YOUR HEART

There must be earnest longing, intense desire, deep passion, fervent faith, behind every petition you present to God. The Lord is unmoved by sleepy, half-hearted, indefinite, apathetic praying. Consider Jesus himself:

> *"...He offered up prayers and petitions with loud cries and tears." He 5:7a (See also Je 29:13; Ac 12:5; Cl 4:12; Ja 5:16-17).*

CONCLUSION

So then...

- knowing the mighty power of prayer;
- knowing the Lord is unquestionably willing to answer your prayer;
- with the peace of God ruling in your heart (Cl 3:15);
- with an inward witness that you are praying in the will of God;
- with all doubt and uncertainty banished;
- come boldly to the throne of grace, and

> *"ASK AND YOU WILL RECEIVE, AND YOU JOY WILL BE COMPLETE."Jn 16:24b*

BOOK SEVEN: THE AMAZING POWER OF FAITH

Introduction to Lesson One
Lesson One **The Importance Of Faith**

Introduction to Lesson Two
Lesson Two - **The Power Of Positive Believing**

Introduction to Lesson Three
Lesson Three - **Your World Of Faith And Authority**

INTRODUCTION TO LESSON ONE

"Jesus said, if you have faith you can throw a mountain into the sea. Obviously this matter of moving mountains must be qualified - we can't go around shifting hills all over the place just to suit our own convenience! The key is to act in harmony with the will of God."[13]

Remember the words of Jesus in John 14:10b:

> *"...The words I say to you are not just my own. Rather it is the Father, living in me, who is doing his work."*

If we follow in the footsteps of Jesus, and determine to do only those things that we are sure are in the will of God, then we will save ourselves from many heartaches.

There are many mountains of fear, unbelief, disease, and opposition from Satan. We need to exercise our faith to remove them from our pathway. Let us determine to learn all we can so that we may be equal to the task. In this lesson we learn that everybody has faith, what that faith is, how it is contrasted with fear, and how to gain deliverance from fear! Truly God is stronger than the devil, and good is stronger than evil!

---

[13] "Sitting on Top of the World;" Ken Chant; Bethany Fellowship, Minneapolis, MN 1972. This ref. pg. 10.

LESSON ONE:
THE IMPORTANCE OF FAITH

In a world that is full of fear and uncertainty it is important for all men and women everywhere to know the power of their own faith in God. Faith, to many people, is a mysterious word with an uncertain meaning. This section will give you an outline of how faith works, what it will do, and how you can use your own faith.

FAITH IS ABSOLUTELY ESSENTIAL

The rightness or wrongness of our believing is something we must all face. The Bible places urgent emphasis on the great need for right believing. It is vitally important that we learn how to have faith in God, and that we learn how to use our faith correctly.

FAITH HAS LIMITLESS POSSIBILITIES

Many times the Lord Jesus Christ spoke of the enormous potential of faith in God! Jesus once said to his disciples,

> *"'I tell you the truth, if you have faith and do not doubt',...'.you can say to this mountain', `Go, throw yourself into the sea,' and it will be done. IF YOU BELIEVE, YOU WILL RECEIVE WHATEVER YOU ASK FOR IN PRAYER." Mt 21:21-22*

It is believing - or faith - that makes all the difference between prayer that moves mountains, and prayer that only beats the air. Jesus said to the Roman centurion;

> *"Go! It will be done just as you believed it would."* Mt 8:13

Nothing will be done for us other than that for which we truly believe. We can gain from God only what our unwavering and confident faith moves the Lord to do.

This Jesus intimated again in his strong word to the woman of Canaan.

> *"Woman, you have great faith! Your request is granted." Mt 15:28a*

Here you will notice that this woman was determined that Jesus would heal her daughter. This determination alone would not move the Lord, but when Christ saw that her determination was coupled with faith, thus creating what Jesus called great faith, he did for her exactly what she wanted.

He will grant your request too if you will have the same great faith. And you can! If this humble woman from Canaan, uninstructed in the ways of the Lord, lacking many advantages that you have, could find great faith in God, so also can you!

On another occasion, a man cried out in desperation for the Lord to heal his son. Jesus did not immediately answer his prayer. The first concern of the Lord was to instruct the man to believe.

> *" 'If you can?' 'Said Jesus'. Everything is possible for him who believes'." Mk 9:23*

Here was a straight forward challenge indeed! Into the face of the man's desperate need, churning into his broken heart, the Lord hurled this stern rebuke, this ringing call to the man's own faith.

Some would have been offended by this response of the Lord, and would have gone away angry and unheard. But out of his passionate love for his son, this father found courage equal to the occasion:

> *"Immediately the boy's father exclaimed, 'I do believe; help me overcome my unbelief!'"* Mk 9:24b

Here is the immediate response of faith that made the heart of Jesus thrill. It drew from him the powerful word that drove the devil out of the boy and healed him completely.

This kind of faith is as effective now as it was then: it will move the compassion of Christ now, as it did then. Dare to believe! to believe for every need! believing will do it! Mark it well,

> *"Everything is possible for him who believes."* Mk 9:23a

EVERYBODY HAS FAITH

Before considering this theme, it may be well to answer an objection that some might make, namely that there is one scripture which says:

> *"...for not everyone has faith."* 2 Th 3:2b

But here the original Greek has the definite article, "THE faith".

The reference here is not to faith as a faculty of the human spirit, but to THE ORIGINAL FAITH, that is the Gospel of Christ and especially to a saving faith in Christ.

But when we say that all people have faith, we mean that everybody has the potential ability to believe God. We all have the capacity for faith. Every man is born with this capacity, and every man makes use of it in some part of his life. The fact that you have

FAITH is proved by the fact that you have FEAR. Fear, when it becomes an overpowering, controlling force, is faith perverted.

There is a legitimate fear of course. It is the natural emotion which arises from our sense of self-preservation, giving an inward warning of actual danger. But fear goes astray when it takes possession of us, and torments us. When this happens fear has mastered our capacity for faith, and has perverted our faith to an overpowering belief that evil will certainly overtake us. When fear is thus allowed to dominate us, it bends the powerful force of our natural faith into a deep dread of the unknown that will ultimately destroy us. The natural emotion of FEAR is intended to tell us that danger lies ahead; but that warning being given, it is then time for FAITH to take control of the situation and to trust God for the way of escape.

God gave you that faith, the ability to believe, that you might use it in him and in his power and provision. The Lord has always endeavoured to guide men to live by the power of an abiding faith. The Bible says:

> *"God has dealt to every man a measure of faith."*
> *Ro 12:3b (KJV)*

However, some make proper use of their faith while others, through doubt or a wavering mind, hinder and cripple faith until it is no longer effective. Jesus said:

> *"If you have faith and do not doubt" Mk 11:23*

Here we see that faith must be purged of all doubt before it can become effective. Great faith is faith in which there is no element of doubt, no uncertainty, no hesitancy. But if these things are present in our believing, and so overshadow our faith, then it may be said that we have only "little faith", or even "no faith".

In one time of danger when the disciples were panic stricken, Jesus rebuked them and sternly asked, "Where is your faith?" They had faith, but somewhere in the turmoil of their fear it had become "lost" that is, it was no longer effective. It was paralysed by fear. Their faith did them no good.

WHAT IS FAITH?

The Bible says that faith is the evidence of things not seen. It is the ability to reach beyond ourselves, to go past the obvious circumstances that surround us. It is our capacity to become convinced of the reality of things that we have not yet seen. It enables us to anticipate things which are not yet perceptible to the natural senses. Faith is the outreach of the human heart to God, an outreach based on unwavering confidence in the integrity of God's word and the ability of his power to meet every need, to overcome every situation.

When that outreach of faith is maintained without doubt or double-mindedness, the power of God is compelled to respond to it. This is great faith; this is faith that moves mountains; this is faith that changes the appearance of things. It is faith which is not in any way influenced by things heard or seen or felt, but it is faith which on the contrary ITSELF INFLUENCES these things and brings them into conformity with its irresistible dictate.

So we repeat, all men have faith - the determining factor, though, is the measure in which we use our faith.

FAITH CONTRASTED WITH FEAR

Never before in the history of mankind has fear exacted such a terrible toll on human happiness as it is doing today. We live in an age that is dominated by two things...the destructive power of the atom, and the even more destructive power of fear. The Lord Jesus

Christ spoke of these atomic days and foretold the devastating tide of fear which nuclear warfare and a collapsing world would produce. He spoke of this fear as a flood tide of powerful human emotion which would take more lives, wreak more havoc, than all the wars of history combined. Concerning these age-ending days the Lord said:

> *"There will be signs in the sun, moon and stars. On the earth, nations will be in anguish and perplexity at the roaring and the tossing of the sea. Men will faint from terror, apprehensive of what is coming on the world, for the heavenly bodies will be shaken." Lu 21:25-26*

But you will notice that in this nuclear age of distress of nations and perplexity, the Lord said the outstanding characteristic of mankind would be that "MEN WILL FAINT FROM FEAR."

The Lord foretold world-wide tension, resulting in deep inward tension, the failure of men's hearts, the desolation of their minds, the breakdown of their lives. Fear is a dreadfully destructive force. Aside from the weapon of lust, Satan probably has no more powerful weapon than fear. Elsewhere the scripture says that fear has torment (1 Jn 4:18 KJV)- torment of mind, torment of body, torment of soul and spirit. Our hospitals and sanatoriums and asylums are filled with stark evidence of the truth of this statement.

We have said that fear in human lives arises from the world situation, and that is true, but there is another aspect also. Jesus brought the matter closer home when he said that men will faint from fear because they are "apprehensive of what is coming on the world." You will notice that it is not the things themselves that cause fear, but the attitude of men and women towards those things. They are "apprehensive of them"...that is, people are living in dread of the future. They exist in fearful anticipation of terrible trouble falling upon them. Fear that has torment, fear that causes men to faint, comes from looking into the future and being afraid that the worst will happen. Seeing only darkness and death and desolation, having no recognition of the overruling sovereignty of God, no trust in the prevailing power of his providence, men's hearts faint. People whose hearts are fainting are people who are living in anxiety of tomorrow, who are burdened down with the care and worry of what they consider lies before them.

But now notice that the Lord said that at this same time, in these same conditions, there would be others who would be "lifting their heads." He said:

> *"When these things begin to take place, stand up and lift up your heads, because your redemption is drawing near." Lu 21:28*

So it is not the surrounding conditions which cause fear, but it arises from our outlook, our attitude toward those conditions. Some are "apprehensive" and their hearts are fainting, they are living in fear: others are "lifting their heads" and their hearts are filled with faith, and they are confident that their redemption is drawing near.

So the only difference between fear and faith is the direction in which they are bent. The one thrusts into the disasters and anxieties and distresses that are coming upon the earth and into the families of men, and is broken down by the overwhelming weight of these things. The other thrusts upward toward God, into the promises of the Gospel, waiting for -

> *"...the blessed hope - the glorious appearing of our great God and Saviour Jesus Christ." Tit 2:13*

They find that the Lord is a strong refuge and defence. People who are governed by faith fear no evil, but believe only in God's prevailing goodness and ultimate triumph.

DELIVERANCE FROM FEAR

We have seen that God gave every man the ability to believe. It was his intention that men should believe in God, and for good. But man has reversed the direction of his believing. Instead of his capacity to believe becoming faith in the unlimited power and resources of God, it has become fear in the negative and destructive forces of Satan. When man disobeyed God, when he believed the devil's lie, when he was cast out of God's presence, his ability to believe became perverted and misdirected. That faith which was to bring us all to God's power and provision was directed into the confused darkness of our own fallen nature, and being bound down by a conviction of sin and weakness it became a tyrant, bringing us all the evil that the devil could offer.

Faith went into reverse and became fear. In other words, fear is our believing toward evil and the devil, whereas our believing should be faith toward God and his goodness. But through the grace of God in the Lord Jesus Christ we can reverse this wrongful tendency and change our deepest anticipations away from the crooked pathways of fear into the confident highway of faith.

Our cry then becomes that of the Psalmist -

> *"My soul finds rest in God alone, my salvation comes from him...my hope comes from him...My salvation and my honour depend on God; he is my mighty rock, my refuge."* Ps 62:1-7

FEAR NOT; BELIEVE ONLY

Jesus used this terse statement to show people how to switch from wrong believing to right believing; from believing in the negative power of Satan to believing in the positive power of God.

People who ask, "How can I have faith in God?" would not think of asking, "How can I fear evil?" We find it so much easier to fear (believe in) evil than we do to have faith in God. This must surely appear as a shameful fact to every child of God!

Christians are afraid to believe God for the best, but never afraid to fear the worst. Yet the former is simply faith in forward motion, and the latter faith in reverse.

FEAR LIKE FAITH, HAS POWER TO ATTRACT AND PRODUCE

> *"Now faith is being sure of what we hope for and certain of what we do not see." He 11:1a*

The Greek text here expresses the idea that faith "brings into reality" the things we hope for. Fear on the other hand "brings into reality" the things we dread.

Job found this to his great sorrow:

> *"What I feared has come upon me; what I dreaded has happened to me." Jb 3:25*

His fears had power to materialise. Jesus said we should switch from fearing to believing, "Don't be afraid; just believe." He meant that we should use the same energy, the same effort, the same powers that we would use in anticipating the worst that the devil can do, but direct them all toward believing in the best that God can do.

Just consider this comparison between fearing and believing.

Turn to these scriptures and read the full context -

> *"The Lord is my shepherd, I shall not be in want..." Ps 23:1*
>
> *"I will fear no evil....for you are with me." Ps 23:4b*
>
> *"Whom shall I fear?...The Lord is my light"... Ps 27:1*
>
> *"For you did not receive a spirit that makes you a slave again to fear...But you received the Spirit of sonship...And by him we cry, `Abba, Father.'..." Ro 8:15*
>
> *"Not a spirit of timidity" "But of power and love and self-discipline. 2 Ti 1:7*
>
> *"Fear has to do with punishment...Perfect love drives out fear." 1 Jn 4:18*

This list could be greatly extended, but it surely serves to demonstrate the contrasting powers of fearing and believing, the negative power of the adversary and the positive power and provision of God.

GOD IS STRONGER THAN THE DEVIL... GOOD IS STRONGER THAN EVIL

Some folk reply to these statements that "the devil is real." They say, "You should not under-rate his power." They remind us that:

> *"Your enemy the devil prowls around like a roaring lion looking for someone to devour." 1 Pe 5:8b*

But like all the scriptures on which the devil thrives, they are only partly quoted or else misquoted. Certainly the devil is real. He most assuredly walks about as a roaring lion. However that Scripture adds,

> *"Resist him, standing firm in the faith..."1 Pe 5: 9a*

In other words,

FEAR NOT THE DEVIL'S POWER; BELIEVE ONLY IN GOD'S POWER.

Your God-given ability to anticipate the unseen or unknown must be rightly directed and expressed as FAITH IN GOD. Otherwise it is misdirected and wrongly expressed as FEAR OF EVIL.

Unmask your fears, identify them, name them, confess them to God. Bring your fears to the light of truth, and you will see that they are founded on the lies of the devil. The serpent's words to Eve in Genesis 3:1 "Did God really say?" are usually the basis of all our fears. Answer your fears with a positive "God really did say!"

God is! His power is almighty. Jesus Christ is alive forever more, and has the keys of hell and death! The Holy Spirit is here, the Comforter, abiding with us until Christ comes again! Angels look on, for they are -

> *"...ministering spirits sent to serve those who will inherit salvation." He 1:14b*

The word of God is true, it lives and abides forever.

"I will fear no evil, for you are with me; your rod and your staff, they comfort me." Ps 23:4b

DO NOT BE AFRAID; JUST BELIEVE, AND (YOU) WILL BE HEALED." Lu 8:50

INTRODUCTION TO LESSON TWO

"Here is the great thing: your own faith can bring you the miracle you need. If you have faith, you will get the result you desire. Faith without result is impossible - like a flame without light, or snow without cold, or love without joy. Faith obtains! Faith possesses! Faith moves the hand of God! Faith captures the promises of God and makes them work! And real faith is always eager to affirm its confidence in Christ, to say what God says, and to declare that the promise of God will come to pass." [14]

Many times in my life God has made his promises of healing come to life for me. I have had many very exciting answers to prayer. Each time, although I have had a solid foundation for my faith, I have had to claim the promises in a new and fresh way. Each time the answer has come differently. Faith in God is something that grows as it is fed by the Word of God and it is something that can grow weak if it is not constantly exercised. If it is used correctly, with a bold affirmation of confidence in Christ, then indeed all things are possible to the one who believes!

In this lesson you will learn the incredible power of your own faith in God. You will learn how much more reasonable it is to believe God than to believe the lies of Satan, and what enormous potential there is in the prayer of faith!

---

[14] "Sitting on Top of the World" Ken Chant. Bethany Fellowship, Minneapolis MN. 1972. This ref. pg. 51.

LESSON TWO:
THE POWER OF POSITIVE BELIEVING

In the Gospels there are established certain clearly defined principles by which people approached the Lord Jesus Christ and claimed his divine power. These principles are the same today. By these principles we can make contact with the Lord of Glory and release in our lives his healing, delivering power, just as surely as people did back in Bible days. Remember the words of Jesus -

> *"Go! It will be done just as you believed it would."*
> Mt 8:13

It will be done...just as you believed! As you believe so it is done to you. As you believe so God will do for you. The thing is determined by your believing - no more no less. No differently, just as you believe. God is all powerful: Jesus Christ is the same yesterday, today, and forever: BUT your needs are met only according to your believing.

Perhaps the greatest discovery concerning faith that anybody can make is this: WE ARE BELIEVING SOMETHING ALL THE TIME. Even unbelief is really a form of believing. Strictly, unbelief is not NON-believing, but WRONG-believing.

When the Bible speaks of human unbelief, it is spoken of from God's point of view. Unbelief is a failure to believe God, or his word, but people are still believing, even when they are not believing God's way. God's way is the RIGHT WAY to believe, but unbelief is the WRONG WAY...and this is the way most of us have been believing most of our lives. There can be no neutrality in our believing. We are believing all the time - either the right way or the wrong way. We are either believing according to God's word or contrary to God's word. Our believing power is always active and productive - whether we are using it rightly or wrongly. Right believing brings its results and so does wrong believing. Wrong believing is what the Bible calls unbelief and it may even become a possessing fear. Right believing is what the Bible calls faith. When we are believing rightly, it means that we have faith in God, full dependence on the power of the Gospel, complete certainty that no evil can befall us as we walk with the Lord.

FAITH is using one's believing power the right way. It is believing what God says: it is believing that God means what he says. Faith is believing that God will do what he has said he will do.

Abraham was a man who knew how to believe God in the face of overwhelming difficulties. God had promised him a son, Isaac, but both Abraham and Sarah were now very old, and it was humanly and naturally impossible for them to have a son. What then was Abraham to believe? Was he to believe in the physical impossibility of a son being born? If he had let himself be influenced by natural considerations, he would have been guilty of WRONG BELIEVING, because he would have been believing contrary to God's promise. But faith is the conviction that God is not a liar; a deep conviction that he will perform what he has promised. So it was with Abraham. We read -

> *"Without weakening his faith, he faced the fact that his body was as good as dead - since he was about a hundred years old - and that Sarah's womb was also dead. Yet he did not waver through unbelief regarding the promise of God, but was strengthened in his faith and gave glory to God, BEING FULLY PERSUADED THAT GOD HAD POWER TO DO WHAT HE HAD PROMISED." Ro 4:19-21*

In this Abraham gave a wonderful demonstration of right believing. He proved himself to be a man who had his believing under control. And if you would tap the supernatural resources of God, you also MUST get your believing under control. You must compel your faith to be directed toward God and the truth that everything is possible for him who believes. You must force your faith away from the consideration of things contrary to God's word, a consideration that will only change faith into devastating fear.

The possibilities of right believing are as unlimited as the promises and power of God. Positive faith in God brings us into vital connection with all the unlimited ability of God to meet our every need. It brings us into co-operation with the Lord. When we begin to properly use our faith it means that we take God's view of things. We think and speak and act as he would, reckoning that all the resources of heaven are ours. Positive believing will give us command over heaven's inexhaustible supply for all our needs, whether they are spiritual, physical, material or financial.

Remember the words of Jesus:

> "Go! It will be done just as you believed it would."

FAITH IS AN INWARD CERTAINTY

> "I write these things to you who believe in the name of the Son of God so that you may know that you have eternal life. This is the confidence we have in approaching God: that if we ask anything according to his will, he hears us. And if we know that he hears us - whatever we ask - we know that we have what we asked of him." 1 Jn 5:13-15

That is a really wonderful passage from the Bible. Notice that three times John uses the word KNOW and once the word CONFIDENCE.

The secrets of faith are packed into those verses - the secrets of answered prayer and of power with God. From these verses we learn faith is KNOWLEDGE - an inward knowledge, an inward certainty, an inward confidence. Faith is NOT thinking or wishing, or hoping. Faith is not reckoning that there is a good chance that "such and such a thing" shall happen.

Hear it again - FAITH IS KNOWLEDGE; FAITH KNOWS WITHOUT A SHADOW OF DOUBT! FAITH KNOWS - it doesn't wish - FAITH KNOWS!

When you have faith for a thing, you KNOW that things is accomplished even before you have any visible evidence of it. When you have visible tangible evidence you don't need faith for it any more. You only need faith before it comes to pass; but you need real faith, and real faith is an inward KNOWLEDGE. Hear it again - faith doesn't hope or guess or wish, FAITH KNOWS.

So we read words like this in the Bible:

> *"Now faith is being sure of what we hope for and certain of what we do not see." He 11:1*

> *"Therefore I tell you, whatever you ask for in prayer, believe that you have received it, and it will be yours." Mk 11:24*

In these two references we are told distinctly that after we pray for something, whatever we pray for, we must in effect believe that IT IS ALREADY OURS, and then it shall be given to us. Jesus said that having prayed, we must believe that we have received what we have asked for, and then we shall have it. The only evidence we need that we have received what we ask for, is faith. Though we can't see it, faith is the evidence of it. Though we can't feel it faith gives substance to it. This is the thought within the text in 1 John 5:13-15. If we know that God has heard us, then we also know that God has given us what we desired of him.

Though as far as our natural senses are concerned, we have no perception of the desired blessing, yet for all that, knowing that God has heard us we also KNOW THAT WE HAVE WHAT WE ASKED OF HIM, and the great truth is this, if we know that God hears, and we know that we have them, then WE SHALL HAVE THEM.

In the Gospel of Matthew there is the story of the woman who received her healing when she touched the hem of her Lord's garment. The record has it: "She said to herself" - she did not boast of a faith which she did not really have. She confessed her faith within herself, and what we find ourselves saying within ourselves is what we really believe. We say many things to other people, but what we say within, in the secrecy of our own hearts, that is the real measure of our faith. And what was the faith of this woman - what was this deep inward conviction that filled her heart? It was a strong certainty, a sure knowledge that if she but touched the hem of her Master's garment she would be healed of her complaint.

Once again, we see that FAITH IS KNOWING for certain that what we ask of God he is both ABLE to give us, and WILL give us. We must pray, then we must believe; and in the period of time between BELIEVING we have received and the MATERIALISATION of our faith, we must not waver, we must not doubt.

THE SOURCE OF FAITH AND STRENGTHENING OF FAITH

While it is true that every human being is born with a faith capacity, it is nevertheless essential that our faith be nourished and strengthened. We may have faith in general terms, but when we are faced with a specific need of healing or supply, we must get hold of a specific faith for that need. A person may have faith in God, and yet not have faith that God will undertake to bring him his particular heart's desire.

The first kind of faith says, "God can move mountains"; the second kind of faith says, "I can move this mountain." The one says, "All things are possible to God"; the other says, "All things are possible to me." The one says, "I believe God did this particular thing in Bible days"; the other says, "I know God will do this particular thing for me now."

Concerning developing a specific faith for a particular need, there are four things we should bear in mind...

1. Faith Born By The Holy Spirit

In the Bible we are told that faith is a gift of the Spirit, and also a fruit of the Spirit. In other words as we live in the anointing of the Holy Spirit of God, and walk in the Spirit day by day, we may expect that our faith will grow stronger and stronger.

As a fruit of the Spirit we understand that our capacity for faith will be constantly enlarged when we live in the Spirit. Faith will become increasingly more prominent in our living, it will grow to be an outstanding characteristic of our Christian experience.

As a gift of the Spirit we understand that when we find ourselves faced with a great mountain of difficulty, the Spirit of God will plant within us the faith of God, so that we can say to the mountain, "Move from here to there!" and it will be done. To live in the Spirit means to live in the anointing of the Holy Spirit, to be active in prayer and praise and fellowship with God: It means to keep ourselves spiritually alert and clean before the Lord. To do this is to ensure that the Spirit of faith will impart his powerful grace to us so that we, believing, shall find nothing impossible.

2. Faith Coming From The Word of God

We read in the Bible these words:

> *"Consequently faith comes from hearing the message, and the message is heard through the word of Christ." Ro 10:17*

Faith comes to us from God's Word because in the Scripture we learn who God is. We discover what his promises are, we are informed of his willingness and ability to back up his promises with his own mighty power. We learn of the things that God has done for others, and so are inspired to believe that he will do the same for us.

But in coming to God's Word we must do more than just read it as a book. Mere head knowledge of the Bible, an intellectual understanding of it, will not serve to bring forth mountain moving faith. You may have a mental grasp of the Bible from cover to cover, and yet be void of faith, or have such faith as is cold and lifeless, not able to effect any mighty works. But, if you will read the Bible in the strong conviction that it is indeed the WORD OF GOD, the living God who cannot lie, and if you will read it with a consciousness of the anointing and revelation of the Holy Spirit, it will become a living book to you. When the Holy Spirit takes hold of the passage you are reading and burns it into your consciousness, then it is that the Word of God gets right down into your heart, you come to an inward conviction of its truth, that certain knowledge which is really faith. We say it again - everyone has the capacity for faith, everyone has the ability to believe, but if this faith is to become a driving dynamic power, you must first of all receive the knowledge of God and his will for your life. Your inward capacity for believing must be supplied with practical material on which to work.

Faith must have a promise to claim, it must have a conviction from which to work. If you are sick, and then you read in God's Word that the Lord said,

> "...I am the Lord who heals you." Ex 15:26b

and you read those words in the deep assurance of their truth, with the Holy Spirit burning them into your soul so that you KNOW THAT GOD IS INDEED THE LORD THAT HEALS YOU, then with a shout of praise and victory your faith can leap out and lay hold of that promise and make it a reality in your life.

So the inward certainty of faith may be planted in your heart by the Holy Spirit, or it may rise from a specific promise in the Word of God.

3. Faith Born Of Desire

There is a third way of receiving faith. It may be born in the deep desires of the heart. Jesus said,

> "...What things soever ye DESIRE, when ye pray, believe that ye receive them and ye shall have them." Mk 11:24 (KJV)

This text begins with DESIRE and concludes with our HAVING the things that we desired. But in between our desiring and having there is our PRAYING until we BELIEVE that we receive them. Here the believing found its foundation in a strong desire. Desire led to fervent prayer and searching out the Word of God until faith flamed forth; the answer was claimed and the Lord heard from heaven.

Some people suggest that we may ask something of the Lord, but that the Lord may answer our prayer by giving us something else! However, that is certainly not what Jesus taught. He said we should RECEIVE the things we desired of the Lord. Still, we do not need to test our desires. We need to check them with the Word of God. We need to be sure they harmonise with the wisdom of God. We need to see that they do not violate the law of love. That is, our desires must not hurt or harm others, but should be for the good of all.

James tells us:

> *"When you ask, you do not receive, because you ask with wrong motives, that you may spend what you get on your pleasures." Ja 4:3*

But if we base our desires on God's Word, then we have made the first step to answered prayer.

What should we desire? Well, conditioned by the fact that we are children of God, the scope is unlimited. "What things soever ye desire."

John said:

> *"If YOU ASK ANYTHING ACCORDING TO HIS WILL..." Jn 15:7*

If we are children of God and familiar with the Word of God so that we are confident that we are not asking anything contrary to God's will as revealed in his Word, then the scope for prayer is very great.

The scripture tells:

> *"How God anointed Jesus of Nazareth with the Holy Spirit and power, and how he went around doing good and healing all who were under the power of the devil, because God was with him." Ac 10:38*

> *"Every good and perfect gift is from above, coming down from the Father of the heavenly lights..." Ja 1:17a*

Here we see that all things that are good and perfect, all things that lead to us being set free from the oppression of the devil are within the Father's will. Jesus said:

> *"Ask and you will receive, and your joy will be complete." Jn 16:24b*

In this we learn that all things which will serve to give us true joy in the Lord may be desired and received.

Paul said:

> *"...my God will meet all your needs according to his glorious riches in Christ Jesus." Ph 4:19*

> *"...If God is for us, who can be against us? He who did not spare his own Son, but gave him up for us all - how will he not also, along with him,*

graciously give up all things?" Ro 8:31-32

These scriptures set before us a tremendous field of prayer. Here are promises embracing our every need, ensuring our rich happiness. We may have them all only so long as we intensely desire them, and out of that desire seek the Lord in fervent prayer until his promises become a burning conviction in our heart, and with unwavering faith we know that we have them.

4. Turning Your Faith Loose

Faith must be released. Faith is not a lifeless thing. It is alive, vital and active. But it will not act of itself. It must be made to make contact with God and it must be sent against the barrier, the mountain that stands in the way. Faith must be snapped into action. Many times in the Bible we see how people set themselves a time and a place when their faith should blaze on forth and bring the desired result.

The Israelites claimed the promise of God and marched around the walls of Jericho. As they marched day by day their expectancy grew more and more fervent, until in a sudden surge of faith, with all their might they blew the trumpets loud and long. The enormous impact of the suddenly released faith of the thousands of soldiers surrounding Jericho shook its walls from top to bottom, and with a resounding roar they came crashing to the ground and the city was conquered.

A WONDERFUL EXAMPLE OF FAITH

The woman who was healed of the issue of blood said to herself,

"If I only touch his cloak, I will be healed." Mt 9:21

Closer and closer she drew to the Lord, inch by inch she pressed through the crowd and jostled and pushed until Jesus was just before her. In a fervour of anticipation she reached out her hand and stretched toward the Lord. Nearer and nearer her reaching fingers came to the hem of his garment. In the mighty moving of her faith she shook and trembled until suddenly her longing fingers touched the Lord. In that moment all of her faith poured forth! It was released from the captivity of her heart, it formed an unbreakable link between her and Christ, so that the Scripture says healing virtue flowed from the Lord into her poor diseased body. And in a moment of time she was made completely whole. She expected to be healed the moment she touched him, and that expectancy was a burning conviction deep in her heart. Touching his garment was the crisis point she had set for her faith. It was the point at which she determined to let loose all of her faith in the healing power of the Lord.

Similarly, many others had a like faith in Christ and we read of several occasions when...

> *"...People brought all their sick to him and begged him to let the sick just touch the edge of his cloak, and all who touched him were healed." Mt 14: 35b-36*

Later on, when the disciples had taken over the healing ministry of the Lord, we read how Peter's shadow became a point of contact for the faith of people who were sick. It says that...

> *"...people brought the sick into the streets and laid them on beds and mats so that at least Peter's shadow might fall on some of them as he passed by...and all of them were healed." Ac 5:15 and 16b*

Once again, as the sick person lying in the street saw Peter coming toward him, his faith built up to a point of tremendous expectancy: it came to a place of great crisis. Then suddenly, as Peter's shadow touched him, all the believing power of the sick one burst forth into living contact with God and in dynamic might against the sickness, and he was healed.

In the same way, your faith must be released. It must reach a point of crisis, and at that point be immediately turned loose toward the Lord and against the problem. Usually in these days that point of crisis is reached by the laying on of hands, for Jesus said,

> *"they will place their hands on sick people, and they will get well." Mk 16:18b*

Then again, within the ministry of the church, if someone should call upon the elders of the church, the expectancy of faith would build up and would reach the point of crisis at the time when the elders anointed the sufferer with oil and prayed over him in the name of the Lord (Ja 5:14). On other occasions faith may reach its point of crisis and release as people take the elements - the bread or the cup - around the Lord's table.

Whatever your need is, and whichever way you choose, your faith must be released. You must open your heart and let your faith touch the power of God.

Remember then, that until you release it, faith remains ineffective.

THE REASONABLENESS OF FAITH

Some people consider that this matter of using one's faith is rather an extra-ordinary experience, a privilege which is reserved only for the favoured few. But on the contrary, there is nothing more reasonable and logical than for a child of God to use his faith in the supernatural power of God to meet his every need. It is reasonable to use your faith because...

1. The Promises Of The Bible Are True

Why do we believe that the Bible is true?

Because the Book itself bears within itself unmistakable evidence of divine authorship; stamped plainly upon the pages of the Bible is the fact that,

> *"...prophecy never had its origin in the will of man, but men spoke from God as they were carried along by the Holy Spirit."* 2Pe 1:21
>
> *"All Scripture is God - breathed and is useful..."* 2 Ti 3:16a

Because nothing has yet been discovered by science or archaeology which disproves anything that the Bible actually states. In fact every present trend of scientific investigation is tending to prove the Bible true in every detail.

Because the miracle of fulfilled prophecy right through the ages, and especially in our time, is thrilling evidence of divine inspiration and unequalled revelation.

Because Jesus unhesitatingly accepted the integrity of the Scriptures (see Mt 23:34-39; Lu 16:31; Lu 24:27; Jn 5:39-40).

Because the apostles likewise accorded the Word of God a unique authority, and based all their claims and ministry upon it (see Ac 2:22-36; 4:23-30; 7:1-53; Ro ch 4 & 5; 2 Ti 3:15-16; 1 Pe 3:20-21; 2 Pe 1:21; etc).

Because of the honour holy men of God placed on it. David cried out,

> *"...I will... praise your name...for you have exalted above all things your name and your word."*
> *Ps 138:2*

Imagine what honour, and praise, and dignity, and glory, and majesty, belongs to the matchless and terrible name of the Lord God almighty, Jehovah of hosts, the King of kings and Lord of lords! Yet God has seen fit to magnify his Word above all this! We can hardly dare to honour it less!

Because the righteousness of God is bound up with his Word. God must first fall before the Bible can be overthrown. His immutable promise is,

> *"...I am watching to see that my word is fulfilled."*
> *Je 1:12b*

Behind the promises of the Bible is the immense power of heaven; they are guaranteed by the highest authority in the entire universe.

Because, and this is the most compelling argument of all, of the amazing miracles of pardon, healing, restoration, renewal and deliverance that have been wrought in the lives of millions as they have simply trusted God's Word.

2. God Is Good and Great

> *"...Not one word has failed of all the good promises he gave..." 1 Ki 8:56b*

- the promise of God is good.
- God is good in his promise.

The promise of God is good because, firstly, it promises good things, not evil; and secondly, it does not mock or deceive, what is seen plainly on the surface of God's promise is what God desires to do.

Also the promise of God is great because the God who promised is well able to perform all that he has spoken. And this God is ever with us -

> "...in him we live and move and have our being."
> Ac 17:28a

> "...Never will I leave you; never will I forsake you."
> He 13:5b

And if God is WITH us, we are told that he is also FOR US - willing to act on our behalf, to see to our welfare, to care for us, to provide for us, to meet our every need.

> "...GOD IS FOR US...(and if he) did not spare his own Son, but gave him up for us all - how will he not also, along with him, graciously give us all things." Ro 8:31b-32

Jesus said also,

> "If you, then, though you are evil, know how to give good gifts to your children, how much more will your Father in heaven give good gifts to those who ask him!" Mt 7:11

> "Every good and perfect gift is from above, coming down from the Father of the heavenly lights, who does not change like shifting shadows." Ja 1:17

Here then, is a God you can trust; and one who demands that you trust him to do good things for you.

3. Christ Is The Same Today

> *"Jesus Christ is the same yesterday and today and forever." He 13:8*

> *"I the Lord do not change." Mal 3:6a*

> *"God is not a man, that he should lie, nor a son of man, that he should change his mind. Does he promise and not fulfil?" Nu 23:19*

- What Christ was: he is!
- What he has done: he will do!
- What he promised to one: he promises to all!
- Believe it! Christ is the same today! And your faith can reach him!

4. The Holy Spirit Is Here

Jesus promised,

> *"And I will ask the Father, and he will give you another Counsellor to be with you forever." Jo 14:16*

The Holy Spirit was sent down on the day of Pentecost, and he will remain on earth, for the comfort and salvation of the redeemed, until Jesus returns in power and glory.

Make bold to claim the promised power of the Holy Spirit in your life. And being filled with the Spirit, you have the sure confidence that,

> *"...the one who is in you is greater than the one who is in the world." 1 Jn 4:4b*

How then can fear grip you? or distrust? or unbelief? What immense encouragement you have to believe in God. Nothing could be more reasonable than to trust him to meet your every need according to his riches in glory by Christ!

5. The Angels Are Here

The angels are,

> *"...ministering spirits sent to serve those who will inherit salvation." He 1:14*

All the hosts of hell may challenge and attack you, but the number of God's holy angels is,

> *"...thousands upon thousand, and ten thousand times ten thousand." Re 5:11b*

And how swift they are to fly to the assistance of every beleaguered saint.

> *"Though an army besiege me, my heart will not fear; though wars break out against me, even then will I be confident" Ps 27:3*

> *"The angel of the Lord encamps around those who fear him, and he delivers them. Taste and see that the Lord is good; blessed is the man who takes refuge in*

him." Ps 34:7-8

On his cross Christ disarmed the powers and authorities, he made a public spectacle of them, triumphing over them (Cl 2:15). Then having totally defeated and utterly routed the forces of evil, he designated the heavenly host as the appointed guardians and helpers of his people.

Here indeed, resting in the providence and protection of God's mighty angels is strong ground for trust!

6. Worry Is Worthless

The Lord God has said that we need never worry. There is nothing whatsoever to be found in life about which we need to be anxious. There is no mountain which cannot be climbed by the pathway of prayer, no cloud through which the sharp arrow of earnest supplication cannot break, nor sorrow which cannot stand before the joy unspeakable and full of glory which fills a heart in tune with God.

Worry is so worthless: in fact, worse, it not only fails to help, but heaps more sorrow and agony onto your burdens. Indeed fear (or fretting worry, or tossing anxiety) torments a person, but the perfect love of God casts out all fear.

Every Christian should have the truth of these words burned into them;

> *"No temptation has seized you except what is common to man. And God is faithful; he will not let you be tempted beyond what you can bear. But when you are tempted, he will also provide a way out so that you can stand up under it." 1 Co 10:13*

Did you note those three mighty words. "GOD IS FAITHFUL?" Faithful to do what? Two things - firstly, God is faithful not to allow any suffering or trial to come your way more than you are able to bear. Secondly, God is faithful in every sorrow or trouble to make a way of escape for you, if you will only look for it. So we read,

> *"Do not be anxious about anything, but in everything, by prayer and petition, with thanksgiving, present your requests to God. And the peace of God, which transcends all understanding, will guard your hearts and your minds in Christ Jesus."*
> *Ph 4:6-7*

See how this scripture refers to those two powerful components of human nature - our affections and our mind. In these two lies the source of all the nervous fret, frustration, fear and failure, to which we are all so prone.

Consider our affections: How many times they have been broken, how deep the injury they have known, how bitter their unsatisfied longings, how terrible the passions that so many times rage and chafe, bite and snarl within us. In the heart of man we find distorted affections that break up homes, turn parents against their children, children against their parents, and lead to all manner of shame and violence. In an effort to conquer the power and effect of the twisted hearts of humanity, men resort to doctors of the body, doctors of the mind, drugs and medicines, social organisations, welfare clubs, education, scores of other means. They are all good and serve their purpose. Yet the simplest remedy of all, and the most effective, is found in the scripture -

> *"You will keep in perfect peace him whose mind is steadfast, because he trusts in you. Trust in the Lord forever, for the Lord, the Lord, is the Rock*

> *eternal." Is 26:3-4*

Consider the mind: Here is the source of all our imagination, of our fear and our faith, of our knowledge of things good and things evil, of strength or of weakness. How much evil and hatred, and defeat, and suggestions of unrighteousness scurry through our mind. It is here we brood over the problems that face us. It is here the devil finds a fertile plot in which to plant his seeds of iniquity. But the scripture says that we must -

> *"... demolish arguments and every pretension that sets itself up against the knowledge of God, and...take captive every thought to make it obedient to Christ." 2 Co 10:5*
>
> *"How great is your goodness, which you have stored up for those who fear you..." Ps 31:19a*

This must be our cry also, not the querulous tones of worry. Like Moses we must shout -

> *"The eternal God is (my) refuge, and underneath are the everlasting arms." De 33:27a*

- Fear not, therefore, but believe only!
- There is power in prayer

We are living at the end of an age. In connection with these last days, and his second advent, the Lord Jesus Christ said,

> *"...when the Son of Man comes, will he find faith on the earth?" Lu 18:8b*

Looking over the centuries that yet lay before, with prophetic insight Christ saw these days in which we live. He saw the far-flung Christian church, the many millions who profess to believe in God; he heard the singing of ten thousand choirs, the sound of many sermons...but he looked in vain to find real faith, faith that would achieve the impossible, faith that would bring the miracle working power of God to bear upon the affairs of men.

This pungent question of the Lord was thrown out as a challenge, and it comes ringing across the years to demand an answer from you and me - when the Son of Man comes, will he find faith - in me!

Now Jesus spoke these words in connection with a parable he told, illustrating the need for prayer.

> *"Jesus told his disciples a parable to show them that they should always pray and not give up."*
> *Lu 18:1*

This parable on prayer concluded with his wondering remark about faith in the last days.

What is this faith of which Christ is speaking? It is faith which moves men, not just religious faith: faith which makes an unrighteous man become righteous; faith which releases the supernatural into human affairs; the faith of which Jesus spoke when he said,

> *"'Have faith in God...I tell you the truth, if anyone says to this mountain, "Go throw yourself into the sea, and does not doubt in his heart but believes that what he says will happen, it will be done for him.'" Mk 11:22-23*

Faith like this is rare: it was so difficult for the prophetic eye of Christ to discover this faith in the churches his gaze roamed over, that he thrust the sharp barb of his condemnation through the space of twenty centuries, to our day. Yet Jesus did not actually say that he would find no faith; he merely expressed a doubt - "will he find faith?" - it remains for us to ensure that, in us at least, when he comes the answer will be a triumphant affirmative! But how can we have this faith?

Jesus said that men should always pray and not give up! It is in prayer that faith which will move mountains is born. When your strength is fast running away, when you feel tempted to lose heart, to surrender to unbelief, to give up the fight of faith, THAT IS THE TIME TO PRAY!

Men and women should always pray! If we do we will not faint. If we do we will have faith in God. If we have faith in God we will be able to face the heaped up mountains that lie before us, and command them to be removed and cast into the engulfing oceans of God's deliverance.

Prayer is your greatest privilege. Pray always! Believe always! Never doubt God's goodness or your own authority in Christ.

INTRODUCTION TO LESSON THREE

We have heavenly authority given to us by Jesus:

> *"I have give you authority to trample on snakes and scorpions and to overcome all the power of the enemy; nothing will harm you." Lu 10:19*

When we are born again, the Lord begins to train us, as we show ourselves trustworthy he gives us authority; just as in our human families we give our children more and more authority over their lives, as they prove themselves trustworthy.

God allowed many years to go by before he was ready to use Moses and during those years he allowed circumstances to mould him into a great man of faith. Even so God still kept on with his training, during the whole time Moses led the people of Israel.

Moses had a rod given to him as a sign of his authority. We have for our rod the Word of God, and the believer's authority.

In this lesson we learn some incredible truths concerning our position in Christ and the power of God which is available to us through Christ. God does not want us to sit passively waiting for him to do everything. He has already done all that he can. Now it is our task to bring his power to those who need him. Let us rise up and claim the authority he has given us and use it for his glory!

LESSON THREE:
YOUR WORD OF
FAITH AND AUTHORITY

In life's disasters there are three things we can do...

- Go under in fear...collapsing without God.
- Go at it fighting...calling on God.
- Go over in faith...conquering with God!

We see this exemplified in Moses and Israel.

With mighty signs and wonders Moses had brought the people of Israel out of Egypt, a great host of some three millions, enriched with the wealth of Egypt (Ex 12:35-36), resplendent with the health and glory of God; there was not one sick or feeble person in that whole mighty host! (Ps 105:37-43).

But when they came to that immense crisis by the Red Sea. See their reactions! They were three-fold; three voices could be plainly heard: there was the voice of the people, a voice of fear - defeated; then above the clamouring crowd Moses spoke out, and his was the voice of hope - waiting; but then God declared himself, and brought forth the voice of faith - triumphant.

The people saw the Red Sea, the desert, the Egyptian army, and in a flood of despair collapsed, defeated by their own fear before the battle was ever joined.

Moses, too, saw the green and rolling waves, the searing desert, and watched the dust haze of the approaching chariots and soldiers. He took stock of all this, remembering the might and mercy of

God, and uttered those words of encouragement and prayer which have unfortunately been admired by countless people across the ages;

> *"Do not be afraid. Stand firm and you will see the deliverance the Lord will bring to you today..."*
> *Ex 14:13a*

ASKING AND ACTING

These words did not ring true. GOD CONDEMNED MOSES FOR THIS PRAYER. It was an error. The words "stand firm" are the key. They reveal that in his heart Moses was defeated! Like the people he was leading, he had seen the danger of the hour and felt that this was beyond their resources. With the voice of hope he commanded the people to stand firm and wait, to face the danger, to fight it out, trusting and hoping that God would deliver them.

No doubt this was true. But had Israel followed his advice, a fierce and bitter battle must have followed, which would have meant the slaughter of thousands of God's people.

Then God spoke.

> *"Why are you crying out to me?..."* *Ex 14:15a*

The Lord rebuked Moses for praying when he should have been doing. There is a time to ask and a time to act. God commanded Moses to speak to the people, to strike the waters with his rod and to go across.

This is the voice of FAITH, COMMANDING AND CONQUERING. There is a time to seek after the Lord, and a time to speak for the Lord!

THE RED SEA AND YOUR ROD OF AUTHORITY

What is the "Red Sea" in your life? Have you reached a place where there seems to be no hope; you are shut in on every side? Do all your past victories seem far away, and the host of howling Egyptians relentlessly bearing down on you? Are you chained and bound by the devil's power of sin, sickness, fear, torment, habit, weakness, lust, hate? Has disaster shattered your hopes and destroyed your dreams, brought you to despair?

In the face of these things what are you doing?

Some people throw their faith to the four winds. The bitter cry of their heart is

> *"...curse God and die!"* Jb 2:9b

Others stand and fight. With great courage and pure trust they grapple with the darkness and wrestle through the long night, standing, hoping, praying, waiting for the salvation of God. Many times this comes, but Oh! with what loss. Some find the battle too hard; becoming embittered, they surrender to the forces of evil.

But God would have us to face squarely at the "Red Sea", and, with triumphant faith, shouting, "I am more than a conqueror through Christ," strike the troubled waters with the rod of God, and march forward.

YOUR POWERFUL WORD OF FAITH

The rod Moses held was the emblem of divine authority. It was given by God as an outward sign that all the power of heaven stood behind him as he spoke in the name of the Lord. To us it was symbolic of the Word of God and the believer's authority in Christ.

Now, many Christians do not know that they have any authority; but see what the Bible says...

1. "I have given you authority...to overcome all the power of the enemy..." Lu 10:19

On his cross the Lord Jesus Christ

> *"...disarmed the powers and authorities, he made a public spectacle of them, triumphing over them by the cross." Cl 2:15*

To every believer is given the right to share in this glorious conquest. Having gained absolute command over Satan and his evil hordes, Christ has now fully conferred his victory and dominion upon his disciples. We must open our eyes to see that we can, by faith, easily crush under foot every wile and work of Satan, the arch-fiend himself!

The authority over the devil that we possess in Christ goes far beyond that which Moses exercised before Pharaoh, and infinitely exceeds all the resources Satan can muster. The powers of evil are compelled to obey us as we stand in the name of Jesus and exert our faith and authority against them. Perhaps these principalities and potentates of iniquity will resist us; perhaps by cunning wile, they will endeavour to turn us aside from our steadfast stand; they will hurl against us all their hatred and malignity; but nevertheless, they must yield.

So long as we stand beneath the precious blood of Jesus, refusing to allow the enemy to bring against us our sin, but holding against him the incomparable name of Jesus, we must prevail, and he will flee in abject misery.

So the scripture says -

> *"They overcame him by the blood of the Lamb and by the word of their testimony." Re 12:11a*

2. "...If God is for us, who can be against us?" Ro 8:31b

Well! Who?

3. "...we are more than conquerors..." Ro 8:37a

The apostle has to resort to repeated superlatives in an effort to depict the immense victory we have in Christ. Satan will try to entice us from this place of sovereignty. He will endeavour to make us burdened, confused, fretful, depressed, self-accusing to a wrongful degree. He will try to turn our eyes on to ourselves and our weakness, and away from God and his infinite might. He will try to centre our affections on this earth rather than on things above.

> *"Since, then, you have been raised with Christ, set your hearts on things above, where Christ is seated at the right hand of God. Set your minds on things above, not on earthly things." Cl 3:1-2*

Rather than allowing us to believe that we are risen with Christ he will try to convince us that we are fallen by sin.

But, so long as we have confessed our sin, we must resolutely believe that we are brought far above Satan's accusations, and are seated in perfect union with Christ; though we were dead in our sins God has made us alive in Christ and has raised us up with him into the place of grace and glory.

> *"...because of his great love for us, God, who is rich in mercy, made us alive with Christ even when we were dead in transgressions - it is by grace you*

have been saved." Ep 2:4-5

Claim the protection and strength of the blood of Jesus; and resting beneath that covering shroud, vigorously resist the enemy and demand your right against him.

4. "But thanks be to God, who always leads us in triumphal procession in Christ..." 2 Co 2:14a

If God's work is to be done in our day, and the church is to stand victorious in this evil hour, it is absolutely essential that every Christian learns how to maintain constant victory in Christ. In one final, furious, desperate effort, Satan is marshalling all his powers for a terrible assault on the church. It is urgent that we now accept, and rejoice in, the provision of total spiritual authority made for us in Christ. We must rise in fearless faith, and in humility and thanksgiving before God, take our seat with Christ in the heavenly realm, and hold the enemy and all his works in complete subjection beneath our word of command.

5. "...be strong in the Lord and in his mighty power." Ep 6:10 (See also 1:19-20, 3:20)

The Lord Jesus Christ is absolute head over all, and is

> *"Far above .all rule and authority, power and dominion, and every title that can be given, not only in the present age but also in the one to come." Ep 1:21*

His control and his government are supreme. Risen from the tomb, and seated now at the right hand of the Majesty on high, he rules far above every other force which may be found in the universe. The rank folly of Satan is discovered in his continuing, yet wholly futile rebellion against our sovereign Lord. The supremacy of

Christ and of those who take their place beside him in full assurance of faith, is unshakable: his, and their, right to rule can never be disputed.

By the grace of God, through the exceeding riches of his kindness toward us, we have been elevated into the honour of heavenly princes; we are all made potential occupiers of the Throne of Christ.

But the final act of being seated beside him depends on the exercise of our own faith in God's Word. We remain here on earth; yet we are not of the earth.

Faith is being sure of what we cannot see - we don't see ourselves in heaven with Christ, yet we believe the declaration of the scripture, and believing it, we count ourselves to be there, and we act accordingly.

By our faith we become identified with Christ; what Christ is we see ourselves to be; we reckon ourselves to be strong with his strength; our power is found in his might.

So we read...

> *"...tremendous is the power available to us who believe in God. That power is the same divine energy which was demonstrated in Christ when he raised him from the dead and gave him the place of supreme honour in heaven - a place that is infinitely superior to any conceivable command, authority, power, or control...(and) now...by his power within us (he) is able to do infinitely more than we ever dare ask or imagine." Ep 1:19-20; 3:20 (Phillips)*

BOOK EIGHT: WATER BAPTISM AND THE LORDS SUPPER

Introduction to Lesson One
Lesson One - **The Greatest Experience After The New Birth**

Introduction to Lesson Two
Lesson Two - **The Lord's Supper**

INTRODUCTION TO LESSON ONE

In making the decision whether or not to be baptised, we cannot ignore the words of Jesus when he came to John (The Baptist) by the river Jordan.

> *"Let it be so now; it is proper for us to do this to fulfil all righteousness." Mt 3:15*

Nor can we ignore the fact that God was pleased with him:

> *"As soon as Jesus was baptised, he went up out of the water. At that moment heaven was opened, and he saw the Spirit of God descending like a dove and lighting on him. And a voice from heaven said, `This is my Son, whom I love; with him I am well pleased.'" Mt 3:16*

Indeed Jesus could say:

> *"....I always do what pleases God." Jn 8:29b*

This was the reason he went down into the waters of baptism: to please his Father; and that is the reason we should be baptised. If we follow in his steps, we also will give pleasure to God.

In a descriptive article written for "The Sword and Trowel", April 1890, speaking of his feelings in "putting on" Christ in baptism, Charles Haddon Spurgeon wrote:

"The wind blew down the river with a cutting blast, as my turn came to wade into the flood; but after I had walked a few steps, and noted the people on the ferry-boat, and in boats, and on either shore, I felt as if heaven and earth and hell might all gaze on me; for I was not ashamed there and then to own myself a follower of the Lamb. Timidity was gone; I have scarcely met with it since. I lost a thousand fears in that river Lark, and found that in keeping of his Commandments there is a great reward. It was a thrice happy day to me. God be praised for the preserving goodness which allows me to write of it with delight at the distance of forty years!"[15]

In this lesson we learn of the importance of baptism and how, when we are baptised, we share in the death, burial, and resurrection of Jesus.

---

[15] "Much Water and Believers Only" Wm. G Channon, Victory Press. London. 1950. This ref. pg. 32.

LESSON ONE:
THE GREATEST EXPERIENCE AFTER THE NEW BIRTH WATER BAPTISM

The Bible promises three great experiences to every person. The first of these is the New Birth. The second is Baptism. The third is the Baptism of the Holy Spirit. We are now concerned with the second of these, Baptism in water.

Baptism is an experience for the Christian; but it is more than a promised experience, it is a definite command. This command and the powerful blessing connected with it occupy our attention now.

DAYS OF CRISIS

Baptism is first mentioned in the Bible against a background of crisis. Israel was crushed under the mighty heel of the Roman Empire; everywhere there was a deep expectancy that the Messiah would soon appear to deliver the people. Into this scene strode John the Baptist, preaching in the wilderness of Judaea and crying to the people,

> *"..The kingdom of heaven is near. Repent..." Mk1:15*

A DIVINE COMMAND

Baptism was included in the last words the Lord Jesus Christ spoke to his disciples, and in the first sermon preached in the Christian church.

Here are the last words of the Lord Jesus Christ to his disciples -

> *"...All authority in heaven and on earth has been given to me. Therefore go and make disciples of all nations, baptising them in the name of the Father and of the Son and of the Holy Spirit, and teaching them to obey everything I have commanded you. And surely I am with you always, to the very end of the age." Mt 28:18-20*

Here are the concluding words of the first sermon ever preached in the church, the powerful and fervent words of the apostle Peter on the day of Pentecost. He followed closely the command of his Lord and exhorted the thousands of listening people to...

> *"...Repent and be baptised, everyone of you, in the name of Jesus Christ for the forgiveness of your sins." Ac 2:38a*

You will notice that in both these passages baptism is closely linked with the mighty power of the Risen Christ. Because Christ has all power in heaven and earth he told the disciples to go and baptise all those who should put their faith in him. And likewise it was against the background of the tremendous events of Pentecost and the mighty outpouring of the Holy Spirit that Peter exhorted every one of the people to repent and be baptised.

Why is this so?

Because baptism is far more than a ceremony, much greater than a mere formality. Baptism, Bible baptism, is a dynamic, living, vital, Christian experience which links the believer with all the mighty power of Christ's Resurrection.

WHY WE BELIEVE IN BAPTISM

(Please read again Jesus' words in Matthew 28:16-20.)

We believe that these words of the Lord Jesus Christ are as applicable today as they were in the primitive church...

1. Because of the greatness of Christ's command.

You will notice from the first verse in the passage that the Lord Jesus Christ directed his disciples to walk all the way from Jerusalem to Galilee. Here was a journey of some one hundred miles laid upon the disciples, a journey that took them many days; and, as each day passed by, excitement and anticipation and anxiety beat more and more fervently within them.

They came to the mountain that Jesus had appointed, and as they laboured upward I can imagine that a fervour of expectation burned hot within them. What would Jesus say to them? What would his last command be? They reached the plateau at the top of the mountain and waited breathlessly for the appearance of the Lord. Suddenly he came and stood before them, and spoke the matchless words -

> "All authority in heaven and on earth has been given to me. Therefore go..."

Go and do what?

Two simple things: preach the gospel, and baptise all those who would believe. We are here concerned only with the second of these.

What an impact this command of the Lord made on the disciples! Consider the greatness of the journey, the grandeur of the mountain top, the eager expectancy of the disciples, the vast importance placed on this simple word to go and baptise. In the light of these things I can never believe that baptism is an insignificant religious formality, an empty ceremony divorced from all power, stripped of all efficacy. Baptism is as great as the journey Christ made the disciples undertake. Its blessings stand as high as the mountain they climbed, its command is surrounded by the Glory of the Risen and Triumphant Christ.

2. Because the command to baptise was given to the whole church.

There are some who say that this word of the Lord was given to the early church only. Others claim that the rite of baptism can be administered solely by an ordained priesthood, having behind them a long line of priestly succession.

But Jesus said to go and make disciples of all nations and that he would be with them even to the very end of the age. It must be very evident that the command to teach and baptise is placed before all men everywhere, and spans every century until Christ comes.

Furthermore, while Jesus had chosen the eleven, he did not limit the number of disciples to them alone. Many other disciples were to be made out of every nation, and these would differ in no way at all from the eleven chosen by Jesus. They would have the same calling, the same authority, the same anointing, for Jesus said they were to teach all nations to obey everything that he had commanded the eleven. But further than this, a close examination of our text shows that these last words of Jesus were spoken to many more than just the eleven disciples. Would you notice particularly the seventeenth verse, where it says;

> *"...When they saw him, they worshipped him; but some doubted." Mt 28:17*

Who were these people who doubted? I am convinced that they were some of the 500 people who also saw the Lord at this time.

> *"After that, he appeared to more than five hundred of the brothers at the same time, most of whom are still living, though some have fallen asleep."*
> 1 Co 15:6

This great crowd of people had heard of the journey of the disciples, and had joined them on the mountain top for the Lord. But some of them doubted because they did not recognise Jesus when he appeared before them as a man. They expected him to come in a blaze of glory, giving a splendid demonstration of his power and majesty. However, as they heard the Lord speak, their doubt turned to strong faith; and when the Lord spoke to the eleven, he spoke to the five hundred also, and laid upon them the same commission.

We are also placed under the same obligation: to go, and make disciples, and baptise.

3. Because Christ has all power.

When Jesus appeared to the crowd of people gathered on the mountain top, some of them doubted whether he was indeed the Lord. But as he spoke in quiet, compelling authority, one and all they recognised him and yielded to his word.

There are many people who stand in a similar place today. They say, "We will be baptised when the Lord gives us a special revelation, when by some sign he shows us he really wants us to be baptised." But the only sign God will give us is the one he gave on the mountain top; namely the straight forward word of the Lord Jesus Christ. Jesus spoke, and he required that those who heard him speak should believe what he said and do what he commanded.

He prefaced his words with the tremendous declaration,

> *"All authority in heaven and on earth has been given to me."*

We dare not resist such authority as this: for such authority to speak alone is sufficient.

Notice also, because he had all authority, therefore they were to go and baptise all who should believe. In this way the Lord showed that baptism is no mere formality; but, rather, a vital necessity. By baptism we come into living contact with the divine power of the Risen and Ascended Christ.

Being baptised in the name of the Father, we acknowledge ourselves to be children of God: we acknowledge that he is our Father and that we are obligated to him for all that we have and for our very life. And, further, we commit ourselves to live as his children, to do nothing unworthy of his name which is given to us.

Being baptised in the name of the son, we show that by baptism we are clothed with Christ.

> *"...for all of you who were baptised into Christ have clothed yourselves with Christ." Ga 3:27*

We clothe ourselves in a new recognition of his righteousness, gaining a new experience of his grace, dedicating ourselves to live as he lived, and do as he did.

Being baptised in the Name of the Holy Spirit, we join ourselves to the mighty power of the resurrection of Christ, for the scripture says -

> *"...having been buried with him in baptism and raised with him through your faith in the power of God, who raised him from the dead." Cl 2:12*

Just as the Spirit of God raised Christ from the dead, so, as we are baptised in the name of the Holy Spirit, that same divine power is wrought within us.

For these three reasons, then, we believe in baptism. Believing it we have experienced it; and being baptised, like the men of old, we have gone on our way rejoicing (Ac 8:39).

THE IMPORTANCE OF BAPTISM

See the mighty things baptism accomplishes in the believer's life.

1. Separation from sin.

Only eight people were saved in the days of Noah. They were kept safe by the Ark as it rode upon the waters which covered the earth.

> *"...and this water symbolises baptism that now saves you also - not the removal of dirt from the body but the pledge of a good conscience toward God. It saves you by the resurrection of Jesus Christ." 1 Pe 3:21*

Everything within us has been corrupted by sin, even the voice of conscience has become warped and unreliable.

> *"let us draw near to God with a sincere heart in full assurance of faith, having our hearts sprinkled to cleanse us from a guilty conscience and having our bodies washed with pure water." He 10:22*

On confession of our faith in Christ, his blood cleanses us of all our sin, and our conscience is made "good". And immediately it begins to cry for holiness of life, godliness in conduct, complete freedom from the outward sway of sin. Baptism is God's strong answer to this cry of conscience.

So it was with Noah. The flood did not save Noah; rather it was a judgment on the whole earth because of sin. The Ark (symbolic of Christ) was the instrument of his family's salvation. But the flood waters did separate Noah from all the sin of the old world. When the waters receded from the earth, Noah was able to make a fresh start.

He had the glorious opportunity of living in a completely new world. Tragically he abused that opportunity and sin very quickly held sway again: but it need not have been so.

Baptism gives a new start in life. It cannot give us salvation, only the blood of Christ can do that, but baptism is able to separate us from all of our old life, and gives us a new start in a new world, with a new power to help us.

It will only be this to us, however, as we lay hold on its promise by faith, and walk consistently before the Lord. The blood of Jesus Christ cleanses us from the stain of sin and removes us from the guilt of sin. Being saved by faith, we have peace with God (Cl 1:20).

In his first sermon Peter said,

> *"Repent and be baptised, everyone of you, in the name of Jesus Christ for the forgiveness of your sins." Ac 2:38*

In the original Greek the word translated "forgiveness" has a stronger meaning that the English term. It goes beyond the simple idea of "pardon" to the actual "sending away" or "dismissal" of sin. It suggests not just release from the guilt of sin, but also from its power. This is brought out better in the KJV by its use of the word "remission" in this verse.

So in baptism we find this additional gift from God of "remission" of sins: that is as we actively and faithfully grasp hold of the promised blessing of freedom from sin, we are loosed from out of the power of sin.

There is an immediate and positive result in the life of every Christian who is baptised, having confident faith in the promise of God.

2. By baptism, the believer "is clothed with Christ"

See again Galatians 3:27.

Phillips translation has it that we have "put on the family likeness of Christ." We are now part of his family, brothers and sisters in him, acknowledging God as our Father and Jesus as our elder brother.

3. In baptism we share with Christ in his...

DEATH

> *"Or don't you know that all of us who were baptised into Christ Jesus were baptised into his death?" Ro 6:3*

BURIAL

> *"We were therefore buried with him through baptism into death in order that, just as Christ was raised from the death through the glory of the Father, we too may live a new life." Ro 6:4*

RESURRECTION

> *"If we have been united with him like this in his death, we will certainly also be united with him in his resurrection." Ro 6:5*

VICTORY OVER SIN

> *"For we know that our old self was crucified with him so that the body of sin might be done away with, that we should no longer be slaves to sin - because anyone who has died has been freed from sin. Now if we died with Christ, we believe that we will also live with him. For we know that since Christ was raised from the dead, he cannot die again: death no longer has mastery over him. The death he died, he died to sin once for all; but the life he lives, he lives to God. In the same way, count yourselves dead to sin but alive to God in Christ Jesus." Ro 6:6-11*

As it is with a person buried in the grave, baptism holds a promise of separating us from all interest in the things of the world and conformity to the way of the world.

As the Lord Jesus Christ was buried, that he might rise again to a new and heavenly life, so we are buried in baptism (that is cut off from the life of sin) that we also may rise again to a new life of faith, and love, and constant victory.

There is perhaps no greater experience in the Christian life than this powerful act of baptism and complete identification with the Lord Jesus Christ in his mighty resurrection life. In speaking of Christ's victory over sin, in which we share through baptism, we can do no better than to quote Weymouth's translation of Romans 6:3-11.

> "This we know - that our old self was nailed to the cross with him, in order that our sinful nature should be neutralised so that we should no longer be the slaves of sin. For he who has died is absolved from his sin. But if we have died with Christ, we believe that we shall also live with him: because we know that Christ, once raised from the dead is now no longer liable to die.
>
> Death has no longer any power over him. For the death that he died, he died once for all to sin but the life that he lives, he lives to God.

So too do you regard yourselves as dead to sin, but as alive in Christ Jesus to God."

The immense spiritual experience portrayed in this passage becomes ours by faith through the obedience of baptism.

WHO SHOULD BE BAPTISED AND HOW?

1. Who should be baptised?

The following groups of people are those whom the Bible names as proper subjects for baptism...

- Disciples, those who are taught of God, in all nations. Mt 28:19
- All who believe and are saved. Mk 16:16
- All who have repented of their sin. Ac 2:38
- Believers, both men and women. Ac 8:12

- Those whose hearts the Lord has opened. Ac 16:14-15
- Those who have heard and believed. Ac 18:8; 8:36-37

From these references it becomes very clear that only mature persons, having definite faith in Christ and being willing to obey his word and receive the tangible blessings connected with baptism, may rightly be baptised.

We see no warrant in the scripture for claiming that the sprinkling of small infants fulfils the Bible command to be baptised. The Ethiopian said to Phillip -

> "...See, here is water; what doth hinder me to be baptised?"

and the answer of Phillip was this -

> "...If thou believest with all thine heart thou mayest" Ac 8:36-37 KJV

Today we say the same. This is the only requirement before baptism, namely that with all his heart a person believes in the Lord Jesus Christ and desires to follow him. But we also say that if this condition is not present then people should indeed be hindered from going through the waters of baptism. In response to Phillip's plain statement, the Ethiopian said - "I believe!" Upon this confession of faith Phillip baptised him and he went on his way rejoicing. (Ac 8:29-39)

It is interesting to notice here also that the scripture merely says that Phillip told him the good news about Jesus yet the first response of the Ethiopian was a desire to be baptised: hence we infer that when Phillip told the good news about Jesus he also preached baptism as being an inseparable and vital part of the gospel of the Lord Jesus Christ.

It becomes plain then that all the persons who were baptised in the early church enjoyed the experience because they had heard the gospel of Christ preached, had believed, had gladly received the Word of God (Ac 2:41), and willingly obeyed the gospel command. Baptism was undertaken only by the deliberate choice of people who had already repented of their sins and placed their trust in Christ as Saviour. Very small children and infants are excluded from this.

How do we explain then the baptism of whole households? (Ac 16:15 and 33; 18:8; 1 Co 1:16). Very simply! In the face of the lack of information to show that small children were involved in these instances, and the plain teaching of the scripture to the contrary, why assume that children were among those baptised? In the majority of homes very small children are not found nor is there any warrant to assume that they were tiny children in the households mentioned. The only reasonable and obvious assumption is that all the members of the households concerned believed the gospel and were accordingly baptised.

What about the passage 1 Co 7:14?

> *"...For the unbelieving husband has been sanctified through his wife, and the unbelieving wife has been sanctified through her believing husband. Otherwise your children would be unclean, but as it is, they are holy..."*

If this text be supposed to give warrant to baptise infants, it must also give the same warrant to baptise, or make eligible for baptism, the unbelieving husband or wife! But as a matter of fact, the very fact that Paul had to write these words shows that many parents were troubled about the position of their children, from which we must conclude that the children were not baptised. Had they been baptised and accepted into the church, all cause for concern would have been removed.

But such a procedure was inadmissible as may be again shown by the apostle's words: had it been possible to baptise these children and so remove the parents' fears he would surely have said so. This text is thus seen to be certain proof against infant baptism.

HOW WE MUST BE BAPTISED

There are two main streams of opinion in the Christian church in this matter, and they are - firstly that baptism is for believers only and must be by full immersion of the whole body in water. Secondly that sprinkling a few drops of water on the forehead is sufficient and that even tiny babies qualify for this rite.

Now in response to these views there are two considerations which may be brought forward and which to my mind fully and finally resolve the whole question.

Firstly, there has never been any contention as to the validity of baptism by immersion. All Christians everywhere accept that a person who has been baptised by immersion, having faith in the Lord Jesus Christ, has fulfilled the biblical requirement. So there is no query as to the genuineness of baptism by immersion. Even those who most ardently advocate sprinkling will admit that immersion is also valid. The argument is only as to the rightness of baptism by sprinkling and concerning this is a large body of Christian people of many denominations strongly refute that baptism may be truly fulfilled by sprinkling. This in itself surely casts a shadow of doubt on the question of sprinkling.

Secondly, it is impossible to find any evidence anywhere in the Bible of people being baptised other than by immersion, or of persons other than genuine believers in the Lord Jesus Christ being baptised. It is impossible to prove that little children, too young to confess faith in Christ, were ever baptised, and it is equally impossible to show that anyone in the Bible was baptised in any way other than plunging right beneath the waters of baptism.

So we find that in the Bible, baptism required...

- Water - Ac 10:47
- Much water - Jn 3:23
- The people concerned going to the water - Mk 1:9; Ac 8:36
- Signifying a burial - Ro 6:4; Cl 2:12
- Those same persons coming up out of the water - Mk 1:10: Ac 8:39
- Signifying the resurrection of Christ - Ro 6:4-5

On the other hand, while sprinkling certainly requires water, in contrast to Bible baptism, it requires only...

- Little water;
- Water being brought to the people;
- The person concerned staying out of the water...

Thus exhibiting in no way at all the burial and resurrection of Christ. Added to this we have the consideration of the meaning of the Greek word translated "to baptise." According to the authoritative Strong's Exhaustive Concordance of the Bible, the word baptise means literally "to make whelmed", that is "fully wet". It is used in the New Testament only in reference to ceremonial washing or "baptism". For example look at the meaning of the word in Mark 7:4 where the word "washing" is literally "baptism".

> *"When they come from the market place they do not eat unless they wash. And they observe many other traditions, such as the washing of cups, pitchers and kettles." Mk 7:4*

Nobody would suggest that cups and pots and kettles were washed by merely sprinkling water over them. Baptism in the Bible was always by total immersion, and no other form will fully satisfy the demands of the scriptures.

Concerning sprinkling, there is a Greek word which specifically means "to sprinkle"; it is the word *"rhantizo"*. This word is used seven times in the New Testament, but it never refers in any way to baptism, but always to the sprinkling of the blood of the old sacrifices, or to the shed blood of the Lord Jesus Christ.

In the Greek language *"rhantizo"* means to sprinkle, and "baptise" means to plunge into. The actions involved are entirely opposite. In the one, water is poured upon the object: in the other, the object is put fully into the water.

The practice of sprinkling, then, rests solely on church tradition and not on the authority of the Bible.

WHY YOU SHOULD BE BAPTISED

Simply, because Jesus commanded that you should. And Jesus said,

> *"If you love me you will obey what I commanded".*
> *Jn 14:15*

The Bible also teaches us that baptism is a righteous act. Christ said to John the Baptist when he was reluctant to baptise the Master -

> "Let it be so now; it is proper for us to do this to fulfil all righteousness." Mt 3:15

In being baptised, the Lord set us a clear example in the importance and manner of baptism. The importance of baptism Jesus showed in the words, "It is proper for us..." - including both himself and all who should believe in the same way. And the Lord also clearly indicated the proper manner of baptism by going down into Jordan and being plunged beneath its waters. He set us an example of righteousness, an example that we are all expected to follow -

> "I have set you an example that you should do as I have done for you." Jn 13:15

and again:

> "To this you were called, because Christ suffered for you, leaving you an example, that you should follow in his steps." 1 Pe 2:21

The apostles instructed every Christian to be baptised. Acts 2:38-41. This was at Jerusalem on the day the Christian church was founded, and from this time on wherever the gospel was preached, those who received the word and believed were baptised. This is clearly shown in the New Testament record where we read of baptised believers in Samaria, Damascus, Gaza, Caesarea, Philippi, Ephesus, Pontius, Galatia, Asia, Cappadocia, Bithynia, Colosse, and Rome.

And again there is a warning connected with baptism: we see it in the example of the Pharisees of old -

> *"(All the people, even tax collectors, when they heard Jesus' words, acknowledged that God's way was right, because they had been baptised by John. But the Pharisees and experts in the law rejected God's purpose for themselves, because they had not been baptised by John)." Lu 7:29-30*

The first public act of the lord Jesus Christ was his baptism in the River Jordan. The last commandment Christ gave to his disciples was to go and teach all nations and baptise all those who should believe.

We conclude with the pungent words that Ananias spoke to Paul just after his conversion and the healing of his blindness -

> *"And now what are you waiting for? Get up, be baptised and wash your sins away, calling on his name." Ac 22:16*

INTRODUCTION TO LESSON TWO

There are four ways of receiving healing from God. The first is through a person with a Gift of Healing. This is the most sensational but has proved to be the least successful, mainly because people who do not know the Word of God come to a large gathering and receive prayer but have no one to teach them how to maintain their faith in the healing power of God. The second is through calling the elders of the church. this is the normal way for people in the church to receive their healing, and it works well. The third is through the laying on of hands by a Christian believer, and mighty things can be done as we learn to appropriate our authority in Christ. There is a fourth way to healing, the least sensational, but perhaps the most successful of all: and that is through the Lord's Supper.

As the church gathers around the Lord's table to confess sin to God and to ask forgiveness from him and from each other, the people can claim physical healing, and have it come immediately.

> *"With his wounds we are healed." Is 53:5b*

In John's gospel Jesus said:

> *"I tell you the truth, unless you eat the flesh of the Son of Man and drink his blood, you have no life in you. Whoever eats my flesh and drinks my blood has eternal life, and I will raise him up at the last day. For my flesh is real food and my blood is real drink. Whoever eats my flesh and drinks my blood remains in me, and I in him. Just as the living Father sent me and I live because of the Father, so*

the one who feeds on me will live because of me. This is the bread that came down from heaven. Your fore fathers ate manna and died, but he who feeds on this bread will live forever." Jn 6:53-58

As we take Communion, we become part of the mystical body of Christ, we become part of him and also part of one another. This is one of the mysteries of the gospel.

In this lesson we examine the Lord's Supper and what it means to us. It is a very solemn sacrament and not to be taken lightly. We need to study it carefully and understand it fully.

LESSON TWO:
THE LORD'S SUPPER

Having dealt with Bible baptism we now come to the second great sacrament of the church - the Lord's Supper, the high water mark of Christian communion.

The ordinance of the Lord's Supper is laid down in 1 Corinthians 11:23-33.

There are many differences of opinion as to the true significance of this observance - some, consider it essential to salvation; others think of it as no more than an act of remembrance; others have dispensed with its observance altogether; some hold it daily, others weekly, or monthly, quarterly, or annually; and so on.

The truth surely must lie mid-way between those who consider this ordinance essential for salvation and those who think of it only as an act of remembrance. We totally reject the idea that the sacrament is unnecessary, and we feel that a weekly observance most conforms to the scriptural pattern.

THIS IS AN ORDINANCE OF CHRIST HIMSELF

The writers of the first three gospels, Matthew, Mark, and Luke, all record the words of Christ when he laid down the pattern his disciples were to follow in remembering his death and resurrection.

> *"...While they were eating, Jesus took bread, gave thanks and broke it, and gave it to his disciples, saying, "Take and eat; this is my body."*

Then he took the cup, gave thanks and offered it to them, saying,

> *"Drink from it all of you. This is my blood of the covenant, which is poured out for many for the forgiveness of sins. I tell you, I will not drink of this fruit of the vine from now on until that day when I drink it anew with you in my Father's kingdom."*
> Mt 27a - 29 (See also Mk 14:22-26; Lu 22:14-20)

In Luke 22:19 Jesus said, "Do this in remembrance of me," and so left no doubt that he expected his disciples to maintain this observance. The early church took the Lord's injunction literally and so we read that they -

> *"...devoted themselves to the apostle's teaching and to the fellowship, to the breaking of bread and to prayer." Ac 2:42*
>
> *...and that they came together on the first day of the week to break bread. (Ac 20:7)*

To this authoritative command and example we can add the words of the apostle Paul, who claimed that he had personally received of the Lord the ordinance which he passed on to the church (1 Co 11:23). So, beyond doubt, the Lord's Supper is a divinely ordained institution which the church is expected to observe regularly.

THE MODE OF ITS ADMINISTRATION

1. The Lord's Supper consists of two elements - the bread, which is a symbol of the broken body of Christ, and the cup, which is a symbol of the shed blood of Christ.

(Note: There is an emphasis on the word "symbol" - we refuse any suggestion that the bread and the cup are miraculously made into the actual body and blood of Christ. When Christ said, "This is my body....this is my blood," he was obviously speaking figuratively, as when he said, "I am the door...I am the way..." etc.)

2. The Lord's Supper, as observed by Jesus and his disciples in the upper room, was closely linked with the Jewish Passover feast, and therefore the bread would have been unleavened and the wine unfermented (Ex 12:15). We consider it desirable to maintain this pattern by using unyeasted bread and pure grape juice. But if these are not available, any bread or biscuit, and any suitable cordial would be acceptable.

3. The scripture references quoted above clearly show that all the members of the early church shared both elements. Therefore we do not agree with those who believe that only the officiating priest can drink the cup. Both the cup and bread should be offered to all who are present.

4. The celebration should be joyous, for we read that Jesus gave thanks and that they sang a hymn and that the early church broke bread with glad and sincere hearts (Mk 14:22-26; Ac 2:46b).

5. This is a church ordinance, delivered to the church, and laid down as an essential part of the corporate worship of the church. Its observance will normally be restricted to such times as the whole church is gathered together. Private observance is therefore unnecessary, but could be permitted if desired by someone cut off from the worship of the church.

6. The scriptures give no definite rule for the frequency of this observance, but they do indicate regular and continual use of the Lord's Supper by the early church, and that the early church broke bread on the first day of the week. In the light of this, we consider a weekly observance, as an integral part of the worship of the church, to be a reasonable requirement.

THE SYMBOLISM OF THE LORD'S SUPPER

The Lord's Supper holds a two-fold meaning - it is a commemoration of the drama of Calvary, and a proclamation of the believer's faith in the promises of the gospel. This can be set out as follows...

COMMEMORATION AND PROCLAMATION

- of the death of the Lord
- of the life we gain from his death
- of the blood of Christ
- of the pardon we gain from his blood
- of the broken body of Christ
- of the healing we gain from his wounds
- of the resurrection of Christ
- of the victory we gain from his triumph
- of the ascension of Christ
- of the hope we have of his glorious return
- of the sacrifice of himself
- of our faith in his deity as the Son of Man and the Son of God

So the observance of the Lord's Supper is an act of simple remembrance; but it is also an act of faith whereby through the elements, we can reach out to the Lord and seize hold of the grace of God to bring us pardon, victory, life, healing and assurance.

ITS PERSONAL SIGNIFICANCE

As we have just seen, the Lord's Supper has a universal symbolism, which embraces the whole church, but it also has a meaning for each individual. This personal significance must be actively appropriated by those who are breaking bread.

1. The act of eating the bread and drinking the cup is an act of humility; it is a confession of our total dependence upon Christ.

By eating and drinking we show that we have no life in us and that we live by Christ alone.

2. The bread and the cup are symbols of our perfect union with Christ.

They show that we are accepted by God only in Christ. All the resources and strength of our spiritual lives stem from this union with Christ. As we eat and drink we should become vividly conscious of this union and, by faith, we should lay hold of all the blessings it provides.

3. The Lord's Supper is also a witness of the union of all those who believe in Christ.

Formerly we were strangers to one another and a barrier stood between us. But now, in Christ, we have become members of the one body of which Christ is the Head. Just as the wine comes from many berries and the bread from many kernels, so we see ourselves as being blended by God into a deep unity with each other member of the church.

> *"...Is not the cup of thanksgiving for which we give thanks a participation in the blood of Christ? And*

> *is not the bread that we break a participation in the body of Christ? Because there is one loaf, we, who are many, are the one body, for we all partake of the one loaf." 1 Co 10:16-17*

Unless we become aware, as we eat and drink, of our oneness with every other member of the body of Christ, we have utterly failed to enter into the real meaning of the Lord's Supper.

4. As we eat we testify in our faith that -

> *"...Man does not live on bread alone, but on every word that comes from the mouth of God." Mt 4:4*

We show our convictions that Christ is the living Word, the true Bread, and that by him alone can we find the nourishment that leads to eternal life. He is the Heavenly Manna by which we are sustained in our journeying through life. And we believe that by sharing in the Lord's Supper we are in a real sense partaking of Christ; - by faith in the grace of God, which operates through the elements, the divine nature is imparted to us.

WE MUST EAT AND DRINK WORTHILY

One passage of scripture clearly answers those who maintain that the Lord's Supper is a commemorative act only, and that no grace can be received from it. That passage is 1 Corinthians 11:27-30.

> *"Therefore, whoever eats the bread or drinks the cup of the Lord in an unworthy manner will be guilty of sinning against the body and blood of the Lord. A man ought to examine himself before he eats of the bread and drinks of the cup. For anyone who eats and drinks without recognising the body of the Lord eats and drinks judgment on himself. That*

> *is why many among you are weak and sick, and a number of you have fallen asleep."*

Here the apostle declares that unworthy eating of the Lord's Supper can lay people open to the judgment of God - they can become weak, or sick, or may even die. These are solemn words and they indicate the great importance God has placed on the communion service.

Now, if unworthy eating can brink the chastisement of God, the converse must hold true, that worthy eating will bring his blessing.

> *"But if we judged ourselves, we would not come under judgment. When we are judged by the Lord, we are being disciplined so that we will not be condemned with the world." 1 Co 11:31-32*

Paul speaks of the Lord's Table in connection with the power of Satan and the strength of God.

> *"You cannot drink the cup of the Lord and the cup of demons too; you cannot have a part in both the Lord's Table and the table of demons. Are we trying to arouse the Lord's jealousy? Are we stronger than he?" 1 Co 10:21-22*

He implies again that a right attitude toward this observance will cause the Lord to make us whole. But a wrong attitude will bring us under his anger.

A wrongful approach to the communion service may lead to sickness, and even death - it will certainly bring weakness to our spiritual lives and well being.

Therefore in contrast a proper approach will bring health and strength, vigor and vitality, to every part of our lives.

Two things are involved in worthy eating...

1. That we judge ourselves (1 Corinthians 11:28, 31).

This means approaching the table of the Lord, not with pride and self-sufficiency, but with humility; not with carelessness, but with concern; not with self-righteousness, but with true repentance and confession to God of all sin; not with self-seeking, but with total surrender to the divine will; not with coldness but with zeal; not with rebellion but with consecration; not with indifference but with love.

2. That we discern the Lord's body (1 Corinthians 11:29).

This means recognising the mystical body of Christ - the church. It means realising that we are all members of that universal body and that Christ is the Head of us all.

> *"Just as each of us has one body with many members, and these members do not all have the same function, so in Christ we who are many form one body, and each member belongs to all the others. Ro 12:4-5 (See also 1 Co 12:12-13, & 27; Ep 1:22-23; 4:12-13)*

Thus, we must put away all strife and jealousy and malice and division as we break bread. Jesus himself laid down the need to make peace with our brother before we presume to stand before the altar.

> *"Therefore, if you are offering your gift at the altar and then remember that your brother has something*

against you, leave your gift there in front of the altar. First go and be reconciled to your brother; then come and offer your gift." Mt 5:23-24 (See also Mt 18:15-17)

It also means looking back to the physical body of Christ and knowing that with his wounds we are healed (Is 53:5b)

In this way we discern that his body was broken on the cross so that we might be made whole, and so we actively and faithfully claim healing and deliverance from God as we eat the bread.

Pardon from his shed blood! Healing from his wounded body! May we discover his full blessing as weak by week we break bread around the table of the Lord.

BOOK NINE: CHRIST IS COMING

Introduction to Lesson One
Lesson One - **The Second Coming**

Introduction to Lesson Two
Lesson Two - **Christ's Return, the Rapture And The Judgment**

INTRODUCTION TO LESSON ONE

One thing we know about the return of Christ is this: it will definitely happen! But we do not and cannot know when it will happen. Jesus himself said:

> *"No one knows about that day or hour, not even the angels in heaven, nor the Son, but only the Father" Mt 24:36.*

How should the Second Coming affect us personally?

First of all we should make sure that we are ready for his coming. We must be certain that we ourselves are Christians, born again by the Spirit of God, living a life that is pleasing to him. Remember, he could come at any time. Secondly, we can hasten his coming by evangelising. Jesus said in Matthew:

> *"...this gospel of the kingdom will be preached in the whole world as a testimony to all nations, and then the end will come'". Mt 24:14*

If we are eager for the return of Christ, then we will be busy telling others of the gospel of the kingdom.

Third, while we are waiting we must not be lazy. Paul urged Thessalonians:

> *"We hear that some among you are idle. They are not busy; they are busybodies. Such people we command and urge in the Lord Jesus Christ, to settle down and earn the bread they eat. And as for*

you, brothers, never tire of doing what is right.
2 Th 3:11-13.

We should be studying, preparing, working, and planning as though Christ were not coming for a thousand years; and yet be ready at any moment to greet him should he come today!

LESSON ONE:
THE SECOND COMING

We are coming now to one of the greatest themes in the entire Bible. For every reference to the birth of the Lord Jesus Christ and his first coming to earth nearly two thousand years ago, the Bible contains eight references to his second coming in power and glory. The glorious return of Christ to the earth is mentioned more than three hundred times in the New Testament alone. So in speaking about his coming we are not talking about a doctrine which is hidden in a corner.

1. THE NECESSITY OF CHRIST'S RETURN

We are plainly taught in the Bible that our redemption would remain incomplete if Christ did not return. Though we have found salvation through the free grace of God in Christ Jesus, it is still true that we live in "corruptible, mortal" bodies. they will not become incorruptible and immortal until the day of resurrection, and there can be no resurrection except Christ comes. Neither have we any hope of entering the kingdom of God unless these mortal bodies of ours are radically changed:

> *"I declare to you, brothers, that flesh and blood cannot inherit the kingdom of God, nor does the perishable inherit the imperishable. Listen, I tell you a mystery: We will not all sleep, but we will all be changed, - in a flash, in the twinkling of an eye, at the last trumpet. For the perishable must clothe itself with the imperishable, and the mortal with immortality." 1 Co 15:50-53*

In another place also the apostle Paul speaks in this way...

> *"But our citizenship is in heaven. And we eagerly await a Saviour from there, the Lord Jesus Christ, who, by the power that enables him to bring everything under his control, will transform our lowly bodies so that they will be like his glorious body." Ph 3:20-21*

Then there are the powerful words of Hebrews...

> *"So Christ was sacrificed once to take away the sins of many people; and he will appear a second time, not to bear sin, but to bring salvation to those who are waiting for him." He 9:28*

The second coming of Christ is closely associated with the great day of resurrection. Paul said,

> *"...If Christ has not been raised, our preaching is useless...you are still in your sins...Then those also who have fallen asleep in Christ are lost. If only for this life we have hope in Christ, we are to be pitied more than all men." 1 Co 15:14a and 17b-19*

Here we are told that the resurrection of the dead is an essential part of our Christian faith. If there is to be no resurrection, then we gain no advantage from Christ, and we may as well "eat and drink for tomorrow we die" 1 Cor 15:32b .

If we are to inherit the Kingdom of God, then we must be raised from the dead, and we must be raised perfect.

This is the great hope of the gospel - that a day is coming when we shall be changed in the twinkling of an eye, released from the confines and the mortality of this world, and made like Christ, "like his glorious body" (Ph 3:21). And then we shall inherit the eternal wealth and splendour of the Kingdom of our God. And this can only be, and must be, realised through a day of resurrection.

How and when will this day be? The Bible tells us: at the second coming of Christ (See 1 Co 15:51-58; 1 Th 4:13-18).

2. THE CERTAINTY OF CHRIST'S RETURN

The sweetest song on the lips of innumerable saints from the earliest times until now, has been the absolute certainty that God would one day establish a personal kingdom among his people. In what is perhaps the oldest book in the world, Job earnestly confesses his definite faith that his redeemer would one day stand upon the earth, and that in his flesh he would see God: He said,

> *"...I myself will see him with my own eyes - I and not another." Jo 19:27*

David sang the same song -

> *"Our God comes and will not be silent; a fire devours before him, and around him a tempest rages. He summons the heavens above, and the earth, that he may judge his people: gather to me my consecrated ones.,...." Ps 50:3-5a*

Daniel saw a resplendent vision of the coming of Christ, and wrote of it in this fashion:

> *"In my vision at night I looked, and there before me was one like a son of man, coming with the clouds of heaven. He approached the Ancient of Days and was led into his presence. He was given authority,*

> *glory and sovereign power; all peoples, nations and men of every language worshiped him. His dominion is an everlasting dominion that will not pass away, and his kingdom is one that will never be destroyed." Da 7:13-14*

And not only Daniel, but many of the prophets of the Old Testament were granted a similar revelation and described the coming of the Lord in terms of immense majesty and awe and grandeur.

The same thrilling theme is continued in the New Testament. The Lord Jesus Christ frequently spoke of his later return to the earth, and he gave due warning concerning false fulfillment's of prophecy, and the true signs which would herald his coming. So the Lord said:

> *"For as the lightning that comes form the east is visible even in the west, so will be the coming of the Son of Man...Therefore keep watch, because you do not know on what day your Lord will come...So you also must be ready, because the Son of Man will come at an hour when you do not expect him." Mt 24:27, 42 & 44*

Then we have the wonderful words of Jesus in the gospel of John -

> *"In my Father's house are many rooms; if it were not so, I would have told you. I am going there to prepare a place for you. And if I go and prepare a place for you, I will come back and take you to be with me that you also may be where I am." Jn 14:2-3*

The disciples of the Lord Jesus Christ again and again spoke of their sure hope in his return. So we have the words of Paul,

> "For the Lord himself will come down from heaven, with a loud command, with the voice of the archangel and with the trumpet call of God, and the dead in Christ will rise first." 1 Th 4:16

> "...when the Lord Jesus is revealed from heaven in blazing fire with his powerful angels. He will punish those who do not know God and do not obey the gospel of our Lord Jesus." 2 Th 1:7b-8

> "When he comes to be glorified in his holy people and to be marveled at among all those who have believed." 2 Th 1:10

James:

> "You too, be patient and stand firm, because the Lord's coming is near." Ja 5:8

Peter:

> "And when the Chief shepherd appears, you will receive the crown of glory that will never fade away." 1 Pe 5:4

John:

> "Dear friends, now we are children of God, and what we will be has not yet been made known. But we know that when he appears, we shall be like him, for we shall see him as he is." 1 Jn 3:2

and Jude:

> "...See, the Lord is coming with thousands upon thousands of his holy ones to judge everyone" Ju 14b-15a

We conclude -

CHRIST WILL COME

THE NATURE OF CHRIST'S COMING

The coming of Christ will be outward and visible. He will return bodily. Possibly the most graphic proof of this statement is found in the following words...

> "...After he said this, he was taken up before their very eyes, and a cloud hid him from their sight. They were looking intently up into the sky as he was going, when suddenly two men dressed in white stood beside them. "Men of Galilee", they said, "why do you stand here looking into the sky? This same Jesus, who has been taken from you into heaven, will come back in the same way you have seen him go into heaven." Ac 1:9-11

1. It is "this same Jesus" who is returning.

The disciples had been intimately associated with Jesus of Nazareth. They had walked with him, followed him, heard his teachings, witnessed his miracles, and had lived in close fellowship with him. They had seen him ascend into heaven, and now they were still gazing longingly into the clouds that had received him out of their sight. Suddenly two angels stood by them, and boldly said - "THIS SAME JESUS, WHO HAS BEEN TAKEN FROM

YOU INTO HEAVEN, WILL COME BACK IN THE SAME WAY..."

If you had heard the words of the angels you would be in no confusion as to what they meant. If you had been numbered among the disciples and had known and loved the Lord Jesus Christ, you would have happily understood that the same Lord he very same Jesus who you had known and adored, would one day return again.

This is exactly what the disciples expected. They fervently and surely believed that the Christ whom they had known in Galilee, the prophet whose mighty words had enthralled them so often, the compassionate healer who had brought deliverance to so many untold thousands, the miracle worker who had stilled the storm, changed the water into wine, asserted his authority over the storm, things of nature and the ways of men, THIS SAME JESUS WOULD BE THE ONE WHO WOULD COME AGAIN.

2. We shall see him coming from heaven.

This is clearly demonstrated by the expression, "will come back in the same way". There are some who claim that the words "in the same way" merely imply that because Christ departed he would also return, and they do not believe that the coming of the Lord will be visible to every eye and splendid beyond imagination. There are many who argue that we cannot expect a literal return of Christ, but that the prophecies of his coming are figurative.

Others make the surprising claim that the prophecies of his coming are fulfilled at the death of a Christian: that every time a Christian dies, Christ returns.

Then there are teachers who say that the predictions relating to the return of Christ were fulfilled on the day of Pentecost. Still others claim that the second coming took place at the destruction of

Jerusalem in 70 AD, or that every time there is a great event in history or some vast disaster or a wide spread revival, Christ has come.

But all of these suppositions play havoc with the plain, simple, obvious meaning of the many prophecies concerning Christ's return. All of them are proved wrong by the three words: "in the same way".

The original Greek phrase (of which those words are the English rendering) occurs several times in the New Testament (See for example Ju 7; Ro 3:2; Hebrews 13:5). The phrase is variously rendered "in a similar way", "every way", "your lives". In all of these references the meaning of the original Greek is brought out which is the "mode" or "style" of action, not merely the action itself. In other words when the angels said, "will come back in the same way", they were, in fact, declaring two things - (1) that as Christ went, so he would come again; (2) that his coming would in all basic respects be identical with his going. The manner in which he went would be the manner in which he would come again.

They SAW him go, we shall SEE him come. Would you take particular notice of the emphasis the scripture places on the act of SEEING the Lord come...

He was taken up BEFORE THEIR VERY EYES...a cloud hid him from their SIGHT...They were LOOKING intently...why do you stand here LOOKING...you have SEEN him go.

The Lord Jesus Christ did not go into heaven in the form of a spirit, neither will he return from heaven as a spirit. He went away in a resurrected body which was visible and tangible. Likewise when he returns he will return in a visible, tangible form.

> *"Look at my hands and my feet. It is I myself!*

> *Touch me and see; a ghost does not have flesh and bones as you see I have." Lu 24:39*

3. He is coming in the clouds of heaven.

In the Bible clouds are spoken of figuratively as God's chariots. The scripture says:

> *"...He makes the clouds his chariot and rides on the wings of the wind." Ps 104:3b*

It was in a cloud that the Lord ascended into heaven - it says:

> *"...a cloud hid him from their sight." Ac 1:9*

In his tremendous vision Daniel saw the Lord coming in like manner and he said;

> *"...I looked, and there before me was one like a son of man, coming with the clouds of heaven." Da 7:13*

Jesus foretold it in these words:

> *"...I say to all of you: In future you will see the Son of Man sitting at the right hand of the Mighty One and coming on the clouds of heaven." Mt 26:64*

Then in another place we read that at the time of his ascension Jesus "passed through the heavens" when he returned to the Father (He 4:14, KJV). He passed through the atmospheric heavens beyond the clouds that rest above us; he passed through the universal heavens, going far beyond all created things; he entered the highest heaven and sat down at the right hand of the majesty on high - but now he is coming again. He will rise from his Father's throne, he will come down through the heavens. The clouds will be rent asunder and will reveal to the sight of the staggering world the magnificent stature of the returning Christ. Jesus said these powerful words:

> "...they will see the Son of Man coming in a cloud with power and great glory." Lu 21:27

And again in the unfolding vision of the Book of Revelation, it is recorded:

> "...Look, he is coming with the clouds, and every eye will see him." Re 1:7a

4. When he comes it will be with the angels and with great power and glory.

The return of Christ will be a glorious even in which the whole host of heaven will participate. It will be a time of unprecedented display of the awful majesty of God. It will be the greatest demonstration of God's power that the universe has ever witnessed.

The prophets record that the earth will reel and shake like a drunken man before the impact of the coming of the Lord of the ages.

Let the Bible speak for itself...

> "...As I looked, thrones were set in place, and the Ancient of Days took his seat. His clothing was as white as snow; the hair of his head was white like wool. His throne was flaming with fire, and its wheels were all ablaze. A river of fire was flowing, coming out from before him. Thousands upon thousands attended him; ten thousand times ten thousand stood before him. The court was seated,

> *and the books were opened." Da 7:9-10*

> *"When the Son of Man comes in his glory, and all the angels with him, he will sit on his throne in heavenly glory" Mt 25:31*

> *"If anyone is ashamed of me and my words, the Son of Man will be ashamed of him when he comes in his glory and in the glory of the Father and of the holy angels." Lu 9:26*

> *"when the Lord Jesus is revealed from heaven in blazing fire with his powerful angels." 2 The 1:7b*

It will be the particular commission of the angels at the time of the coming of the Lord to gather the whole church together around the Lord as he comes:

> *"...And he will send his angels with a loud trumpet call, and they will gather his elect from the four winds, from one end of the heavens to the other." Mt 24:31*

And mark the enormous power and glory which will be revealed on this stupendous day. There will be no resemblance in the second coming of Christ to his first appearing on the earth. He will not come as a babe to Bethlehem, to be despised and rejected by men; a man of sorrows, and familiar with suffering (Is 53:3). Not this time the shame of the cross.

The Son of God will return to this world as King of kings, and Lord of lords, Sovereign Ruler of the princes of the earth.

He will be crowned with many crowns, he will carry the sceptre of world dominion. So awe-inspiring and overwhelming will this event be that the apostle Paul informs us that every knee will be compelled to bow, and every tongue be made to confess that Jesus is the Christ to the glory of God the Father.

> *"At that time the sign of the Son of Man will appear in the sky, and all the nations of the earth will mourn. They will see the Son of Man coming on the clouds of the sky, with power and great glory." Mt 24:30*

Then again there is the magnificent description given in the book of Revelation...

> *"I saw heaven standing open and there before me was a white horse, whose rider is called Faithful and True. With justice he judges and makes war. His eyes are like blazing fire, and on his head are many crowns. He has a name written on him that no one knows but he himself. He is dressed in a robe dipped in blood, and his name is the Word of God. The armies of heaven were following him, riding on white horses and dressed in fine linen, white and clean. Out of his mouth comes a sharp sword with which to strike down the nations. He will rule them with an iron scepter. He treads the winepress of the fury of the wrath of God Almighty. On his robe and on his thigh he has this name written. KING OF KINGS AND LORD OF LORDS." Rev 19:11-16*

5. Christ will return to the earth and to the city of Jerusalem.

There are many scriptures which positively declare that Christ is to return to this present earth. But they also declare that his return will be associated with world-wide upheaval, and will be preceded by a period of great tribulation across the whole earth.

The return of Christ will alter the establishment of every nation on earth and will result in the final defeat of the forces of evil. (See Is 63:1-4; Joel 3:13-16; Lu 21:25-27; 2 Th 2;8; Re 19:1).

But in particular, when Christ comes he will sweep across the heavens as the lightning from the east to the west, finally to descend upon the Mount of Olives. The prophecies clearly reveal that Christ is to set foot on the Mount of Olives and that when he does so, the Jewish people will then indeed look upon him whom they have pierced and they shall mourn for him. (Re 1:7).

The descent of Christ on the Mount of Olives will be followed by cataclysmic changes in the geography of the whole land, and in fact all the countries surrounding Palestine. (See Zc 2:10-13; Zc 12:9-14; 14:1-7; Is 2:2: Mt 24:6-14; Re 1:7).

It is then that the King will make Jerusalem his capital and the Holy City will become the center of the whole earth, the focal point of all nations. (See Is 2:3-4; 33:20-22; Zc 2:1-4; 14:8-11; 16:21; Ps 48:1-8.

INTRODUCTION TO LESSON TWO

"Caedmon, the old English poet drew a picture in one of his poems about the day of Judgment. He imagined the Cross set in the midst of the world; and from the cross there streamed a strange light which had a penetrating x-ray quality about it, and which stripped the disguises from things and showed them as they are. It is Paul's belief that when the ultimate judgment comes, the man who is in Christ can meet even it unafraid, because he will be clothed not in his own merits but in the merits of Christ, so that none will be able to impeach him." [16]

How wonderful to know that when we stand before the judgment seat of Christ we will be able to claim his covering, because of his sacrifice on Calvary. He suffered for us that we might go free! As you study the great theme of the Rapture and the Judgment, your heart should be stirred by a great excitement. Each day that passes should find you waiting for that blessed hope, even the glorious appearing of our wonderful Saviour Jesus Christ, who is King of kings and Lord of lords.

But do not forget that while we are waiting we have been given a task. Our commission from Jesus our King is to share the "Good News" with everyone who will listen. In the words of Jude:

> *"But you, dear friends, build yourselves up in your most holy faith and pray in the Holy Spirit. Keep yourselves in God's love as you wait for the mercy*

---

[16] "The Daily Study Bible" William Barclay, 17 vols. St. Andrew Press, Edinburgh 1964. This ref from The Letters to the Corinthians" pg. 14.

of our Lord Jesus Christ to bring you to eternal life. Be merciful to those who doubt; snatch others from the fire and save them; to others show mercy, mixed with fear - hating even the clothing stained by corrupted flesh" Jude 20-23.

LESSON TWO:
CHRIST'S RETURN, THE RAPTURE, AND THE JUDGMENT

At the time of the second coming the rapture, or translation of the Church will take place.

1. THE DEAD IN CHRIST WILL BE RESURRECTED.

This is the great hope of every child of God. His faith is in Christ as Saviour and Keeper. Did he not promise in John 6:39 to raise every believer?

> *"And this is the will of him who sent me that I shall lose none at all that he has given me, but raise them up at the last day."*

The apostle Paul confirms that wonderful truth in 1 Thessalonians 4:13-16,

> *"Brothers we do not want you to be ignorant about those who fall asleep or to grieve like the rest of men, who have no hope. We believe that Jesus died and rose again and so we believe that God will bring with Jesus those who have fallen asleep in him. According to the Lord's own word, we tell you that we who are still alive, who are left till the coming of the Lord, will certainly not precede those who have fallen asleep. For the Lord himself will come down from heaven, with a loud command, with the voice of the archangel and with the trumpet call of God, AND THE DEAD IN CHRIST WILL*

RISE FIRST."

The Thessalonian Christians had been sorrowing because their loved ones were dying. Paul had taught them about the return of Christ, but they had apparently not understood the truth of the resurrection of believers at the time. Now he writes to comfort them with the assurance that living believers, at the time of Christ's return, will have no advantage over the "dead in Christ". He explains that those who are alive "will certainly not precede those who have fallen asleep" but rather "the dead in Christ will rise first".

Paul also wrote in 1 Corinthians 15:21-24 as follows:

> *"For since death came through a man, the resurrection of the dead comes also through a man. For as in Adam all die, so in Christ all will be made alive. But each in his own turn: Christ, the first fruits; then, when he comes, those who belong to him. Then the end will come, when he hands over the kingdom to God the Father after he has destroyed all dominion, authority and power". (when the rest of the dead are raised for the final judgment - Re 20:5, 12-15).*

Thus those who are Christ's will be raised from the dead when he comes again. Little wonder the apostle Paul could fearlessly address death, and say:

> *"Where, O death is your victory? Where, O death is your sting?" 1 Co 15:55*

2. LIVING BELIEVERS WILL BE CHANGED

The church is "the whole family in heaven and on earth" (Ep 3:15), and Christ is "Lord of both the dead and the living." (Ro 14:9), therefore it would not be possible for the dead in Christ to be clothed in immortality and the living believers to remain unchanged.

Thus we read in the words of the apostle Paul in 1 Corinthians 15:51-52:

> *"Listen, I tell you a mystery: We will not all sleep, but we will all be changed - in a flash, in the twinkling of an eye, at the last trumpet. For the trumpet will sound, the dead will be raised imperishable, and we will be changed."*

This raising of the dead in Christ and changing of the living in Christ, that they should be "caught up (together) with them in the clouds to meet the Lord in the air" (1 Th 4:17b) is said to take place at the LAST TRUMPET The Seer of Patmos describes the sounding of the seventh, and last trumpet as follows:

> *"The seventh angel sounded his trumpet and there were loud voices in heaven, which said: "The kingdom of the world has become the kingdom of our Lord and of his Christ, and he will reign for ever and ever" Re 11:15*

> *".The nations were angry: and your wrath has come. The time has come for judging the dead, (see 2 Co 5:10) and for REWARDING YOUR SERVANTS THE PROPHETS AND YOUR SAINTS and those who reverence your name, both small and*

> *great - and for destroying those who destroy the earth." Re 11:12*

These scriptures make it clear that at the last trumpet, Christ will return to reign, the dead will be raised, living believers will be changed, and judgments will be brought upon the ungodly world and the nations that fight against the Lord.

3. THIS RESURRECTION WILL BE A TREMENDOUS EVENT FOR EVERY CHRISTIAN.

But note, only those who are truly "in Christ" will take part in this first resurrection. The scripture says,

> *"...Blessed and holy are those who have part in this first resurrection." (The rest of the dead did not come to life until the thousand years were ended.) Re 20:6*

The resurrection which will take place at the coming of Christ will concern only those who have died in Christ or are born again at the time of his coming. Those who died outside of Christ across the ages will one and all remain in the darkness of death until the thousand years of his millennial kingdom are ended. They will then be raised from the dead to stand before Christ in the great day of judgment. (See Re 20:1-6).

> *"Then I saw a great white throne and him who was seated on it. Earth and sky fled from his presence, and there was no place for them. And I saw the dead, great and small, standing before the throne, and books were opened. Another book was opened, which is the book of life. The dead were judged according to what they had done as recorded in the books." Re 20:11-12*

Concerning the first resurrection, involving those who believe in and love the Lord Jesus Christ, we are told that it will be for us a wonderful release from the confines and limitations of this present world and from our mortal and corruptible bodies:

> *"(He) will transform our lowly bodies so that they will be like his glorious body." Ph 3:21*

> *"Meanwhile we groan, longing to be clothed with our heavenly dwelling." 2 Co 5:2*

In the resurrection we shall find liberty from all persecution, corruption, sin and pain. The apostle Paul shouted:

> *"I consider that our present sufferings are not worth comparing with the glory that will be revealed in us." Ro 8:18*

And then he goes on to speak about the longing of the whole creation as it strains toward the mighty day of resurrection.

THE GLORIES OF THE RESURRECTION

The resurrection will be a time of great gathering, as all the redeemed of all ages are brought together to stand in praise and exultation around the throne of Christ. For the first time in all history, all the members of the church will be united with each other and with their glorious Head. The promise of the Lord is that he will gather the whole church:

> *"...and to present her to himself as a radiant church, without stain or wrinkle or any other blemish, but holy and blameless." Ep 5:27*

All this will take place in a moment of time, so the apostle said:

> *"...Listen I tell you a mystery: We will not all sleep, but we will all be changed - in a flash, in the twinkling of an eye, at the last trumpet. For the trumpet will sound, the dead will be raised imperishable, and we will be changed." 1 Co 15:51-53*

And what a glorious change that will be, and how we long for it! How eagerly those who love the lord saw with the apostle Paul:

> *"while we wait for the BLESSED HOPE - the GLORIOUS APPEARING of our great God and Saviour, Jesus Christ." Tit 2:13*

The abundant happiness, the indescribable joy that will fill the heart of every child of God at that hour is graphically foretold in the words of Isaiah...

> *"But your dead will live; their bodies will rise. You who dwell in the dust, wake up and shout for joy. Your dew is like the dew of the morning; the earth will give birth to her dead." Is 26:19*

> *"...and the ransomed of the Lord will return. They will enter Zion with singing; EVERLASTING JOY WILL CROWN THEIR HEADS. GLADNESS AND JOY WILL OVERTAKE THEM, and sorrow and sighing will flee away." Is 35:10*

> *"The ransomed of the Lord will return. They will enter Zion with SINGING: EVERLASTING JOY WILL CROWN THEIR HEADS. GLADNESS AND JOY WILL OVERTAKE THEM, and sorrow and sighing will flee away." Is 51:11*

JUDGMENT AT CHRIST'S RETURN

1. THE UNGODLY WILL BE BANISHED FROM HIS PRESENCE

Many, solemn and powerful prophecies of the Old Testament portray the physical desolation that will come upon the earth, and the punishment of the ungodly that will take place at the coming of Christ. This will not be the final judgment, but a physical judgment on the nations of the earth, causing death, devastation of property, untold destruction everywhere. It will not be a complete annihilation of all the wicked, but rather a part demonstration of the wrath of God against all ungodliness. It is intended to be a tremendous demonstration to the whole world of the holiness of the Lord, an example that will have a lasting impact and influence on the peoples of the earth. In fact the lesson of this great judgment will restrain men from open disobedience to the Lord throughout the entire length of the Millennium. There will be no more open rebellion against God until, at the end of the thousand years, Satan is loosed again, and in his violent hatred stirs up the nations to their last great conflict with the God of heaven. Many pages would be required to set down all the prophecies relative to these events, but their meaning is summed up in the two following scriptures:

> *"Enoch, the seventh from Adam, prophesied about these men: "See, the Lord is coming with thousands upon thousands of his holy ones to judge everyone, and to convict all the ungodly of all the ungodly acts they have done in the ungodly way, and of all the harsh words ungodly sinners have spoken against him." Ju 14-15*

> *"...when the Lord Jesus is revealed from heaven in blazing fire with his powerful angels, He will punish*

> *those who do not know God and do not obey the gospel of our Lord Jesus. They will be punished with everlasting destruction and shut out from the presence of the Lord and from the majesty of his power on the day he comes to be glorified in his holy people and to be marveled at among all those who have believed." 2 Th 1:7b-10a*

Here we have a graphic demonstration of the vindication of the church and the judgment of her persecutors at the return of the Lord. The burning wrath of God will fall heavily upon those who KNOW NOT GOD, that is the atheistic, anti-God nations of the world: and his anger will also burn against those who DO NOT OBEY THE GOSPEL, that is, those who have deliberately rejected the Lord Jesus Christ. Their punishment will be banishment from the presence of the Lord when he establishes his glorious kingdom on this earth. They will be excluded from the wonderful happiness of the millennial kingdom and will be chained in utter darkness waiting the final day of judgment. But in contrast with this,

THE SAINTS -

THOSE WHO HAVE LOVED AND TRUSTED THE LORD JESUS CHRIST - will find themselves exalted to a place of incredible honour, for it says -

> *The Lord will be "glorified in his holy people and to be marveled at among all those who have believed." 2 Th 1:10a*

2. THERE WILL BE A JUDGMENT OF ALL NATIONS.

The revelation of this mighty day of international judgment is given to us in both the Old and New Testaments:

> "In those days and at that time, when I restore the fortunes of Judah and Jerusalem, I will gather all nations and bring them down to the valley of Jehoshaphat." Joel 3:1-2 (See also 3:11-12; Re 19:11-16)

But the most vivid and comprehensive picture is found in the words of the Lord Jesus Christ (Mt 25:31-46 - Compare Jer 4: 11-31).

The Lord spoke of the day immediately after his return when he, as King of kings would judge the living nations of the earth. It will not be a judgment based on the state of affairs prevailing at the actual time of Christ's return. Christ will sit on the throne of glory which will be situated in the "Valley of Jehoshaphat" and all the nations of the earth will be compelled to stand before him, acknowledge his sovereignty and receive his judgment. It is here that the Lord Jesus Christ will take to himself the total authority of earthly government. Here his kingdom rule will begin: and the first act of the great King will be to utterly obliterate all present national boundaries, to disband every present earthly government, to unseat every existing royalty.

Two classes only will be recognised on the day - the "sheep" and the "goats". The basis of reward or judgment will be the treatment the nations have meted out to the brethren of Christ. Some consider that these people are the Jews, who are several times spoken of in the scripture as his brethren - he was born of their family, he was of them and came to them. Others claim that the reference is rather to the church and to those nations who have on the one hand received the church, or on the other hand persecuted the church. Either teaching may be correct, and probably they are both true.

The "sheep" nations will find entrance to the visible kingdom of God, will be covered with blessings, will, as nations, be converted, and for the first time in history there will be a world of truly Christian nations, and truly righteous civilisations. The "goat" nations on the other hand, will be forcibly excluded from the kingdom, and remain under the wrath of God awaiting the final day of judgment.

THE FINAL CONSUMMATION

CHRIST WILL REIGN UPON THE THRONE OF DAVID

In words of deep majesty, Isaiah said:

> *"Of the increase of his government and peace there will be no end. He will reign on David's throne and over his kingdom, establishing and upholding it with justice and righteousness from that time on and forever." Is 9:7*

Then we have a remarkable confirmation of this prophecy in the words of the angel to Mary concerning the birth of Jesus:

> *"You will be with child and give birth to a son, and you are to give him the name Jesus. He will be great and will be called the Son of the Most High. The Lord God will give him THE THRONE OF HIS FATHER DAVID, and he will reign over the house of Jacob for ever; his kingdom will never end." Lu 1:31-33*

The first coming of Christ is now an established historical fact; and it is clear that the record of this fact tells nothing of the throne of David being given to him then. At this present moment, the Bible says that Christ is reigning in heaven, seated in divine glory at the right hand of the Majesty on High. But nowhere are we told that he yet occupies the throne of David. On the contrary, the Lord is seated on the throne of heaven. However, Christ has promised that the overcoming Christians will one day share HIS THRONE, when he comes to occupy it.

So we read:

> *"...To him who overcomes, I will give the right to sit with me on my throne, just as I overcame and sat down with my Father on his throne." Re 3:21*

Thus it is made clear that Christ now shares his Father's throne in heaven: but at his second coming he will take the throne of David, and the overcoming saints will be privileged to reign with him, sharing in the authority and splendour of that royal throne. Moreover as the scripture declared, he will reign primarily over the HOUSE OF JACOB (that is the re-united twelve tribes of the kingdom of Israel).

Many thrilling passages in the Bible foretell the restoration of Israel as a twelve tribed kingdom inhabiting the earth under the sovereignty of Christ (See Is 11:11-16; 33:20-24; Je 3:17-18; Ez 36:21-28; 37:12-28).

This glorious kingdom of the Lord will endure for one thousand years, during which time the devil will be bound in the bottomless pit. For a thousand years Christ and his glorified saints will reign over the peaceful and prosperous earth (See Re 20:1-6).

The order of the millennial theocracy will be something like this...

CHRIST THE KING

Will be reigning on the throne of his glory along with

THE OVERCOMING CHURCH

Who will share in the splendour and authority of the royal throne of their Lord, and with him will govern?

THE REUNITED KINGDOM OF ISRAEL.

Israel in turn will have authority over the remaining nations of the earth with a commission to evangelise them until

> *"THE EARTH WILL BE FULL OF THE KNOWLEDGE OF THE LORD AS THE WATERS COVER THE SEA." Is 11:9b*

So Christ will reign over his saints for one thousand years over an earth from which all sickness and warfare and poverty and injustice have been removed.

With the removal of Satan from the earth and the establishment of the perfect government of Christ, and his church, through a purified and powerful Israel, it is impossible to conceive what heights of spiritual, intellectual and physical perfection humanity will reach.

This will indeed be the golden age of mankind, and our prayer is that God will hasten it according to his promise

Other Books By Ken & Alison Chant

Angelology
A study of the splendours of the heavenly realm

Attributes of Splendour
Reflections on the nature, being, and glory of God

Authenticity and Authority of the Bible
The Authenticity and Authority of scripture

Better than Revival
A Pragmatic look at Christian Ministry and the Idea of Revival

Building the Church God Wants
Not goal-setting, nor statistics, but faithfulness

Christian Life
A positive and creative approach to life.

Clothed with Power
A Pentecostal Theology of Holy Spirit baptism.

Corinthians
Studies in 1 Corinthians

Dazzling Secrets
For Despondent Saints the causes and the cure of depression.

Demonology
Understanding and overcoming our dark enemy

Discovery
Learning and living the will of God

Dynamic Christian Foundations
Studies in Foundational Christian Truths

Emmanuel 1
Jesus: Son of Man.

Emmanuel 2
Jesus: Man who is God.

Equipped to Serve
Understanding, receiving, & using the charismata to Serve

Faith Dynamics
The limitless power of faith in God

Great Words of the Gospel
The major themes of salvation and holiness.

Healing in the New Testament
The healing covenant now.

Healing in the Old Testament
The healing covenant then.

Highly Exalted
The ascension and heavenly ministry of Christ

Mountain Movers
Secrets of mountain-moving prayer

Royal Priesthood
The priesthood of all believers.

Songs to Live By
Studies in the Psalms and Christian worship.

Strong Reasons
The Bible & Science, and the Proofs of God.

The Cross and the Crown
The passion and resurrection of Christ.

The Pentecostal Pulpit
The art of preaching in the power of the Holy Spirit.

The Worlds Greatest Story
The dramatic first millennium of church history

Throne Rights
Our position and spiritual authority in Christ.

Understanding Your Bible
Studies in biblical hermeneutics.

Unsung Heroines
Sage counsel for women in leadership in the church.

When the Trumpet Sounds
Studies in the Return of Christ.

Walking in the Spirit
The Apostle Paul offers as the key to successful Christian living the instruction to "walk in the Spirit".

www.ingramcontent.com/pod-product-compliance
Lightning Source LLC
Chambersburg PA
CBHW050536170426
43201CB00011B/1450